THOMAS WATERS

MAGICK

DECODING THE VISUAL
CULTURE OF SPELLS, ILLUSIONS
AND PSYCHIC POWERS

CONTENTS

CONTENTS

Canon a 3

INTRODUCTION

> 'I DEFINE MAGIC AS ATTEMPTING TO CAUSE THE PHYSICALLY UNUSUAL.'
>
> GERALD GARDNER, *THE MEANING OF WITCHCRAFT* (1959)

Magic is mystical power, seemingly controlled using rituals, objects and mental acts. Worldwide, many of its basic ideas and practices are remarkably similar. Low magic soothes common problems with superstitions, personal rites and help from community experts. High magic is complex, incorporating the impressive ceremonies of magicians, illusionists and some rulers. Alternative magic is countercultural mysticism like mesmerism, spiritualism, psychic powers, revived traditions and New Age practices. Since prehistory, magic has played many roles. Above all, it helps people cope with stress and misfortune.

INTRODUCTION

Magic is the secret ingredient of human life. It is everywhere and multipurpose, yet so familiar that it often goes unnoticed. Timeless and borderless, magic enchants most people in some form. Many of us perform lucky superstitions – often 'just in case'. Magic-infused fantasy and science fiction are among the most popular entertainment genres in movies, television, books and games. More subtly, magic shapes our speech and thoughts, with expressions like 'cursed', 'demonized', 'ghosted' and 'trolled' being commonplace.

Magic saturates our human past. You could say that it helped civilization begin, because magical thinking inspired or featured in much of the oldest known art, language and writing. The earliest surviving paintings and sculptured figurines, made by our prehistoric ancestors around 40,000 to 51,200 years ago, are plausibly magical. One of the oldest pieces of recorded literature, the Mesopotamian advice text known as *The Instructions of Shuruppak* (*c.* 2600 BCE), gives the warning: 'You should not curse strongly: it rebounds on you.' Magic also inspired the earliest known examples of the ancestor of Chinese characters: oracle script was written on bones used for divination rituals by the Shang dynasty more than 3,000 years ago. The Derveni papyrus (340–320 BCE), probably the most ancient surviving Greek literary papyrus, records magical ideas. And the longest text in the ancient Gaulish language – the Larzac tablet, a lead cursing plaque created in *c.* 100 CE – is entirely magical. The great psychoanalyst Sigmund Freud (1856–1939) thought that humanity's general capacity for language may stem, in the first place, from magical intent. 'Words were originally magic,' he wrote in *A General Introduction to Psychoanalysis* (1920). This is unverifiable speculation. Yet judging by the magical roots of many other cultural forms, Freud may well have been right.

Some evolutionary psychologists suggest that humans are instinctively predisposed to magical thinking. Maybe, in a way, we are born to believe in magic, principally because it helps us cope with stress and anxiety. Literal belief in magic is certainly far more widespread than many of us realize. A 2024 Pew

< *page 8*
'Dagol the Prince of Darkness', from *Compendium Rarissimum Totius Artis Magicae* (*A Rare Summary of the Entire Magical Art*), *c.* 1775
The demon Dagol seems to be unique to this book of magic and the name does not appear in other spirit lists. Dagol may be a corruption of Algol, a star in the Perseus constellation also known as the Demon Star.

Magical pendant made of gold, hessonite garnet, peridot and sapphire, England, 1540–60

Early modern Europeans believed that the magical properties of stones and other materials could benefit the wearer. Gold was thought to cleanse evil, strengthen the heart and soothe unwanted passions. Sapphire was supposed to counteract poison and prevent fevers.

Palm reading in Sumatra, Indonesia, 1989
Indonesian palm readers often use large diagrams to entice and communicate with customers, both locals and tourists. Curiosity motivates some clients. Others seek guidance with specific uncertainties.

survey of adults from thirty-five countries found that 45 per cent of people worldwide believe spells, curses and other magic can influence our lives. The portion of believers varied widely across cultures and nations, from a low of 20 per cent in Sweden through to a high of 87 per cent of people in Ghana. Ideas about the existence of uncanny and anomalous powers, which defy natural laws, are even more widespread. Polls consistently find that between two-thirds and three-quarters of Americans hold at least one paranormal belief. Around two-thirds also report having mystical experiences, ranging from personally encountering a demon (10 per cent of Americans sampled answered 'Yes' to this in a 2022 survey) to feeling an abnormal presence or energy (37 per cent of respondents). According to another 2024 Pew survey, 30 per cent of US adults consult astrology, tarot cards or fortune-tellers at least once or twice a year.

Magic is thus a great human universal. A common thread, tying together distant peoples, places and

Amulet, Sudan, 19th century
This ink and paper amulet protects against the evil eye: a culturally widespread idea that an evil or envious look can cause harm or misfortune to the object or being to whom it is directed. Note the pentagrams (five-pointed stars), a common magical symbol in Europe, Asia, the Americas, Africa and beyond.

periods. From prehistory to the present, from the Stone Age to the Internet. From desert through countryside to city and suburb. From caves to tower blocks. Our world simply abounds with magical beliefs, concepts, stories, practices, objects and images. No topic is so spellbinding, mysterious and fascinating. No idea is so familiar, widespread and evergreen. Why?

Magic is the original superpower. The most accessible, too. You don't need to be born with it or belong to a special family. You don't even need many resources or much education, although these may help. Magic attempts to control mystical forces for any reason you desire. To have, in a small way and for a brief time, the supernatural power of a god. If you follow the rites. If you believe strongly enough. If you keep the secret. If you do the trick right or tell the story well. If you take your mind beyond rational, cynical thinking. Perhaps then, extraordinary powers could work for you.

Results may vary. But whatever your views on the literal existence of mystical forces, there is no doubt

PROFILE MAGICAL FAIRY-TALE ITEMS

In fairy tales, magical items make dreams come true. Humble characters, experiencing relatable struggles, use enchanted objects to get rich, find love and escape danger. Magical items are associated with supreme fantasies, but they also teach proper behaviour.

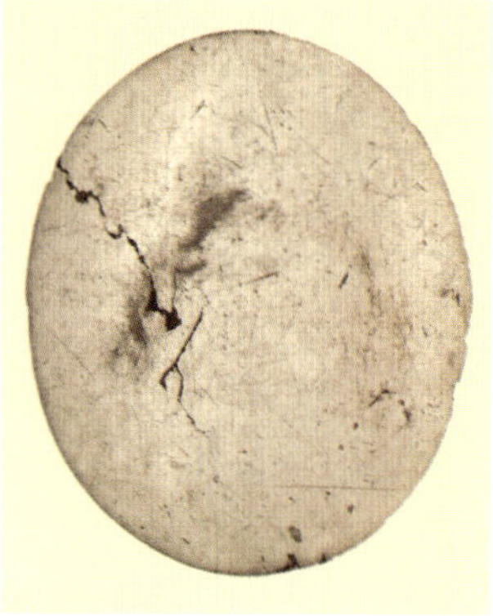

MIRROR
Diviners worldwide utilize mirrors like this Peruvian anthracite disc (900–600 BCE). In *Snow White*, words from the queen's mirror inspire conflict. In *Beauty and the Beast*, a mirror reconnects Belle with her family.

GOURD
Legends worldwide depict the calabash or gourd as an enchanted object. In Taoism, the Immortal Li Tieguai carries magical elixirs in a bottle gourd, linking the object with healing and prosperity.

LAMP
In Arabian folk tales, genies (a Western term for jinn) are contained in objects such as jars, rings, bottles and lamps. This reflects actual magical practice: sorcerers attempted to trap spirits in such objects.

MAGIC CARPET
Flying rugs, as depicted here by Russian painter Viktor Vasnetsov in *c.* 1920, are found in fairy tales across Eurasia. From Arabia, in tales about Aladdin and Prince Ahmed, the motif spread to neighbouring regions.

SPINNING WHEEL
Magicians reputedly weaved spells using textile technology. In *Sleeping Beauty*, a spinning wheel (depicted here by Nicolaes Maes in 1655) conveys a curse. In *Rumpelstiltskin*, it spins straw into gold.

HANDSOME PRINCE
Fairy tales magically produce handsome men who are rich, honourable and powerful. Love, care or a kiss transforms slimy frogs and terrifying beasts. This illustration is from a 1913 edition of *The Fairy Book*.

As Soviet folklorist Vladimir Propp (1895–1970) noted, ‘donor’ characters usually give magical fairy tale items in gratitude for a good turn – but also with warnings about correct usage. Like magic generally, magical fairy tale items are closely connected with women.

DRUM
In West African folk tales, magical drums create food when beaten. As in genuine magical practice, the instruments must be used carefully, following strict taboos and rules.

COMB
Combs such as this 1880s example are magical items in Slavic tales of Baba Yaga and German stories of water spirits. In one story, the comb is thrown on the floor and becomes a mountain that slows down a supernatural pursuer.

BRUSH
The Chinese tale of a young man called Ma Liang tells of a magical paintbrush that brings art to life. However, the brush must be used justly, to benefit the needy and not enrich the greedy.

RICHES
Wealth magically appears in many stories, from Aesop’s *The Goose That Laid the Golden Eggs* (illustrated here by Harry Rountree in *c.* 1930) to Irish tales of returning coins. Indiscretion or greed usually breaks the spell.

INVISIBILITY CLOAK
In *The Worn Out Dancing Shoes*, collected by the Brothers Grimm, a soldier uses an invisibility cloak to follow twelve princesses. In 1700s Europe, soldiers were known to use concealment magic.

BEANS
Many European fairy tales, such as *Jack and the Beanstalk* (above), feature magic beans and peas, partly because these were once multifunctional magical items. Ancient Romans exorcized evil spirits using broad beans.

that magic can induce powerful psychosomatic effects on human minds and bodies. Effects that really do heal, harm, scare, soothe, shock, energize, reassure, inspire and sometimes kill. Make-believe stories and conjuring tricks are powerfully enchanting. Literal and non-literal magic takes us far beyond the limits of ordinary life. Magic provides not just escape and fantasy but hope, creativity, insight and perspective. Above all, it teaches us about the art and power of belief.

Historians, anthropologists, folklorists, theologians and other scholars, as well as magical practitioners themselves, have never agreed upon a simple definition of magic. 'After a lifetime's career as a professional anthropologist, I have almost reached the conclusion that the word has no meaning whatsoever,' wrote Cambridge University's Edmund Leach (1910–89) in frustration. The difficulty in defining magic stems primarily from the fact that, like people, it is immensely diverse, colourful and strange, and in some ways varied. However, the ease with which magic moves and migrates across cultures suggests that, under the surface, it has common and compatible core features.

Since antiquity, magical beliefs and practices have been imported from distant lands by curious people seeking exotic powers. Four thousand years ago, Mesopotamians in what is now Iraq were casting spells in foreign languages such as Elamite. During the Middle Ages, translated Islamic texts conveyed astrological magic from Arabia and India into European Christendom. In recent years, Western shamans have sometimes been accused of culturally appropriating indigenous and sacred traditions. However, these contemporary practitioners are continuing well-established conventions of magical borrowing.

The lure of foreign mysticism helped to create the very words 'magic' and 'magick' (a variant from 15th-century English). 'Magus' and 'magi' were Old Persian names for Zoroastrian priests. These ritual specialists were obviously very impressive because they fascinated people a thousand miles west, around the ancient Mediterranean. Detailed descriptions feature in *The Histories* of Greek writer Herodotus (*c.* 440 BCE).

'Magical treasure hunting', from *Compendium Rarissimum Totius Artis Magicae* (*A Rare Summary of the Entire Magical Art*), c. 1775

The magicians depicted here look remarkably cheerful, considering the macabre events. The work is one of thirty-one watercolours illustrating a Latin and German manuscript that explains how to summon and command powerful demons. Like many grimoires, the book is falsely dated, in this case to 1057.

Hieronymus Bosch,
The Adoration of the Magi,
***c.* 1475**
Bosch follows the medieval tradition of depicting the magi as kings rather than as astrologers or Persian priests. In this detail, the magi represent the three continents of Asia, Africa and Europe.

Magical information about them appears in the Derveni papyrus, which describes the magi appeasing ancestor spirits with sacrifices and prayers, while using incantations to drive away harmful daimons (lesser spirits, between gods and humans) from the underworld. Three magi memorably feature in the New Testament's Gospel of St Matthew. These astrologers (in later Christian tradition they are portrayed as kings) follow a star to pay homage to baby Jesus. By the era of the New Testament, however, some Greek speakers were using their version of the term 'magi' to mean much more than a Persian priest. A *mágos* had become a general soothsayer, astrologer and conjurer. A dealer both in illusionary tricks and genuine occult arts. From this usage descends our word 'magic'.

Basic magical concepts or archetypes are extremely widespread. Harmful spells, luck, mediums, witches, wizards, spirits, mystical healing, love magic, war magic, divination, house protection and everyday superstitions occur internationally and throughout history. Hybrids, half-person and half-animal beings who fizz with magical power, are transcultural. Figurines are not only used to harm and help in vodou (a highly practical spiritual system created by Africans

‹ **Siren statuette, Greece, 3rd–1st century** BCE
In mythology, sirens were dangerous female-bird hybrids who used enchanting songs to lure sailors to their death. Statuettes like this one were used in funerals and rituals, as mourners, tomb guardians, guides for the dead and votive offerings to the gods.

› **Bronze amulet, Rome, 1st century** CE
This phallic amulet features testicles and an offensive hand gesture. Since the ancient world, such amulets have been used to protect against dangers such as the evil eye. In Rome, they were worn by both adults and children.

and their descendants in the Caribbean and Americas), but in almost all magical traditions. Mystical amulets span prehistory to the present. Curses and oaths, mingling religion and magic, calling on gods to deliver supernatural punishment in certain circumstances, exist worldwide. In Homer's *Odyssey* (*c.* 700 BCE), they evoke Zeus. In the Bible and Quran, it is the God of Abraham. Presiding deities change. The forms of curse and oath persist. For millennia, enchanting narratives have spread across borders, from ancient myths to folk tales of Baba Yaga and *The Arabian Nights* (first published in English between *c.* 1706 and 1721), to modern stories about characters like Harry Potter and the KPop Demon Hunters. No matter where you are from, the magical ideas underlying these tales are easy to translate and understand.

Beyond these near-universal concepts, several dynamics commonly mark magic. Secrecy quite often reigns. Many spells, wishes and charms do not work if you speak about them. Embarrassment, and concerns about being seen to know too much, keep magic quiet. Believers may worry that directly naming fearful powers somehow tempts fate to make them appear. If you must refer to magical powers, use respectful euphemisms. 'Generous ones', not 'jinn' (spirits from Islamic and Middle Eastern tradition). 'Good people',

PROFILE
MAGICAL GODS

Throughout history, magical practitioners have often asked their god or gods for assistance, praying for divine help to make spells succeed, amulets power up and charms take effect. In this respect, all deities are magical. Certain gods, however, are themselves great magicians. Most share special, magic-friendly characteristics. Some magician deities are tricksters or boundary-crossers. Others possess special knowledge. Several are linked with the deathly spirit realm or the great time of magic: night. Above all, magical gods are frequently females, with expertise in love, healing, divination and protection.

CIRCE
This 5th-century BCE vase portrays Circe, wand in hand. In Homer's *Odyssey*, Circe uses drugs to turn men into animals. Despite eating protective herbs, Odysseus is bewitched by her seductive powers.

HERMES
Depicted in this marble relief (27 BCE–68 CE) is Greek messenger and healer Hermes, who was renowned for magic. In Homer's *Odyssey*, Hermes uses his magic rod or staff more often than any other god.

HECATE
This marble sculpture (1st–2nd century CE) depicts Hecate, who was associated with liminal areas such as the moon, night, crossroads and magic. In ancient Greece and Rome, she was often portrayed with three faces.

TEZCATLIPOCA
This ornament (1400–1521) is thought to represent Tezcatlipoca, Aztec god of night (hence the black mosaic), war, sorcery and hurricanes. Using magic, he shaped weather, altered fate and shapeshifted.

ODIN
This 18th-century statue of the Norse god Odin shows him with his characteristically long beard. Odin was able to shapeshift, spirit-summon, influence and prophesy, and was often invoked to activate magical runes.

FREYA
Freya was a Norse divinity who specialized in the magical craft of *seiðr* or *seidr*. Around her shoulders in this Viking pendant is the Brísingamen necklace, said to be made for her by four dwarfs.

HEKA
Ancient Egyptian magic took divine form in Heka, who is sometimes depicted with a lion on his head (broken off in this 664–332 BCE figurine). Heka was the name for both a god and the supernatural power of magic.

THOTH
Ancient Egyptians knew Thoth, usually depicted with a baboon's or ibis's head, as the 'Lord of Divine Words'. He was called upon in spells for protection, healing, writing and safe passage through the afterlife.

ISIS
In ancient Egypt and beyond, Isis was a divine sorceress known as 'Weret Hekau' (Great of Magic). On her head in this amulet (332–30 BCE) is a throne, which is the hieroglyph that represents her name.

< **Nepalese woman, Kathmandu Durbar Square, Nepal, 2025**
In Nepalese Hindu and Buddhist traditions, devotees light butter lamps as offerings to deities for good fortune, healing, peace and prosperity.

> **Sōhei (Buddhist warrior monk), Japan, 1893**
During Japan's medieval period (10th to 17th centuries), sōhei were feared warriors who used mystical rituals, prayers and objects to protect themselves and harm enemies.

not 'fairies'. Magic also frequently involves belief, faith or at least an accepting mindset. The psychological act of willed belief can be difficult: for many, it is not easy to accept that mystical powers exist and can be controlled by humans. Regardless of your position in normal times, at key moments, when a magic spell is said or magic object created, you are supposed to summon up faith. Even if it is temporary, willed belief can make the experience of doing magic feel soothing, empowering, healing or electrifying. However, willingness to believe in fantastical things can also foster some of the problems associated with magic, such as paying excessive amounts of money for purportedly magical services or accusing other people of wielding harmful powers.

Magic has an intricate and intense relationship with religion. All faiths have protective supernatural practices, using pious words, holy symbols, sacred rites and blessed objects. Divination, healing and cursing can also be found in many religious traditions, such as tantric Buddhism. If you are not part of the faith in question, practical religion can look seriously magical. Accepting (although not necessarily endorsing) the

Holed mollusc shells, Blombos Cave, South Africa, 76,000 years ago
These shells - some bearing traces of red ochre clay - may have been worn as talismans of protection or power.

reality of some types of magic has functioned as an article of faith in many religions. To abandon believing in witches was effectively to give up believing the Bible, said the founder of Methodism John Wesley (1703–91), echoing a long-held view among Christians.

Religious institutions and people have often criticized, prohibited and occasionally persecuted types of magic deemed impious or unholy. Yet despite the hostility of some clerics, magicians tend to make immense use of religion. Gods, angels, devils, spirits and other supernatural beings are often called on to make rites and rituals succeed. In Japan, for example, the powerful magical tradition of Shugendō mixes esoteric Buddhism, Taoism, folk belief and Shintoism. Practitioners, known as Yamabushi or Shugenja, train in mountains to attain spiritual enlightenment, which in turn creates supernatural powers to heal, protect, exorcize and divine. They use fire ceremonies to ward off danger, and also hand signs, amulets, mantras, meditation, spells, charms, text recitals and other rituals. Shugendō first emerged in the Nara period, during the 7th century, but was banned in 1872. Today, after the easing of suppression from the mid-1940s, Shugendō is practised by a few thousand Yamabushi.

Magic probably emerged somewhere within the Middle Paleolithic (300,000 to 50,000 years ago). The earliest evidence is indirect and comprises the basic elements of magic: rituals, special objects, symbolism and perhaps a conception of a spirit world. Perforated

Engraved ochre plaque, Blombos Cave, South Africa, *c.* 75,000 to 100,000 years ago
Zigzag and diamond symbols are found quite widely on prehistoric artefacts, from amulets and figurines to shells dating back more than 500,000 years. They were perhaps thought to provide protection or power. Ochre may also have been symbolically important because its ruddy colour evoked blood.

shells, seemingly worn by humans using caves in Morocco 142,000 to 150,000 years ago, may be the first evidence of talismans (although they could also have been worn for decoration or to signify group membership). Intentional burials, with deposited shells and body painting, which occurred at Qafzeh Cave in Israel between 90,000 and 130,000 years ago, may be among the earliest evidence of a spirit world and afterlife.

Geometric symbolism comes from Blombos Cave in South Africa, where archaeologists discovered pieces of ochre that were etched with zigzag, diamond or cross-hatch patterns about 75,000 to 100,000 years ago. These may be among the earliest examples of magical markings or sacred geometry, because similar patterns were used on later prehistoric figurines and amulets. In Botswana's Tsodilo Hills, a huge rock shaped like a python's head is littered with carefully carved stone markings, made around 70,000 years ago, in what seems to be ritual. Prehistoric people could have done all these things for many reasons. But by this time, it seems they had created the essential ingredients of magic.

Evidence of magic becomes stronger and more direct during the Upper Paleolithic (50,000 to 12,000 years ago). Prehistoric cave paintings from this period

< **Female Venus figurine, Hohle Fels Cave, Germany, *c.* 41,000 years ago**
This figurine is carved from a woolly mammoth tusk, with incisions on the body and arms. The protrusion in place of the head may have allowed it to be worn as an amulet.

> **Woman-fish hybrid figurine, Vinča culture, Serbia, 4,500–3,500 BCE**
Featuring very large eyes, a fish tail and a swollen belly, this figurine is decorated with red paint. Two amulet holes indicate that it was worn.

may have been a form of hunting magic. As of 2026, the oldest known rock art of this type was created at least 51,200 years ago, on the Indonesian island of Sulawesi (examples from France and Spain have been dated back to around 36,000 to 40,000 years ago). Most Paleolithic cave paintings like these depict pigs, bulls, horses, lions, bears, deer, bison, rhinos and birds, as well as other large mammals. There tends to be few environmental objects such as trees or rocks, but lots of heads or full animals, portrayed sideways on with emphasized sensory features. Some of the creatures are pock-marked, as if attacked artistically to kill them. Hunters figure in other scenes, along with a smattering of half-human, half-beast hybrids, possessing heads of birds, bison and red deer. These hybrids have often been interpreted to be shamans, magicians or other ritual specialists. However, they could also be cautionary and threatening beings, like the nature spirits and cryptids said, in folklore worldwide, to stalk dangerous locations.

Figurines with plausibly magical uses date back 35,000 to 41,000 years. The earliest were carved from mammoth ivory and come from caves in the Swabian

DECODING LAMASHTU PLAQUE

Lamashtu plaques were magical healing devices from the Neo-Assyrian Empire (911–609 BCE). Made of metal, clay or stone, they were used to exorcize Lamashtu, a terrifying female demon said to feast on critically ill people, especially mothers and children.

1.

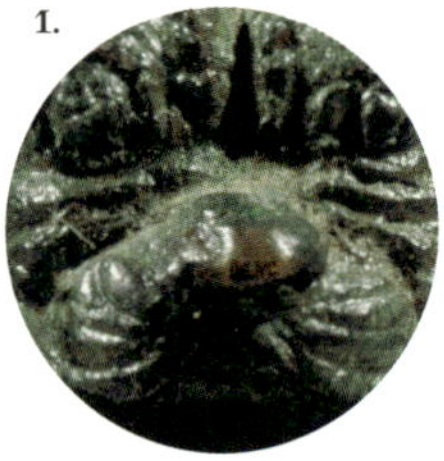

PAZUZU
King of the wind demons, Pazuzu was powerful and watchful. He grips the plaque with sharp claws, his dog-like head featuring a gaping mouth, huge bulging eyes and a prominent nose.

2.

DIVINE SYMBOLS
The symbols include the eight-pointed star, the owl of Ishtar (goddess of fertility) and the inverted crescent moon of Sin (god of wisdom). These gods and goddesses were invoked for aid.

3.

APKALLŪ
These animal-headed beings were endowed by the gods with great wisdom and power. Apkallū feature on other magical objects and reliefs: seemingly, their image alone provided protection.

4.

LAMP
The Mesopotamian god of light and fire, Nuska, is symbolized by the lamp, depicted here on a stand or tripod. Nuska is called upon to protect the sick and vulnerable from demons such as Lamashtu.

5.

EXORCISTS
Two fish-cloaked figures holding buckets (*banduddû*) flank the patient. They are performing rituals to expel Lamashtu. Similar characters feature on many Mesopotamian protective objects.

6.

THE SICK PERSON
Towards the centre of the plaque, the patient lies on a raised bed, their hands lifted in prayer and supplication. The fish-cloaked figures also raise their hands to perform the exorcism.

7.

LAMASHTU
The terrifying demonic daughter of sky god An was cast from heaven for devouring human flesh. With a lion's head, naked breasts and claws, she rides a donkey aboard a boat through the underworld.

8.

PAZUZU CHASES LASHMANTU
Pazuzu appears again at the bottom of the plaque on the left, actively driving his enemy Lamashtu back to the netherworld. His body is scaly and he has a scorpion-like tail.

Small Lamashtu plaques functioned as protective amulets. Large versions, often bronze, were hung at a patient's bedside, while an āšipu or exorcist conducted rituals designed to send Lamashtu back to the netherworld.

Carved figure and cave imagery, Ice Age

The carved ivory mammoth (top) is from Vogelherd Cave, Germany, and is 40,000 years old. Zigzag patterns like this can also found on later figurines and amulets. The cave painting of a wild pig (above) with hand stencils is from the Leang Karampuang limestone cave in Sulawesi, Indonesia, and it dates to c. 49, 200 BCE. Perhaps the hands were reaching into the spirit world to grab the pig's soul.

Jura region of Germany. Many figurines are horses, lions, bison, birds, bears, deer and mammoths. Some are voluptuous women and male sex organs. A few are hybrids, awesomely mingling person with beast, like the Lion-Person of Hohlenstein-Stadel. Some prehistoric figurines were deliberately smashed or damaged with ritual kill marks. Later clay examples were intentionally destroyed during the firing process. This looks like symbolic destruction, to mystically or magically harm animals and people. Other figurines inspired reverence, such as the mermaid-like, fish-woman statues made from clay by the Vinca culture of the Balkans and Central Europe some 4,000 to 8,000 years ago. Painted red, with huge eyes and fish tails, these figurines have amulet holes, indicating they were worn in rituals. Many prehistoric figurines like these were carried, stroked or hung around people's necks, presumably because they served a helpful purpose. Some animal figurines were etched with diamond or zigzag patterns around the flanks or face. The little markings would not always have been visible to anyone beyond the holder or the wearer, suggesting they had a non-aesthetic and non-status purpose, perhaps associated with magical power. Prehistoric wearables (animal teeth, bones and shells) were likewise holed, reused and damaged, as if what they looked like was of secondary importance.

Magic wands, rods and pointers may be prehistoric. The oldest candidate is 30,000 to 32,000 years old, found in the Paviland Cave in Wales. Twenty fragments of ivory rod were placed in a grave around a red painted partial skeleton of a man. An instrument made of polished horse bone was also interred, along with holed shells. Was this, perhaps, a prehistoric magician? Prehistory also contains plausible evidence of dangerous magical forces and drastic countermeasures, from 10,000 years ago, in the form of trepanning or trephination, which removes small parts of the human skull. This worldwide technique may have been designed to cure mental illness by releasing evil spirits or harmful powers. As human life became more complex, so did the practice of magic.

Ivory rod fragments, Paviland Cave, Wales, *c.* 30,000–32,000 years ago
These fragments were buried around the skeleton of a man in his twenties. Some theories suggest they could be the earliest known magic wands.

Herbs, figurines, symbols and ritual burying were combined into demanding, multistage rites 5,000 years ago at settlements of the Cucuteni–Trypillia culture, in what is now Eastern Romania.

Elaborate war magic may have emerged during the later parts of the Stone Age, when humans formed settled but rival communities. A particularly bloodthirsty version of conflict-focused mysticism seems to have been practised at Herxheim, in Germany's Rhineland, around 7,000 years ago. Over a period of about fifty years, this prehistoric group buried in ditches the partial skeletal remains of at least 450 people (archaeologists speculate the total number may be as high as 1,300 to 1,500), along with deliberately broken high-value items such as pottery, small animals and a few other artefacts including amulets. The deceased were not local, genetic testing reveals, but were captured elsewhere then transported to Herxheim to be ritualistically killed, dismembered, cannibalized and buried. The partial skeletons were not eaten by animals, strongly suggesting they were contained in a guarded and highly supervised ritual environment. Heads were singled out for special treatment, with many skinned and split vertically, then later buried together or stacked on top of each other, rather than being randomly thrown into the trenches. What was the purpose of these rituals of death,

cannibalism and desecration? Ritual cannibalism, as recorded in both history and anthropology, is often motivated by beliefs about transferring positive powers while extinguishing vengeful spirits. Perhaps the Herxheim cannibals believed they were mystically empowering themselves or assuaging terrible beings.

With the invention of writing, magic bloomed in the ancient civilizations. In Mesopotamia, magicians used cuneiform text on clay tablets to enumerate hundreds of stones with mystical and magical qualities. The Mesopotamians made great lists of demons, who were deemed responsible for all manner of physical and mental problems. Fighting evil with evil, they buried, displayed and wore amulet figurines of demons such as Pazuzu, fearsome king of the wind demons, who featured in the 1973 movie (and 1971 book) *The Exorcist*. Medical texts diagnosed numerous illnesses as caused by harmful ghosts. Writing also facilitated the development of hours-long anti-witchcraft rituals to cure people suffering from ailments attributed to harmful sorcery, which ranged from bad sleep and anxiety to failing relationships and poor health.

In ancient China, magic developed different points of emphasis. Ancestor spirits were thought to determine a person's fate. If displeased, ancestors might bring their descendants bad fortune, but well-disposed spirits could ensure fine harvests, safe travel,

< **Cuneiform tablet, Mesopotamia, 1st millennium BCE**
This tablet lists 303 magical stones. Some stones were worn to relieve attacks from demons or gods such as Marduk and Sîn. Others protected the wearer from plague and bad dreams or brought joy, riches and strength. Often, multiple magical stones were worn across a single necklace.

> **Bronze Pazuzu head, Mesopotamia, 800–600 BCE**
This head of the king of the wind demons would have been worn as a protective amulet.

Oracle bone, China,
***c.* 1300–1050 BCE**
Under the Shang dynasty, ox shoulder blades and turtle plastrons were engraved with questions. The bones were then heated, and the cracks that formed were interpreted, providing answers to the questions. Topics ranged from rainfall and hunting to travel and marriage.

sound health and good luck. Chinese mysticism also stressed the importance of a mystical, impersonal and powerful energy: qi, which means 'breath', 'life force' and 'vital energy'. Ancient texts such as the Daoist *Zhuangzi* (4th–3rd century BCE) argued that qi's presence created life while its absence brought death. Later theories stressed the importance of ordered flow, and the ability of specialists to control qi, such as those trained in martial arts like tai chi. In China, as across the globe, various service magicians assisted laypeople with natural and supernatural problems, for a price. For example, a fangxiangshi was an exorcist who conducted regular rituals to expel demons from houses and graves. Figurines of these powerful experts sometimes served as tomb guardians.

In ancient Egypt, magic (known as *ḥkꜣ* or *heka*) was not only pervasive in daily life but also highly focused on the dead. Mummification and funeral magic helped elite Egyptians journey through grim death to be reborn in the glorious afterlife. Many magical amulets were created and rituals performed to assist the dead, but the most important item was a bespoke magical papyrus called *Spells of Coming Forth By Day*, which was read by priests and relatives at funerals. Sometimes it was inscribed on tomb walls or placed directly on the mummy, as an empowering talisman. Within the elaborate text, drawings showed the deceased enjoying themselves as a spirit, while spells and prayers besought the aid of gods such as Thoth, Horus and Osiris.

Antiquity created many imposing, intriguing and intricate magical traditions. The druids of Celtic Britain and Gaul (today's Western and Central France) were so distinctive that foreign observers gave them their unique name, derived from Celtic terminology. Like Persia's magi, these seemingly awesome practitioners became renowned in distant lands. The oldest known reference to druidic magic occurs in *Magikos* (*c.* 380–300 BCE), a now lost Greek magical text falsely attributed to Aristotle. However, we know little for certain about the druids, because most evidence of them comes from unverified Roman observers. Julius Caesar's account of the Gallic Wars (58–50 BCE) explains that the druids kept their secrets close and passed on knowledge only by word of mouth. Apparently, they were responsible for law, religion, philosophy and human sacrifices, including mass burnings of people bound inside huge figures of woven wood (a detail that inspired the 1973 movie *The Wicker Man*). Tacitus's *Annals* (*c.* 109 CE) describe awesome druid battle magic. On the shores of Anglesey, last island bastion of Celtic resistance,

Jasper and gold heart scarab, Egypt, *c.* 1590 BCE
This scarab, placed on the mummy of Sobekemsaf II, is the earliest known example produced for a king. Like other heart scarabs, it was a magical safeguard that helped the deceased in the afterlife by ensuring that the heart did not testify against its owner. The underside (right) contains a spell for this purpose. The inscription omits the legs of the hieroglyphic birds to prevent them attacking the deceased.

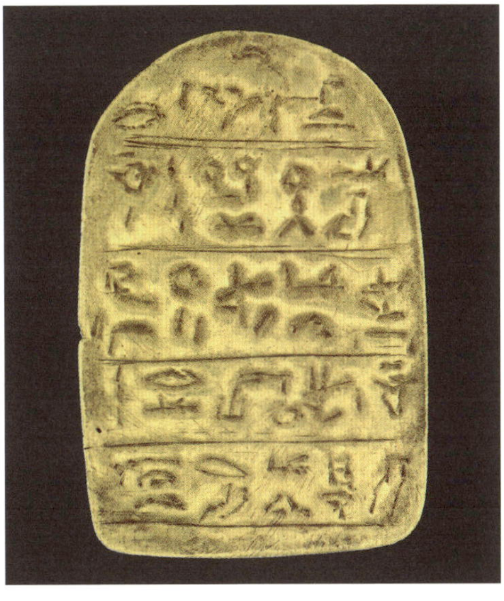

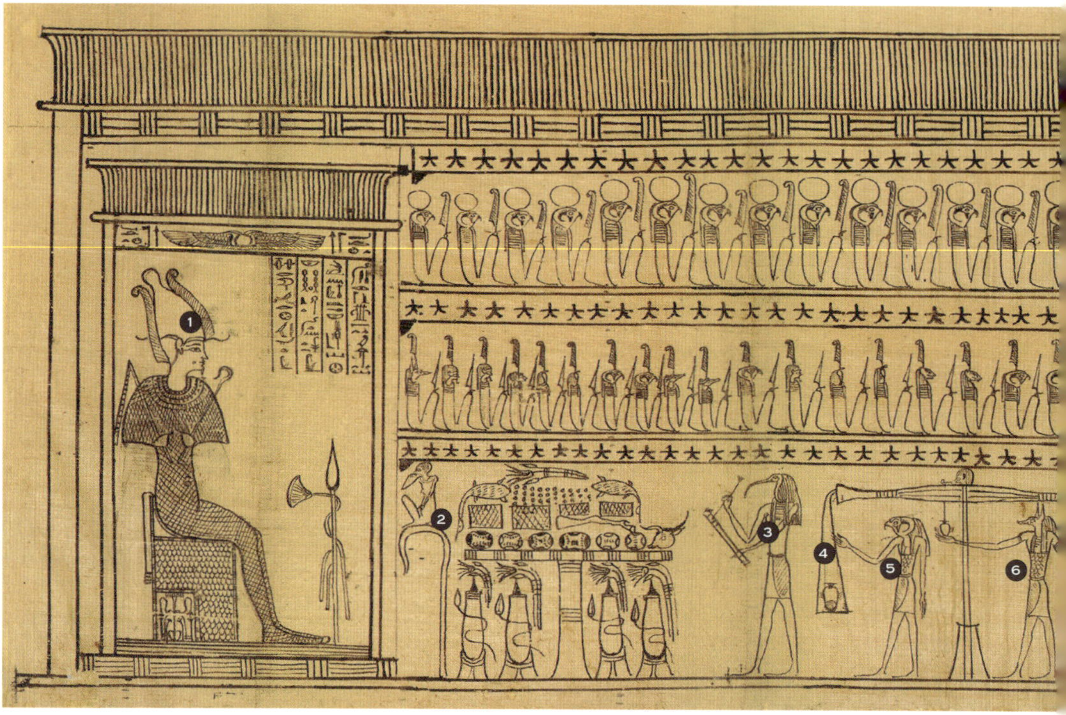

1.

2.

3.

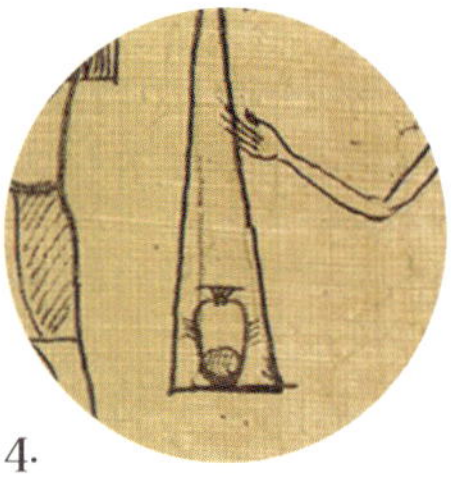

4.

DECODING SPELLS OF COMING FORTH BY DAY (BOOK OF THE DEAD)

Spells of Coming Forth By Day, known today as *The Egyptian Book of the Dead*, was a funerary text that helped mummified Egyptians journey through the underworld to be reborn in the afterlife. This example, for a priest named Imhotep (332–200 BCE), is unusually complete. A vast papyrus written primarily in hieratic cursive script, it contains 182 columns of spells, prayers and incantations. This scene depicts the 'judgment of the heart'. It determined whether the deceased's spirit could leave the tomb either to enter paradise, visit the mortal world or follow the sun god Ra through the sky.

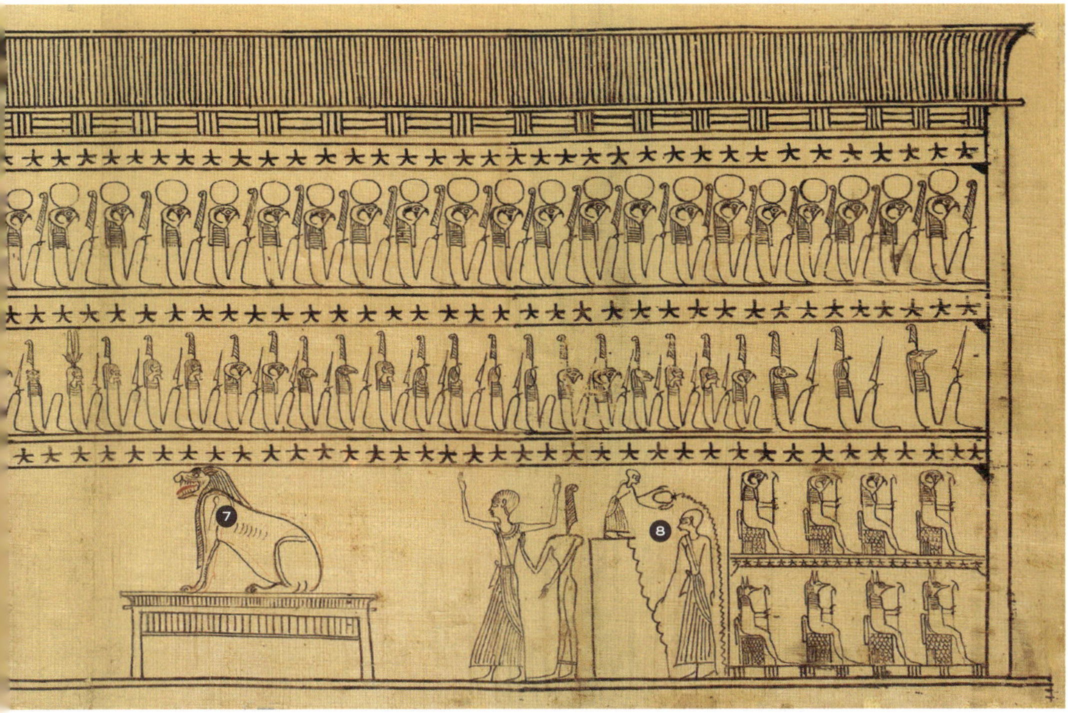

5.

6.

7.

8.

1. Osiris: the god of resurrection and the afterlife sits in judgment.
2. Ba: a bird-headed human represents the deceased's 'ba' or spirit. They stand in front of a table of offerings.
3. Thoth: the ibis-headed god of writing and magic records the result.
4. Heart: Imhotep's heart is weighed against the feather of Maat, the god of justice. If the deceased's heart weighs more than the feather, the spirit will not achieve eternal life.
5. Horus: the falcon-headed god of rule and protection assists in the judgment.
6. Anubis: the jackal-headed god of mummification and funerary rites weighs the heart. He is protector of tombs and also the guide who leads souls into the underworld.
7. Ammit: the crocodile, lion and hippo hybrid-monster waits, mouth open and tongue out, on an offering table. He will eat the heart if its owner is deemed unworthy and Imhotep will die forever.
8. Imhotep: the deceased is depicted being purified with water before raising his arms in supplication as he enters the scene of judgment.

Druid wicker colossus engraving, from *Magasin Pittoresque*, France, 1833

According to Julius Caesar, the druids of ancient Gaul and Britain made sacrifices of people and animals trapped inside huge figures made of woven wood, which were then set alight.

the druids supposedly raised their arms skywards, calling down showers of curses on the Romans. The invaders were briefly awestruck and exposed, until the generals began a rally. It is possible this event happened: magicians have played important roles in many anti-colonial struggles and in battles generally in traditional societies, as British anthropologist Neil L. Whitehead (1956–2012) discovered when he studied war shamanism in 1990s Guyana.

Ancient Indians developed the magical connections between astrology and precious stones. Around 3,000 years ago, Hindus also created a corpus of everyday religious devotions mixed with magic in the form of the Atharvaveda or Atharva Veda. Its 20 books, 6,000 verses and more than 700 hymns contain a wealth of healing charms, curses and prayers, as well as defensive and love magic. In the 21st century, we can still feel the universal relevance of many of these rites. Some incantations address anger, bullying and jealousy in families and communities: 'Indra, overcome the plan and mind of the jealous.' Many maintain health and combat illness. Others ensure prosperity and success: 'May that generous man be our friend.' Elsewhere across South and East Asia, tantric varieties of Buddhism developed elaborate forms of magical divination, cursing, healing and protection.

Magical traditions were mixed and debated in the ancient civilizations of Greece and Rome. Details of Greek, Egyptian, Roman and other practices were combined to create the complex texts known today as the Greek magical papyri, between about 100 BCE and 400 CE. Supernatural powers were widely credited, but doubts existed, too, in constant dialogue with belief. Homer's *Odyssey* voices uncertainties about omens. Aristotle (384–322 BCE) was sceptical of allegedly prophetic dreams. Cicero's dialogue *On Divination* (44–45 BCE) gives arguments for and against using supernatural means to gain insight into the future, leaving it up to readers to decide. In this debating culture, unappealing and unreliable forms of magic were abandoned. Cicero (106–43 BCE) thought that divination from observing the behaviour of birds (augury) was less used in his day than it had been in earlier periods.

Judaism and Christianity attacked several styles of ancient magic. The Old Testament denounced harmful witchcraft, soothsaying and spirit summoning. According to the New Testament's Acts of the Apostles, Jesus's followers repeatedly challenged powerful magicians. After Roman emperor Constantine converted to Christianity in 312 CE, he tightened existing prohibitions against higher forms of magic. In *The City of God* (*c.* 413–*c.* 426 CE), St Augustine of Hippo argued that magic was satanic because it was done with the explicit or implicit assistance of demons. Yet despite these assaults, magic thrived. Particularly victimized forms went underground while new versions of magic emerged, rich with ingredients from Judaism and Christianity. King Solomon the Wise, builder of the First Temple in Jerusalem, was famed for his magical learning, while his six-pointed star became a powerful magical symbol. Angels, saints, holy figures and prayers to the God of Abraham entered the repertoire of magic.

By the Middle Ages, magic was enormously diverse. Divination alone contained endless sub-categories. Aeromancy interpreted sneezes and winds. Pyromancy saw signs in fire. Hydromancy perceived mystical

Corinthian column krater (mixing bowl), Greece, *c.* 575–550 BCE
This large krater depicts a boar being hunted with spears and hounds attacking it from the front and back. The bird flying above the boar is an augury: a divinatory sign of hunting success.

‹ **Malnazar and Aghap'ir, *Solomon Writing*, 1630s**
This work from the Persian illuminated manuscript titled Bible *depicts Solomon, fourth king of Israel, who was famed for his magical learning.*

› **Masonic Seal of the Grand Chapter of London, 1769–1817**
Formed of two interlaced triangles, the Seal of Solomon was an influential magical and mystical symbol.

knowledge in water. Geomancy involved earth and dice. Scapulimancy used shoulder blades and bones. Medieval religious and secular laws officially prohibited many types of magic, especially the most profane (demon summoning) and anti-social (harmful witchcraft). Yet these laws were not often enacted. Magic was largely ignored, by states and religions: the major creators of grimoires (books of magic) were clerics and priests.

On the cusp of the modern age, the suppression of magic increased. Between the 15th and 18th centuries, harmful witchcraft became more feared and persecuted across Europe and colonial America. Around 70,000 to 100,000 people, mostly women, were tried for crimes of sorcery. Around half were found guilty and executed: 35,000 to 50,000 people. Professional magicians, selling magical services to help clients, were not often persecuted; grimoires were not the main target. But clerics started to become less involved in producing magical texts and providing magical services, as did elites generally.

Magic gradually became more alternative and less mainstream. As it did, authorities began suppressing the trade in magical services on the grounds that it

DECODING WITCHES' SABBATH

The Witches' Sabbath (1607) by Frans II Francken depicts a debauched nocturnal revel in which harmful magicians meet with their demonic masters. Night witches, who supposedly convened under cover of darkness to practise magic and immorality, were feared by people worldwide, from antiquity to contemporary sub-Saharan Africa. Among early modern Europeans, during the period of the witch trials, the witches' sabbath inspired elaborate fantasies and terrors. Witches were depicted in starkly binary terms, as the negative of everything good, moral, pious, normal, rational and orderly. Their sabbaths were orgies of magic, depravity and chaos.

1. Rays: luminous beams depict the magical forces unleashed by the witches' spells.
2. Flight: flying was supposedly enabled by demons and enchanted objects smeared with magical ointment.
3. Bleeding post: witches were said to syphon milk from their neighbours' cows with a blade stuck in a wooded post. Some witch trials heard that the same method was used to torment human victims.
4. Rich witch: wearing fine clothes and jewelry, she represents the early modern fear that witches exist throughout society. Uncovered hair and an exposed chest convey uncontrolled sexuality.
5. Hand of Glory: made from a hanged-man's hand, this charm was supposed to paralyse or shut the eyes of the victims of theft.
6. Toads: poisonous animals were closely linked with harmful witchcraft. Toads especially were connected with witches, as familiars and spell ingredients.
7. Cauldron weather magic: witches were sometimes blamed for causing storms, hail, snow and other harmful weather events.
8. Executioner witch: witches were sometimes accused of cannibalism and using human body parts in spells.
9. Magical ointment: witches were accused of creating magical ointment from human body parts.
10. Child witch: some said harmful

witches were inducted into the wicked craft by their parents and grandparents, as with this little girl.

11. Women: across the vast majority of early modern Europe, witches were thought to be more commonly women. Misogynistic tropes portrayed women as more sexual, envious and easily misled by demons.
12. Shapeshifter: witches were supposed to have the power to change form, often into aggressive or nocturnal animals. This allowed them to secretly spread their magic.
13. Demons: the idea that witchcraft was satanic, performed with the assistance of demons, became particularly prominent in Europe during the period of the witch trials.
14. Naked witches: witches were supposed to break every rule, including conventions of female sexual modesty and restraint.
15. Syphoning: demons steal souls and life force. Witches and their familiars were regarded as vampire-like, not only harming victims but also taking their health and wealth.
16. Grimoires: witches used books of spells for instructions and to inscribe powerful symbols during their rites.
17. Magic circle: witches were believed to use complex symbols, herbs and figurines for evil magic. Blood spiriting represents the life force the witches are extracting from victims.
18. Shears and sieve: these items were commonly used for divination and fortune-telling.

was false and fraudulent. England's Witchcraft Act of 1736 did not criminalize harmful witchcraft, but it did outlaw the selling of 'pretend' magical spells by wise-women, fortune-tellers, cunning-folk and wizards. Between the early and mid-1900s, governments and agencies worldwide began cracking down on mystical and magical healing. In South Korea, folk healers worked underground between the 1950s and 1970s. The World Health Organization embodied the rationalist spirit. Its first director-general, Canadian psychiatrist Dr George Brock Chisholm (1896–1971), appointed in 1948, severely criticized folklore and superstition, including Santa and lucky number 13.

Magic was too appealing and deeply rooted in human culture to be totally suppressed. From the 1700s, periodic occult revivals created new magical artworks and novel mystical traditions, many of which mingled magic with science. From the 1960s or 1970s, magic and mysticism underwent a particularly global and long-lived advance. The massive growth of academic scholarship about magic, which this book draws upon, is one manifestation of growing interest and acceptance. From the 1970s, the World Health Organization began promoting traditional and complementary medicine as an economical and effective form of health care, when pursued alongside clinical medicine. Anti-magic laws went unenforced or were repealed. Legislation prohibiting the Caribbean service magic of *obeah*, for example, was repealed in Anguilla (1980), Barbados (1998), Trinidad and Tobago (2000) and St Lucia (2004). Across the world, growing acknowledgment of human rights and particularly freedom of religion and conscience has made magical belief seem more legitimate. Feminism and ecology swelled interest. The Internet has made magical knowledge and magical services more available. As living standards have declined, particularly for younger generations during the early 21st century, interest in magical lifestyles and mystical therapies has grown. There will always be magic, but it grows when normal solutions are insufficient and conventional remedies fail.

Advert for an astrologer and psychic, New York City, USA, 2021

Magic explains and solves problems holistically across many areas of life, from love and money to education and divorce. Note the service advertised here for removing bad luck, black magic and curses.

I

1

EVERYDAY MAGIC

2

COMMUNITY EXPERTS

3

LOCAL MAGIC

LOW MAGIC

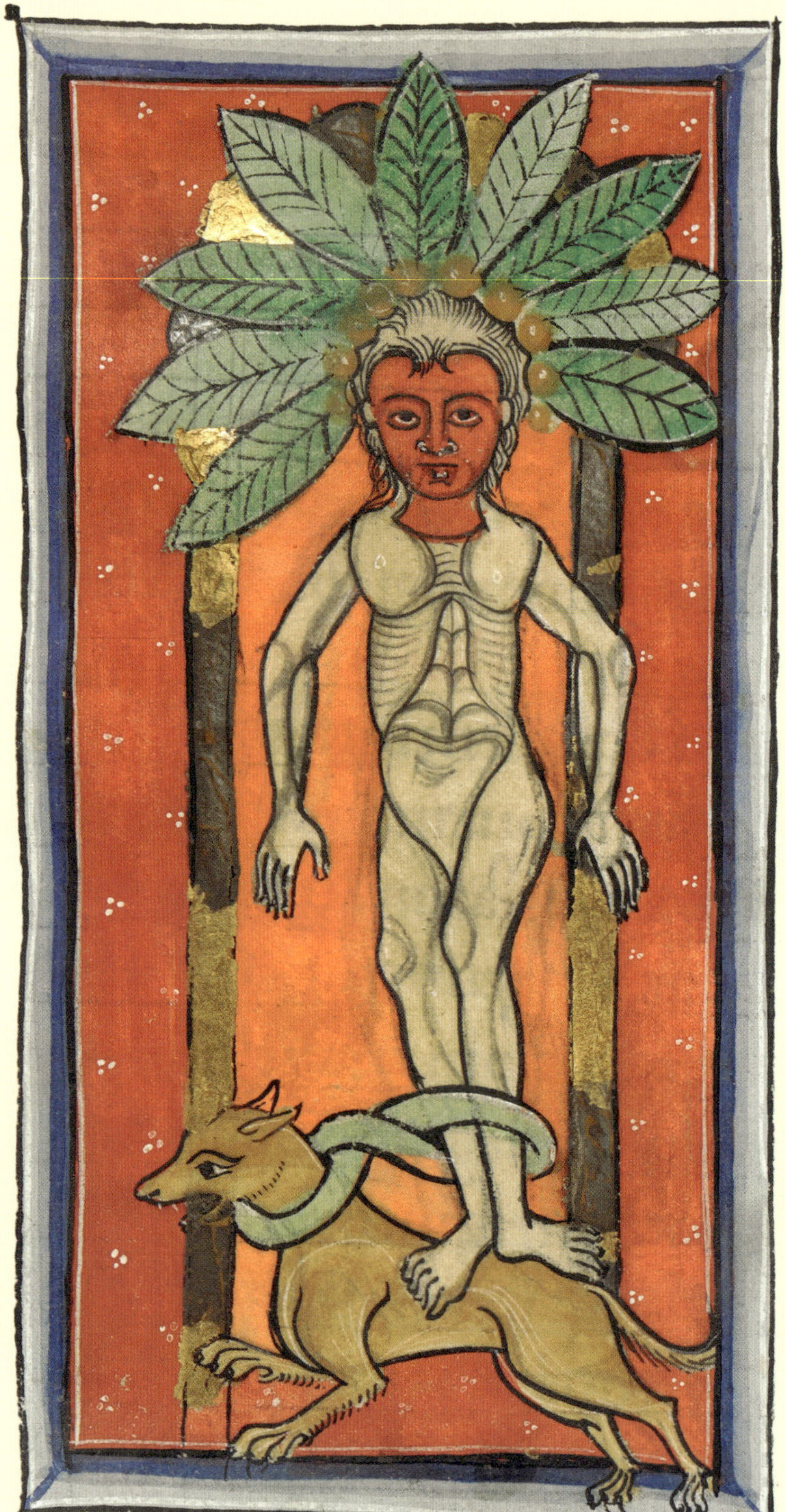

'IT WILL SCARCELY BE CONCEIVED HOW GREAT A NUMBER OF SUPERSTITIOUS NOTIONS AND PRACTICES ARE STILL REMAINING.'

FRANCIS GROSE,
A PROVINCIAL GLOSSARY (1787)

Everyday magic directs mystical powers towards common problems, anxieties and ambitions. Practical, unpretentious and solution-focused, this style of magic draws on many different sources, including oral folklore, accessible texts, religious ideas, expert teachings and, in recent decades, the Internet. Everyday magic is mainly practised by amateur magicians, often, although not always, women. Its principal focus is protecting self, home and family. However, everyday magic can also be used to look into the future, gain information, heal, foster romance, control, bind and do harm.

Today, as in the past, many ordinary people use magical rituals, charms, objects and spells to assist with common but tricky problems. Men often employ magic for their advantage, such as by performing luck-generating superstitions for occupations with anxious and risky outcomes like gambling, fishing, mining, hunting, fighting and sports. Certain magical gifts are associated with males in particular: in Scottish tradition, men were far more likely to possess 'second sight' to see ghosts and fairies. Men can be great magicians, yet in numerous cultures women tend to be highly adept at everyday magic, which they typically do on behalf of their loved ones as well as themselves. This female propensity for magic, combined unfortunately with misogynistic derision, is why common superstitions are often known by feminine names such as 'old wives' tales' in English, or 'grandmother tales' in Russian.

As a very broad generalization, it is probably fair to say that the primary purpose of everyday magic is defensive: to protect your mind, body, loved ones, home, property and future. Traditionally, safeguarding children was paramount, because these precious humans were especially vulnerable to natural dangers and supernatural threats, such as jinn, harmful witches, trolls and evil spirits. Historically, night was regarded as the key period for raising magical defences. Mystical forces were heightened, for good and ill, after the sun set and darkness fell. 'In darkness my children take most delight,' the English poet Lord Byron (1788–1824) made the Devil say. For anyone wishing to try more ambitious magic, night was the time.

Many cultures have warded off supernatural evil using recurrent magical and religious rituals. In Japan, at Setsubun on 3 February, people cast soybeans in a ceremony called *mamemaki* to attract good luck and repel evil spirits. During the holy month of Ramadan, many Muslims believe that some otherwise dangerous jinn spirits are prevented from pursuing their conflict with humanity. Seasonal protections or defences and special forms of divination sometimes go together. In Britain, this occurs at Halloween (31 October), the

« *page 44*
The Love Charm,
15th century
In this German oil painting, a naked woman enacts a love spell. She simultaneously strikes a flint and squeezes a sponge, so that sparks and water fall on a wax heart.

‹ *page 46*
Illuminated miniature of a mandrake plant (*Mandragora*) with a human-form root being pulled from the ground by a dog, from a Latin herbal and medical text, England or France, 12th century
Mandrake berries and roots have been widely associated with magic since ancient Mesopotamia. Many ancient writers, including Rome's Pliny the Elder, recorded that elaborate rituals were needed to harvest the mandrake plant.

Bean scattering (*mamemaki*), Yasaka Shrine Setsubun festival, Kyoto, Japan, 2024

Performers and crowds chant: 'Oni wa soto! Fuku wa uchi!' ('Out with the demons! In with good fortune!') while throwing the beans. The roasted and scattered soybeans are supposed to drive away demons and bring good fortune. After the ritual, it is considered lucky to eat the number of beans equal to your age plus one.

PROFILE
SUPERSTITIONS

The portion of people judged superstitious ranges from around one-third (a 2023 British poll counting people who described themselves as 'very' or 'somewhat' superstitious) to more than 90 per cent (a 2024 Israeli study that includes people who said they believed and unbelievers who still performed superstitions). Superstitions, which are mostly associated with luck, can be recent inventions or derived from the deep past. They can feel silly or embarrassing, yet superstitions also increase confidence, reduce negative expectations and soothe stressful moments by bringing touches of magic into everyday life.

1. *CROSSED FINGERS*
Crossing your fingers for good luck is so widespread in English-speaking countries that people say 'fingers crossed' without doing the gesture. Until the early 20th century, many people crossed legs, too. Central Europeans mostly press thumbs instead.

2. *SPILLING SALT*
In Europe, the Americas, Australasia and parts of Asia it is unlucky to spill salt. To negate ill-luck, throw salt over your left shoulder, because the Devil stands there. During the Renaissance, Jesus's betrayer, Judas Iscariot, was often depicted spilling salt.

3. *NEW BRIDE CARRIED OVER THE THRESHOLD*
A practice noted in Plutarch's *Roman Questions* (*c.* 100 CE), although the Greco-Roman historian did not know its origins. Some 19th-century Scots said that carrying a new bride over the threshold protected her against witchcraft.

4. *FOUR-LEAF CLOVER*
Now a lucky object worldwide, the superstition probably originated in Britain, where finding a four-leaf clover has been lucky since the Middle Ages. In 19th-century folklore, it was said that those bearing a four-leaf clover could see fairies.

5. *BLACK CAT*
A black cat is lucky to meet but unlucky to drive or chase away (because you would be driving away good fortune), according to English folklore. During the 17th and 18th centuries, many magical cures for witchcraft and other ailments used the bodies, blood or fur of black cats.

6. *MAGPIE*
The magpie is a bird of joy and prosperity in China and Korea. Among English-speaking peoples, seeing a single magpie has been bad luck ('one for sorrow') since medieval times. A chattering magpie, however, supposedly portended that a stranger would visit.

7. *STEPPING ON CRACKS*
Today, stepping on a pavement crack is unlucky or likely to break your mother's back. This notion evolved from a racist 19th-century superstition in England and the USA that warned that people who stepped on pavement cracks would have interracial relationships.

8. *WALKING UNDER A LADDER*
Though its origin is unknown, walking under a ladder is notoriously unlucky. In England, until the early 20th century, doing so meant you would not marry this year or you would be hanged. Spitting afterwards supposedly nullified the effect.

9. *LUCKY TOUCH*
From Russia to Latin America, many cultures knock on or touch wood or metal as a good luck gesture and to avert misfortune. The idea may have ancient origins, but some folklorists think that it stems from an early 19th-century children's game.

1.

2.

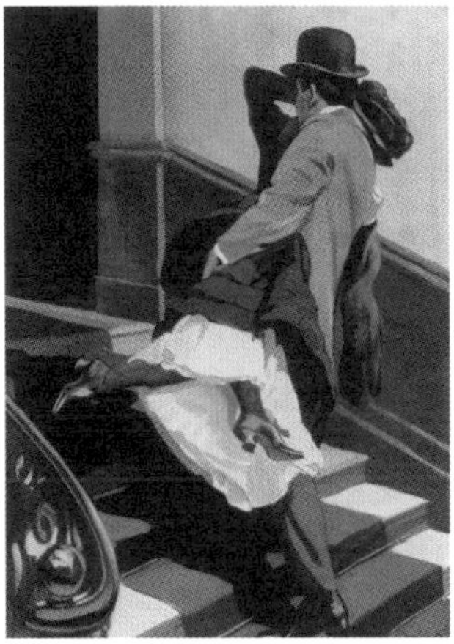

3.

4.

5.

6.

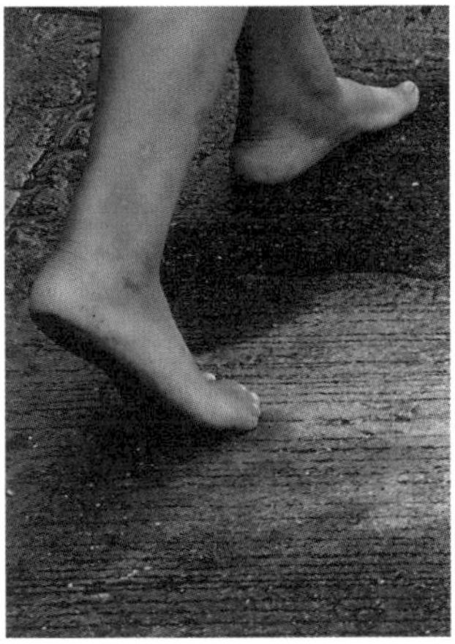

7.

8.

9.

Konstantin Makovsky, *Christmastide Divination*, *c.* 1905
A group of young women take part in the festive tradition of alectryomancy, or divination by rooster. They watch as the bird pecks grains, thereby answering their questions about marriage prospects.

night before All Souls Day (1 November). Contrary to a recent cliché, Halloween is not a modern invention. As historians of the ritual year such as Ronald Hutton (b. 1953) have shown, although there is little evidence that convincingly traces Halloween back to ancient pagan festivals, by the medieval period the peoples of both Ireland and Scotland saw Halloween as a time of heightened activity for fairies and other dangerous magical forces. During the 19th century, many people still conducted evil-repelling rites on Halloween, while gathering for stories and drinks around the fire. It was also a time for a special type of marriage divination. Blindfolded, you must select from three different dishes or pails, for clues about your future spouse. If the water is clean, they will be young. Dirty water means an old partner. And no water means no partner at all.

Everyday magic does far more than divine and defend. Among proactive and ambitious magical acts, perhaps the most enduring focus is love. We can see this in an accessible book of magic from 18th-century France: *Secrets Merveilleux de la Magie Naturelle et*

‹ **Pendant made from animal bone or tooth, Scotland, 7,000–4,000 BCE**
The crossed markings presumably gave this talisman particular power.

› **Vodou talisman, Haiti, 20th century**
This talisman is connected to the Gede family of loa *spirits, who are linked with death and fertility. It may have been used as a ritual focal point, to repel harm or to provide enhanced powers.*

Cabalistique du Petit Albert (*c.* 1702), known for short as the *Petit Albert*. To make someone love you is the aim of the first eleven spells, because there is nothing more natural 'than to love and be loved'. One typically grim rite involves drawing a little of your own blood on a Friday in spring, then drying it in the oven in a small pot along with two hare's testicles and a dove's liver. This mixture should be reduced to a fine powder then secretly put into the drink of the person 'on whom you have some design'. After dealing with love magic, the *Petit Albert* moves on to spells for making people dance naked, divining who you will marry, and causing and curing impotence. After that come spells for gambling and riches. Romance and prosperity are as important in magic as they are in life.

Amulets are the most common magical objects. According to a 2018 YouGov poll, a quarter of American adults wear some form of talisman or lucky charm. Some amulets are displayed openly; most though are worn secretly. Historically, many have been made of cheap perishable material, although others were amazingly ornate and enduring. Often amulets are purchased from magical experts, who make these potent items from various types of supernatural

Written charm to cure toothache, Scotland, late 1800s
This charm was purchased from a female magician at Kishorn in northern Scotland, then worn around the neck by a shepherd.

material. In the syncretic tradition of vodou in Haiti and Louisiana, manbos (priestesses), houngans (priests) and bokos (spellcasters) specialize in making 'gris-gris' amulet bags from herbs, written spells, hair, nails and animal bones. Of all magical items, nothing is so versatile as the amulet. Typically, it only requires two things: first, to be worn close to the body; second, to have faith in its power.

The most persistent adornment in the history of our species must surely be the magical amulet made of animal tooth, ivory, shell or bone. People wore these during much of human prehistory. In the ancient world, they were widely respected by great scholars and also common people. Pliny the Elder (23–79 CE) notes in his multivolume *Natural History* how 'bones, attached to the body as an amulet, are productive of advantageous effects.' Tooth and bone amulets remained extremely popular in the medieval and early modern periods, but they have faded somewhat in recent years because of a growing distaste for the suffering of animals.

Probably the most widespread protective amulets mix magic and religion. Many are holy words or charms, written either by clerics or service magicians. Sometimes, these pieces are worn temporarily, when a problem persists. For example, a written charm to cure toothache may be folded up, placed in a bag with a necklace and worn while the pain continues. Other written charms are folded and kept close to the

< **Emerald and gold amulet with magical symbols, Europe, 16th or 17th century**
Emeralds were supposed to provide protection and enhance cognitive powers. The symbols appear to be the sigil of Haagenti, President of Hell and master of alchemy.

> **Tumar triangular amulet holder, Central Asia or Iran, late 19th or early 20th century**
This silver and carnelian amulet holder contains a Quranic scroll. Amulets such as this were worn for protection by wealthy women among the nomadic Turkmen peoples in Central Asia.

sufferers, inside a pocket or underclothes. Text-based amulets, containing passages and prayers from the Quran and Hadith, are popular among Muslims worldwide. Some include additional magical symbols or even depictions of bound jinn, handcuffed and shackled, so they cannot do harm. Miniature Qurans, in octagonal amulet holders, were popular with Islamic warriors during the medieval and early modern eras.

The third major type of magical amulet features gems. Conventionally, the magi of Persia were supposed to have first imparted to humankind the knowledge of precious stones. In the final chapter of his *Natural History*, Pliny the Elder complains that those great priests credited too many mysterious powers to gemstones. Yet Pliny was not a complete sceptic. He wrote that amber benefits babies when attached to them as an amulet, and also related how other authors thought that amber necklaces protect people of all ages against fever and disease. According to a 15th-century English lapidary manuscript held in the library at Peterborough Cathedral, UK, emerald increases riches, guards against gout and makes the bearer's words 'feared'. Black jet, the same text notes,

PROFILE
AMULETS OF RELIGION AND MAGIC

Many amulets mingle religion with magic because together they are more powerful than magic or religion alone. Religious symbolism also sanctifies amulets, legitimating objects that otherwise may attract criticism. Religious amulets often contain magically significant colours or substances such as threads,

BES
This dwarf amulet from *c.* 1070–712 BCE protected the living and dead by frightening away dangers. Blue glaze symbolizes life and growth, providing it with additional power.

ST ROCH
During the Middle Ages, St Roch (1295–1327) was thought to protect and cure plague. In the 19th century, he acquired new abilities, including in amulets worn to protect against cholera.

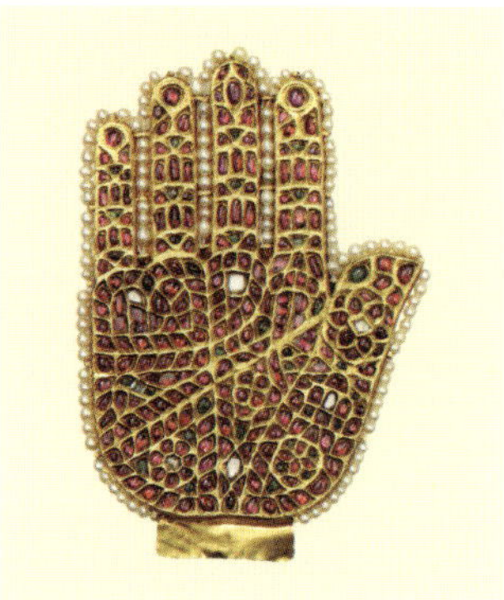

HAMSA
Also known as the 'hand of Fatima', this late 18th- or early 19th-century jewelled hamsa from India protected against dangers natural and supernatural.

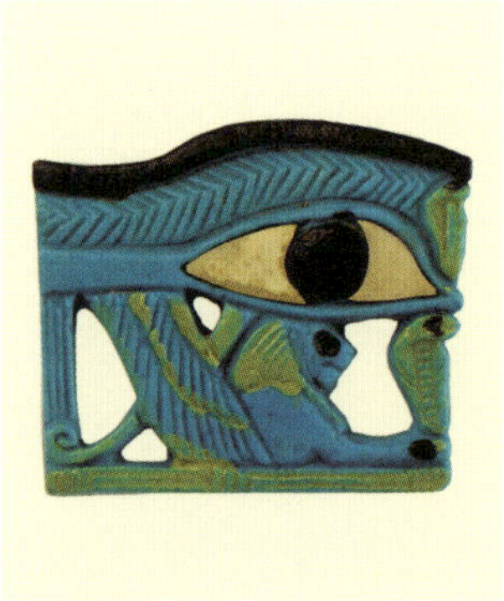

WEDJAT EYE
Known today as the 'Eye of Horus', this amulet (*c.* 1070–664 BCE) represents the falcon-headed god's eye, stolen by Seth but restored by Thoth. It evokes magical powers of healing.

HIPPO
This tomb figurine (*c.* 1961–1878 BCE) partly represents the protective ancient Egyptian goddess Taweret. Three broken legs stop the hippo harming the deceased in the afterlife.

HATHOR
The ancient Egyptian goddess Hathor is here depicted as a cow (*c.* 1070–656 BCE). Women often wore her amulets for fertility enhancement or protection during pregnancy and birth.

animal teeth, gems, shells or metals. Even amulets made from holy scriptures reflect magical beliefs about the supernatural powers of written text. Known as 'phylacteries' in Judaism and 'taviz' or 'taweez' in Islam, textual amulets can be found in most faiths.

ELECTROGALVANIC PENDANT
This American pendant from *c.* 1881 used the apparent healing power of electric currents to cure the wearer of a range of ailments.

ANKH
This ancient Egyptian wooden ankh dates to *c.* 1981–1802 BCE. The symbol was used in hieroglyphs to mean 'life', 'live' and 'alive', and it remains a potent symbol of life.

CIPPI OF HORUS
Cippi of Horus protected and healed against feral animals. This stela (*c.* 664–30 BCE) shows Horus standing on a crocodile, holding dangerous animals including scorpions.

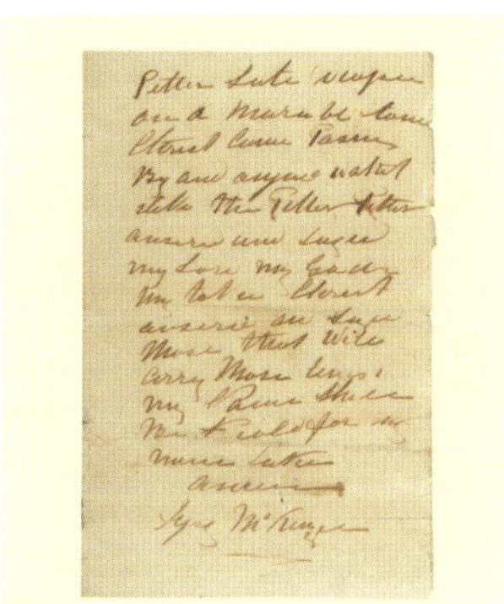

TOOTHACHE CURE
This 1869 charm, which features text telling an apocryphal biblical story about St Peter and Jesus, was made by a female charmer for a domestic servant in Dingwall, Scotland.

JAUNDICE CURE
This 18th-century European kabbalistic amulet would have been folded up and worn close to the body. Kabbalah experts catered to Jews and clients of other faiths.

PLAGUE PROTECTION
This Bavarian amulet (*c.* 1700) protects against disease by combining religious medallions, written prayers and images of Christian saints with magically potent seeds, threads and seals.

‹ ***Penca de balangandã*, Brazil, 19th century**
This penca is made of tin-plated copper, raffia palm nut, boar's tooth and wood. The grapes, fish, pineapple and mandarin evoke fertility. The cashew apple probably denotes vitality, and the dark wooden hand perhaps provides protection against the evil eye.

› **Woman wearing a *penca de balangandã*, Brazil, 1885**
This noisy and eye-catching accessory, attached at the waist, was both a store of value and a source of magical powers. Pencas were said to provide strength, fertility, wealth, protection and more.

cures swellings, repels harmful witchcraft and can be immersed in water to produce a drink that helps women in labour. Turquoise, with its light and milky-blue colour, has often been thought to protect against the evil eye. In Central Asia in *c.* 1000 CE, it was commonly said that a turquoise gemstone pendant would burst or crack if someone with the evil eye looked at the wearer.

Between the 17th and 19th centuries, kidnapped people of African heritage devised new amulets to fortify themselves against the struggles of slavery, and to cope with life's general troubles. In Brazil, Africans and their descendants created the *penca de balangandã*. Made by local artisans, a *penca* (meaning 'bouquet') *de balangandã* (an onomatopoetic term evoking the sound of charms jangling) was worn for adornment and also wealth-storage (they were passed through generations and are mentioned in wills). Yet its primary purpose was magical, often for protection, but also for power, success and love. *Penca de balangandã* mixed African, Catholic and indigenous traditions. Multiple charms mingled together, generating various desirable magical effects.

〈 **Silver engraved amulet, USA, *c.* 1776**
According to tradition, this amulet was made to hold the caul or amniotic sac of Samuel Moffatt of Portsmouth, New Hampshire. The caul was believed to secure luck, strength and protection from drowning.

〉 **Gold finger ring with red stone and runic inscription, Denmark, *c.* 1100**
The ring is inscribed with the words: 'AROTA AGLAGALA LAGA'. Arota comes from the Greek word for virtue (areté). Agla is formed from a Hebrew phrase meaning 'You are strong for eternity, Lord!'.

Gruesome magical amulets can be made from human body parts. Among the least grizzly are those associated with the amniotic sac or caul. Around one in 80,000 babies are born while still inside the amniotic sac: they have often been said to possess enhanced powers, to be lucky and to be able to avoid death by drowning. During the 17th-century age of naval warfare and World War I, cauls sold for considerable sums. Over the centuries, some caul bearers made them into amulets, to keep close and provide enduring protection. In recent years, some African hospitals have been accused of selling human remains to *muti* (a South African term for traditional medicine) amulet makers. In horrifying cases, people with albinism and others have been murdered for this appalling trade.

Rings, usually worn on a finger (rather than an ear, toe or arm), have for millennia served many magical functions. The circle is a unique symbol of protection and wholeness: perhaps, this is why 'a mysterious significance has been associated with rings from the earliest periods', as Victorian antiquarian William Jones (1817–85) notes in his study *Finger-ring Lore* (1877). During the 19th century, some English people believed that a ring made of silver sixpences begged from unmarried men could prevent fits. However, it only worked 'if worn with faith', a folklorist working in

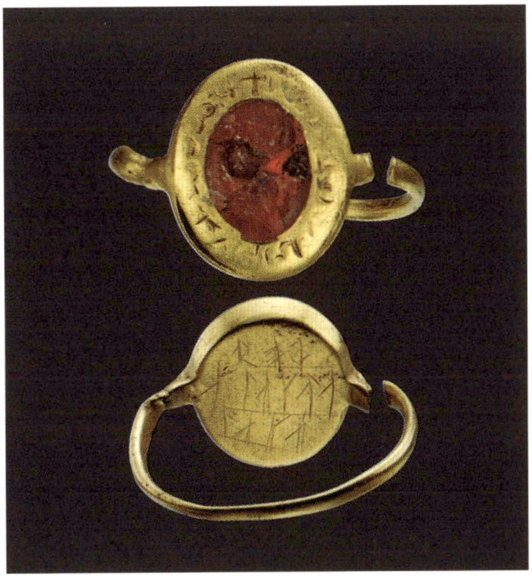

Gold, enamel and toadstone finger rings, Europe, 16th or 17th century
Toadstone, made from fossilized fish teeth, was widely believed to protect against poison, fever and supernatural harm. As the 'king of metals,' gold was said to help wearers resist disease.

the county of Sussex noted. Rings were also used in common spells for purposes like divination: to find out how long you would be married, you should attach a ring to a hair or thread then count the number of times the ring oscillates in a glass. In 19th-century Slavic folklore, meanwhile, a broken wedding ring was a terrible omen that meant one of the couple would soon die.

Tales of powerful rings have peppered myth and legend since classical times. In the *Republic* (*c.* 375 BCE), Plato (*c.* 428–423–*c.* 348/347 BCE) explores the concept of virtue by telling the story of the Ring of Gyges, which grants invisibility. In ancient Greece and Rome, many rings were engraved with gods such as Hermes or Mercury, who was not only a messenger but also a healer and magician. Deities like Fortune or Victory were useful during dangerous times of war and conflict. The Vikings and Anglo Saxons used runic inscriptions to enhance talismanic rings with scriptural references and magically potent words. Among Muslims, protective rings often bore holy verses. Some were also marked with the Seal of Solomon, the Israelite king, who – according to Islamic tradition – could command jinn. Church fathers including Gregory of Nyssa (*c.* 335–395 CE) advised Christians to preserve themselves from evil by wearing rings featuring sacred items like the sign of the cross or fragments of Holy Wood. Throughout medieval Christendom, images of Solomon and other holy figures were commonly

  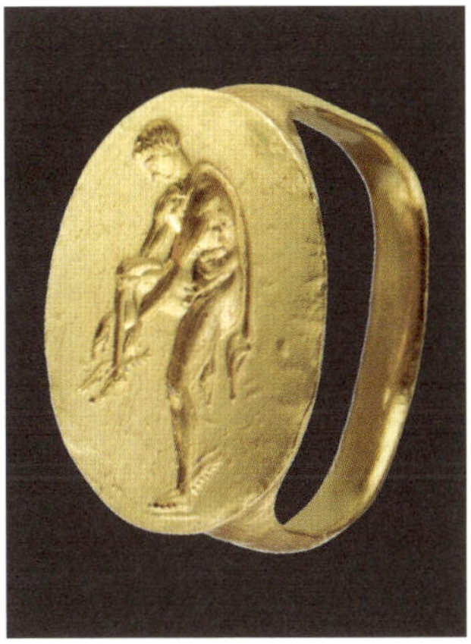

< **Gold finger rings with Christian and other symbolism**
These medieval rings from Denmark (left and centre) were worn to avert harm on many levels. The ring on the left (1375–1425), from Helgenæs cemetery, Jutland, shows the crucifixion. The rope-effect decoration on the central ring, which is from Lynge, North Zealand, was said to evoke fidelity and protection.

> **Gold ring of Hermes, Greek Southern Italy, 4th century BCE**
The messenger god is depicted lacing his sandals at dawn, symbolizing divine speed, readiness and vigilance.

inscribed on ring metal and gemstones, for protection and healing.

Gold, in medieval and early modern Europe, was regarded as magical. It purified the body, strengthened the heart, limited fever and more, according to many authorities. Rubies, diamonds, emeralds and especially sapphires were regarded as multifunctional but particularly protective against poison, whether natural or supernatural. These gemstones, however, were dizzyingly expensive. Partly for this reason, protective rings were often set with a cheaper but magically potent material called toadstone. Also known in the past as 'crappot' and 'crapaudine', toadstone was said to come from the head of a toad. In reality, it was the rounded and fossilized teeth of the *Lepidotes* fish. Insect stings, venom, kidney disease, poison, witchcraft, fairies, demons and more were all supposed to be diverted into the ruddy brown fossil. Touching toadstone, on a ring or amulet, gave additional protection at key moments. Some believed that it gave off heat, cracked or changed colour if its wearer was infected with poison, whether normal or magical. Toadstone was also supposed to have empowering effects. According to a 15th-century manuscript held at Peterborough Cathedral, the stone made men and women 'mighty'.

Clothes, weapons, armour, belts and other jewelry all have defensive magical functions for some. Among

DECODING HILYA

Islamic hilyas are talismanic scrolls containing descriptions of the Prophet Muhammad, blessed names of God and magical iconography. They were sometimes given as housewarming gifts and the scrolls were believed to help prevent misfortune in this and the next world. Many were created as talismans, to be folded, enclosed in an amulet and worn close to the body. Making hilyas developed into an art form during the Ottoman Empire, from around the 17th century. This example was made by master calligrapher al-Haj Musa in Istanbul in April or May 1712, using ink and gold on paper, backed with green silk.

1.

CRESCENT SHAPES
There are two crescents with text describing the person and character of Muhammad: the upper is in Arabic; the lower is in Ottoman Turkish.

2.

CENTRAL CIRCLE
The central circle details this hilya's particular powers: to gain the release of hostages and provide protection against accidents and illnesses.

3.

FOLD LINES
Pronounced creases indicate that this hilya was folded up and placed into an amulet, to be worn for protection and assistance.

4.

QURANIC VERSES
Square panels at each corner contain Quranic verses invoking the Prophet and his companions, and more of the ninety-nine names.

5.

HAND OF FATIMA
The hand of Fatima, also known as the 'hamsa', is drawn on the lower crescent. This symbol was, and is, widely believed to repel danger.

6.

NINETY-NINE NAMES
The border of panels is filled with numbers, several of which give some of the ninety-nine names of Allah in numerical or alphabetical form.

ابو بكر
عمر
عثمان
علي
1
2
3
4
5
6

Kris dagger, Java, 12th to 15th century (above); kris dagger, Bali, 16th to 19th century (below)
These asymmetrical daggers were used as both weapons and magical objects that brought good luck, protection, influence, strength and more.

medieval Muslim soldiers, blades and chainmail were sometimes inscribed with Quranic verses and mysterious symbols. In Java, an asymmetrical dagger called a kris conferred upon its bearer magical protection, luck and other benefits. Earrings could hold magical symbols, like the Star of Solomon, or gems, such as turquoise, for protection. Since the 1980s, the red thread of Kabbalah has spread from Jewish folk magic to the wider New Age scene: tied around the left wrist, it is supposed to provide luck and strength against the evil eye. Some advocates trace the practice back to the Book of Genesis, to a midwife who tied scarlet thread around Zerah. Maybe. But thread generally, and red thread especially, has long been used in protective magic, from China to Africa and beyond.

House protection is a huge part of everyday magic. In the Irish countryside until the early 1900s, some people drew circled crosses on cottages or walls around fields to repel fairies. Respectful offerings, echoing sacrifices made long ago to ancient gods, were another strategy. A little milk, some potatoes, a drop of whisky or just a bowl of water would keep the fairies happy, at least for now. Plants, trees and herbs were often used for magical defence. Hanging

< **Tomb guardian figurine, China, 8th century**
Such figurines were supposed to protect the deceased from malevolent spirits. They were meticulously placed in the entrances of tombs belonging to rulers and other elites.

> **Glazed earthenware demon tile, China, 6th or 7th century**
This is one of a number of tiles that probably lined the walls of a tomb to protect the deceased from harmful powers.

rosemary, ivy and mistletoe in a house was commonly reckoned to be good against witchcraft, as noted by English astrologer William Drage (*c.* 1636–69) in his treatise of 1665 about practical magic. Across Europe, rosemary bushes were (and perhaps still are) planted in front gardens for magical defence. Traditionally, they were supposed to keep nocturnal witches too busy to enter the house, because they would be stuck counting every leaf until sunrise, when they would be forced to leave. Similarly, African Americans living in the American South in the early 1900s left brooms near entrances, in the hope that witches would count every straw, and sieves, so that they would count every hole. Red pepper was put in shoes or hung on doors as a counter-charm against hoodoo in early 20th-century Mississippi. Salt was also scattered around houses to repel evil.

Vast stores of magical items protect buildings and the people inside. China has a beautiful but slightly macabre tradition of earthenware tile decorations featuring frightening demons. Demonic faces look out from ancient tomb doors to scare off would-be robbers. If anyone gets past them, terrifying little earthenware

PROFILE
HOUSE PROTECTION

Innumerable objects, symbols and spells have been used to magically protect homes and gardens. The following examples, taken from the folklore of Europe and its diaspora, were widely observed between the early modern era and the 19th century.

WITCH BOTTLES
Filled with hair, nails, bent pins and cloth images, these bottles were heated, buried or placed up the chimney to break harmful spells through magical retaliation.

HAG STONES
These stones were hung on beds to stop nightmares, which were associated with witchcraft, or placed around buildings and gardens for protection.

ROWAN CROSSES
Fixed on doors, windows and chimneys to keep out evil. These crosses were more effective if made on magically special days, such as May Eve.

WITCH POSTS
Carved with a diagonal cross and located near hearths, witch posts were used in North Yorkshire, England, between the 17th and 19th centuries to repel harmful spirits.

HEXAFOILS
This symbol was found in Europe and beyond from the Bronze Age. Later, it was carved on beams, walls and doors to protect buildings and their inhabitants.

WITCH MARKS
For protection, two interlocking Vs – likely derived from a medieval term for St Mary, *Virgo Virginum* (Virgin of Virgins) – were etched into beams or walls.

WITCH STONES
On the Channel Island of Jersey, stones added to chimneys acted as resting places for flying witches. Some protective magic placated evildoers.

WITCH CHIMNEYS
In Spain's Aragon region, in the 17th and 18th centuries, geometric shapes on chimney flutes were commonly used to confuse witches.

PLANTS
Some plants were said to protect if grown in gardens or hung up. Rosemary, bay and ivy were used in Europe. Chilli peppers were popular in the USA.

‹ **Holed stone or hag stone, Britain, 19th century**
Hag stones were supposed to protect against harmful witchcraft and bad dreams.

› **Marian or witch mark, Ireland, 1619**
This mark on the beam of the former St Mary's Church, Kilkenny, was made to repel evil.

demon models await inside. Homes were protected by hanging scrolls of lucky or evil-repelling themes, such as Zhong Kui the fearsome demon queller.

A horseshoe was seen as an easy way to repel witchcraft and bring good luck throughout Europe and its diasporas. Also useful was a holed stone, known in Britain as a hag stone. A large hag stone could be placed in a field or near buildings. Or an example could be dangled from the roof or rafters of a barn to stop witches magically syphoning off the milk and cream from the cows. If hung on a bed, a hag stone was supposed to stop nightmares. Across Europe and its colonies, old shoes were deposited in roofs and walls for magical defence. For the same purpose, written charms were sometimes hidden in rafters, silver spoons placed within walls and open scissors left near windows.

Magical markings are relatively easy forms of house protection. Five- and six-pointed stars were scratched into mortar and carved on wooden beams. Interlocking Vs, sometimes today known as witch marks, were meant to provide protection from harmful witches and other dangers. According to British archaeologist Brian Hoggard (b. 1971), the letter Vs probably derive from a Latin holy phrase, meaning 'Virgin of Virgins'. Another powerful symbol, found throughout Europe

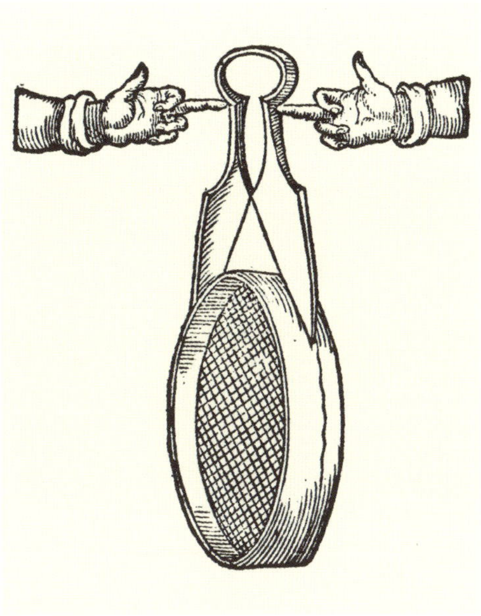

‹ **James Walker, *The Spell, or Hobnelia*, 1783**
This print depicts a popular divination rite, involving a snail drawing a trail to form a future husband's initials.

› **Illustration from the work of Cornelius Agrippa, Europe, 1530s**
This illustration shows the practice of coscinomancy, or divination with a sieve.

and colonial America, was a circle containing six ellipses: the hexafoil or daisy wheel. It forms the basis of the flower of life symbol, widely used today in crystal healing and protective magic.

Omens, based on happenings in the natural and human world, were supposed to help people glimpse the future. In 18th-century England, 1 May was a customary day for blindfolded girls to search for slugs and snails to place on a surface covered with flour or ashes. The molluscs' slimy trails were supposed to form the initials of a future lover's name. Fortune-telling offered greater insight, typically using questions that could be answered with 'Yes' or 'No'. Specific divination methods were endless, but many included the gentle turning of an object. One particularly ancient and enduring form of this was coscinomancy – fortune-telling by turning a sieve. It goes back at least to ancient Greece and was mentioned in the Salem witch trials of 1691. The exact method remains mysterious, but the best indication is provided by an image in the work of Renaissance occultist Cornelius Agrippa (1486–1535). Seemingly, the sieve is suspended in a pair of shears, held upright by two single fingers of two different people. A charm was said, too, at Salem: 'By Saint Peter and Saint Paul, if Hagget be dead, let this sieve turn around.'

If illness struck, natural or unnatural, herbs were a solution. They were not merely pharmacological remedies. Herbs supposedly interacted with the planets, and picking them at certain times increased or enabled their potency. This was explained by texts such as *Complete Herbal* by English physician Nicholas Culpeper (1616–54), which featured on many everyday magicians' bookshelves, between its publication in 1653 and the 1800s. It notes that a bay tree in the garden protects from witchcraft, the Devil and lightning. Betony (*Stachys officinalis*) is good against liver disease, epidemics and witchcraft, while the vine known as bittersweet nightshade (*Solanum dulcamara*) is also effective against harmful sorcery.

If disasters persisted and conventional remedies failed, people sometimes began to suspect that harmful witchcraft was the cause. In early modern Europe, sufferers and their families quite often attempted to force alleged evildoers to renounce their spells and pronounce blessings on the supposed victim. Another alternative was to send harmful magic back to the purported witch. One basic way of doing this involved subjecting bewitched property to fire or red-hot implements. Some people made witch bottles, containing the afflicted person's urine, nails, hair and bent pins, which were then buried or heated over a fire. It was supposed to leave the witch in agony, unable to relieve themselves and forced to relent.

Others tried to kill their witch with magic. Stabbing pins into an animal's heart was a method of deadly counter-magic practised across Europe until the early 20th century. It had to be done with ceremony, and at night (preferably at midnight), with all windows and doors closed. Everyone in the house was forced to listen to biblical curses being read while the animal's heart was stuck with pins and roasted. However, if the situation was so bad that murderous counter-magic was necessary, perhaps the assistance of a magical expert would be required.

> *pages 72–73*
Jules Breton, *The Feast of Saint John*, 1875
Across historical Europe and beyond, one of the most magical nights was St John's Eve (23 June), before the feast of John the Baptist (24 June). Demons, fairies and other evil powers supposedly went forth. To ward off these dangers, people danced, built fires, made amulets and conducted protective rituals. Because magical powers were heightened, St John's Eve was also a time for divination and herbalism.

Charm against witchcraft, Scotland, 19th century

This calf's heart was stuck with pins then roasted, probably while denunciatory biblical psalms were read. The aim was to harm or kill a witch who was supposedly responsible for wrongdoing.

'COULD YOU HAVE CURED HIM?'

'CERTAINLY, UP TO THE LAST DAY. BUT I HAVE TO BE BELIEVED IN … HE DIED BECAUSE HE WOULDN'T BELIEVE IN IT.'

JEANNE FAVRET-SAADA, *DEADLY WORDS: WITCHCRAFT IN THE BOCAGE*, TRANS. CATHERINE CULLEN (1980)

Community experts provide powerful magic to anxious, suffering and desperate clients – often for a fee, although not always. Service magicians span very many traditions and styles. Shamans and medicine people use music and rhythm in public rituals. By contrast, historical Europe's cunning-folk mostly worked magic privately. Worldwide, community experts supply magic for broadly similar purposes, including divination, healing, exorcism, defence, anti-witchcraft, love and success. Experiences vary, yet clients of the best community experts find their magic empowering, helpful and therapeutic.

2 COMMUNITY EXPERTS 2

Community experts provide supercharged magical assistance. They are called upon when things go badly wrong, when serious dilemmas arise and when desires or needs cannot be met by conventional methods. In desperate, anxious or hopeless moments. When normal techniques have failed, other avenues are closed, and amateur magic is not enough. During deeply trying times, service magicians offer to use strange and powerful abilities on their clients' behalf. Usually they charge a fee. Occasionally, it is quite a significant sum. Some magical experts are paid in kind, while a few give away their services at low or no charge to poor clients whom they deem worthy.

Service magicians belong to innumerable traditions. Some experts are highly religious priestly figures, who provide a strictly white sort of magic that is concerned with defence and healing. In China, a fashi was a Daoist ritual master who made healing talismans, exorcized evil spirits, conducted funeral rites and performed *jiao* (offerings) for community harmony. Other service magicians sell grey varieties of magic that control or black spells that harm. Some community experts offer more targeted and specific services, like the ubiquitous street and store fortune-tellers of historical and contemporary East Asia.

Despite many differences, community experts tend to ask clients to adopt a mindset that is at least open to the process. Healers of harmful witchcraft, working in Western France during the 1960s, would say that the clients who believed the most were the easiest to heal. By contrast, as anthropologist Jeanne Favret-Saada (b. 1934) observed, patients who could not bring themselves to fully believe in a magician's treatment were often blamed for its failure.

Across much of the world, magicians and magician-priests use their powers for public benefit. Kongolese banganga (ritual specialists) create *nkisi* statues to protect villages from evildoers. Shamans and medicine people from Siberia to the Americas employ magic to assist hunting and war parties, control the weather and defend their communities against other magicians. In the wake of Haiti's earthquake in 2010, vodou

< *page 74*
Sangoma (Zulu and African healer and medium) wearing traditional costume, Lesotho, *c.* 2009
Sangomas often wear vibrant clothes to signify their special role in connecting the living with the spirit world. Animal skins evoke courage, authority, protection and power. Beads and colours likewise have spiritual meaning. White typically denotes peace and healing, while red represents blood and sacrifice.

Ceremony for the vodou spirit Baron Samedi and his Gede family, Port-au-Prince, Haiti, 2021

The Fèt Gede is celebrated on 2 November. Some people believe that assistance given by the Gede family must be acknowledged or repaid by this date, or punishment will follow. The family has various powers, many of which are linked to death, fertility and healing.

‹ **Masked dancer, Botswana, late 19th or early 20th century**
Among peoples such as the Bangwato of Botswana's Serowe region, ritual dancers wore frightening headdresses and performed in ceremonies designed to bring protection and prosperity, by warding off or appeasing dangerous spirits and harmful powers.

› **Pustaha book of magic, Sumatra, Indonesia, late 19th or early 20th century**
In this pustaha, a spiritual and magical specialist known as a datu would have recorded his knowledge of his predecessors. Datus were among a revered minority of Batak people in Indonesia who possessed writing skills.

priests helped their communities by providing healing, consolation and visions of a better future. Some publicly advocated for wider distribution of aid.

What do you need to become a community expert in magic? In some traditions, mysterious powers choose you. Among Tungusic peoples in North Asia, shamanism is not a mere job or profession, but a profound calling. Conventionally, it was resisted. But then, following a psychological or health crisis and recovery, shamans embraced their destiny, using ritual drums, ornamental dress, public performance and spirit helpers to aid individuals and the wider community with an extensive range of magical problems.

Spirits call the leaders of Haitian vodou. Messages from the *lwa* or *loa* (spirits) may inspire someone to become a houngan (male priest), manbo (female priest) or boko (spellcaster). Some *loa* have dual identities that combine African or Haitian traditions with Christianity. A few are particularly associated with magic. Baron Samedi, a zombie-like spirit of death with a penchant for rum and cigars, may help if a boko wanted to raise a dead body to serve as their zombie. Kalfu, a dangerous and violent *loa*, could assist with controlling evil spirits and harmful

Raising Evil Spirits, **satirical print published by Laurie & Whittle, England, 1795**
This satire is about a cunning-man commanding demons for the benefit of his clients. Interestingly, in this image, the wizard's magic is not false and fraudulent but absurd and ridiculous. Caricatures of these community experts in magic were quite common, during the 18th and early 19th centuries. Hanging crocodiles always featured alongside other magical paraphernalia.

magic. All *loa* need to be properly summoned, with acceptable offerings, proper reverence, perhaps music and dance, and the right *vèvè* symbols drawn in corn flour on the floor.

In Europe until the early 1900s, some spirit-summoning magicians wore robes and gowns featuring occult symbols around the fringes. Medicine people across sub-Saharan African used, and in some cases still use, massive teeth necklaces and animal pelts. Among Inuit people, magicians wore costumes of long-nailed creatures for certain rituals, to exorcize and scare away harmful spirits. Shamans of Central Asia and Siberia had (and have) perhaps the most impressive dress of all, with full body suits and hats, brimming with decoration. Musical performances using drum and rattle gave (and give) immense power to the magic of shamans, magicians and medicine people over a very wide area of the world, in Central Asia and Siberia, Northern Scandinavia, Africa and the Americas. The Sami shaman's ritual drum was a powerful magical item, played with ritual hammers

Medicine man, Zimbabwe, *c.* 1900

This community expert uses ceremonial costume to enhance his powers and signify his identity. The medicine man's hat is a wild animal's pelt fastened with a goat's gallbladder, a sacred item of magical power and protection. His necklace, made from hollowed-out black buck horns, contains medicines.

and bearing symbols of people, animals, plants, the heavens and other powers. During healing rituals, outdoors and with public participation, the drums were periodically placed on the patient's body.

Between the early modern era and the early 1900s, European practitioners working within the loose tradition known as the cunning-craft decorated their offices with half a dozen or so widely recognized occult items. These included books of magic, such as the 16th-century *Fourth Book of Occult Philosophy* attributed to Cornelius Agrippa, perhaps shelved with some dusty tomes in Arabic, Latin and Greek. Ceremonial candles and braziers were kept on desks and shelves, as were various bottles and phials. A pack of cards was essential, along with a mystical-seeming animal (alive or stuffed). Some practitioners had a human skeleton or skull. In Ireland, fairy doctors (cunning-folk with powers to heal injuries caused by the 'good people') often decorated their consulting room with magically useful herbs as well as more macabre objects.

Books of magic were (and are) central to the work of community experts worldwide. Among Batak people in Indonesia, priest magicians named datus created magnificent books called pustahas, bound in wooden covers carved with the figure of a gecko, representing the helpful earth god Ilik or Boraspati. In Europe, folk tales were told about magicians possessing powerful black books, which thundered when opened and needed to be padlocked shut. Some cunning-folk used books from the grimoire tradition, such as the 17th-century *Lesser Key of Solomon*. From this material, they learned complex blessings, intricate talismans and sigils, secret names of angels and God, and details of numerous demons and spirits who could (hopefully) be commanded to do their magical bidding.

Today, some community experts use flyers or advertisements in newspapers and on Internet marketplaces. Many get clients through word-of-mouth, by cultivating a local reputation. Historically, Inuit angakkuit (spiritual and shamanic practitioners)

***Tupilaq* figurine, Greenland, *c.* 1905**
Tupilaqs *were supposedly created and animated by Inuit shamans or angakkuit. This figurine depicting the dangerous* tupilaq *monster was carved by Mitsuarnanga, a renowned angakkuq. Apparently, a* tupilaq *once haunted his family, and its defeat probably influenced Mitsuarnanga's reputation as a great magician.*

in Greenland spread stories of creating and fighting terrifying monsters called *tupilaqs*. Practitioners apparently made the monsters to terrorize enemies and seek revenge, with rival angakkuit being prime targets. Using secret rituals, *tupilaqs* were made from parts of plants, animals and even dead children. This was a dangerous magical act, because if a *tupilaq* were sent after someone with greater magical power, it could be diverted back to attack its creator.

Other community experts get their power and reputation from a unique magical object. Between the Middle Ages and the 19th century, quite a few European magicians based their practice and local reputation on unique crystals, passed down the generations, with fantastical origin myths. In Scotland, these crystals were called charm stones. In Ireland, they were luck stones. Charm and luck stones were applied to the body of a sufferer or hung around their neck while a ritual was performed. Often, they were dipped in water, transferring a little bit of their magical power to the liquid, which the client then drank or used for bathing.

Many community experts create supercharged amulets. Charm makers across ancient Greece and Rome sold healing and protection amulets, with long prayers and magic words etched on rolled-up tablets of lead, silver and occasionally gold. Talismans for popularity, prosperity, attraction, strength and more

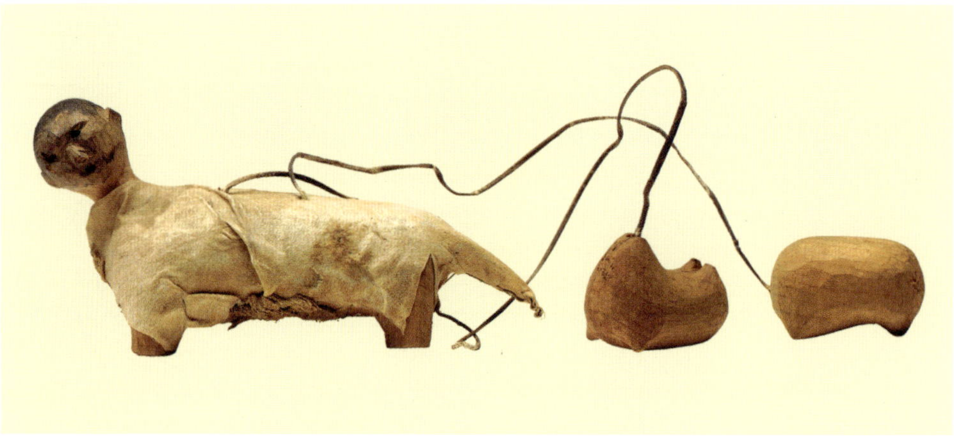

< **Archer-Butler Luck Stone, Ireland, 1600s**
This luck stone was used to cure unwell cattle by dipping it in their water or hanging it around their neck. Its custodians were the Butler family of Garnavilla, County Tipperary, who possessed it between the 17th and 19th centuries.

> **Seller of magical charms and herbs, Southern USA, 1965**
Indigenous American experts were notable for making and selling herb mixtures and bags with magical powers for protection, luck, love and success. Nettle supposedly repelled evil eyes and bad dreams, while tiger lily and basil attracted prosperity.

were (and are) made by magicians from numerous traditions, including hoodoo doctors in the USA and cunning-folk across Europe. Enhanced magical house protection is also sold by many community specialists. In 19th-century Ethiopia, unordained clerics named däbtära created scrolls and rituals for healing that were rich with religious imagery, but also contained various magical symbols and ideas. Mesopotamian magicians, both male and female, made incantation bowls to repel demons and witchcraft, as discovered by Israeli researcher Dorit Kedar (b. 1948). Between 300 and 800 CE, Mesopotamians filled bowls with concentric inscriptions that mingled Rabbinic formulae, Babylonian spells, biblical quotes and references to Mesopotamian deities, such as Šamaš the god of sun and Sîn the god of moon. In the middle, some incantation bowls pictured demons like Lilith, bound and naked, legs and hands outstretched, with big eyes and sometimes wings. Many of these bowls were then buried face down, to trap the demon or witch within a magic circle or send them to the netherworld.

Community experts carefully tailor divination to their clients' precise needs. Early modern European elites commissioned learned astrologers to draw charts of the heavens that revealed past, present and future. 'Nativities' mapped the stars and planets at

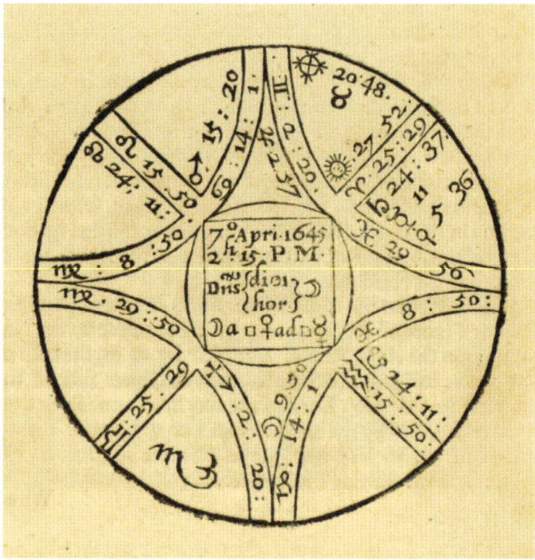

< **Incantation bowl, Iraq, 6th to 8th century**
Incantation bowls were popular defensive magical items. Many of them protected against Lilith, said to be particularly dangerous to women and children, by depicting the demon in the centre with bound arms and legs, as seen here. For incantation bowls to be effective, it was not necessary for the magical text and prayers to be legible.

> **William Lilly, horary astrological chart, from *Christian Astrology*, 1647**
In the text accompanying this chart, Lilly explains that he correctly predicted the baby would be male and that it would arrive in about fourteen weeks (the mother gave birth thirteen weeks and four days after the chart was drawn up).

the moment of a client's birth, and could be used to predict lifetime prospects as well as the coming year. 'Elections' compared nativity horoscopes with current maps of the skies, to establish the best times to carry out important actions. Horary astrology was the most controversial practice: it answered specific questions by drawing horoscopes at the moment the query was posed. In England, Elizabeth I (1533–1603) tasked her advisor John Dee (1527–1608) to undertake an astrological election to determine the most fitting date for her coronation. The event took place on 15 January 1559, perhaps because Dee thought that a glorious reign should begin when the sun was in the youthful and future-orientated air sign of Aquarius, while the moon was in Aries, a fire element and the zodiac's first sign. Magicians from ancient Greece and Rome to Africa have revealed their clients' troubles and prospects by drawing and casting dice, pebbles, knucklebones or other similar objects. One classical method drew oracle bones, each marked with a different letter of the Greek alphabet, which in turn corresponded to a particular outcome. Before the ritual began, prayers had to be said to gods such as Hermes and Apollo, asking for the oracle to work excellently. With a charismatic magician posing sensitive and perceptive questions, divination like this can help tease out concerns, develop plans, reassure and build confidence for the future. It can be intensely stress-relieving, which is why today a small but important number of customers find themselves becoming addicted to fortune-telling.

Community experts in magic specialize in forms of holistic healing that encompass mental and physical health, prosperity and relationship problems. Rituals are often tactile and intimate, with laying-on of hands and special breathing. In several traditions, magicians use their mouths to somehow suck out evil from their client. Ordering the evil to leave, with great authority, is another basic technique, used by Jesus and others when exorcising. Magical healing can also be a long-term process, in which experts demand changes in behaviour and mindset. Many clients find this approach encouraging or invigorating because it gives them a powerful sense of agency. Jeanne Favret-Saada, working in rural Brittany and Normandy in the 1960s, found that French matriarchs from misfortune-blighted farms enthusiastically followed rules issued

Henry Meynell Rheam, *The Fortune Teller*, 1891
This late Victorian social realist painting captures how successful community experts in magic carefully observe, understand and empathize with their clients. Here, the client looks at the cards, but the fortune-teller stares intently at the client.

PROFILE COMMUNITY EXPERTS AROUND THE WORLD

Community experts in magic are important therapists worldwide. Although they have striking differences in style and magical practice, these charismatic

MEXICAN CURANDERO
Using herbs, prayers and spiritual cleansings, curanderos heal problems conceptualized as 'soul loss', where traumatic events cause a portion of the client's soul to leave their body.

AFRICAN SANGOMA
In southern Africa, sangomas use shells and bones to divine whether witchcraft or ancestor spirits are responsible for harm. They then provide solutions using herbs and magic.

BOLIVIAN YATIRI
Yatiri undertake divination by reading coca leaves. They support health and the harvest by making offerings to Pachamama, the Mother Earth goddess of the Aymara and Quechua peoples.

CHINESE FORTUNE-TELLER
In China, fortune-tellers consider a client's fate using the divination manual the *I Ching* or astrological calculations known as the Four Pillars of Destiny.

HAITIAN HOUNGAN AND MANBO
Houngans and manbos lead vodou ceremonies, using powerful performances and offerings to invoke *loa* spirits to provide guidance and insight.

JAPANESE ITAKO
Itako are blind, predominantly female, shamans. They heal, exorcize, contact the dead for bereaved families, and communicate with Shinto spirits. Training is intense.

characters share a holistic approach to addressing and caring for their clients' physical, emotional and spiritual problems.

ABORIGINAL CLEVERMAN
Clevermen were, and are, healers, leaders and keepers of culture among Aboriginal Australians. Many use herbs, spirit communication and magical rituals to heal problems.

INDIGENOUS AMERICAN MEDICINE PEOPLE
These medicine people support health, fortune, fertility and the wider environment, using herbs, private and communal rites, sacred music and more.

KOREAN MUDANG
Conventionally women, Korean mudang appease spirits, divine fortunes and heal illnesses of the soul. They enter a state known as 'Mu-A', a mystically powerful ecstasy or trance.

HOODOO EXPERT
Also known as 'root doctors', hoodoo experts dispense potent blends of West African spirituality, indigenous American botanical knowledge, European-derived folklore, Christianity and more.

SIBERIAN SHAMAN
Among the Tungus of Siberia, shamans enter altered states, often using drums and chants. They journey into the spirit world to heal, divine, take revenge or provide protection.

INUIT ANGAKKUQ
Angakkuit ensure good weather for hunting, retrieve lost souls, heal and enforce community taboos. For centuries, they helped Inuit people survive harsh environments.

Spiritual healers performing a ritual, India, 1862
This highly posed photograph is part of a series of colonial views of India compiled for a British audience. Images of spiritual healers were used to illustrate the alleged exoticness and cultural backwardness of India. These stereotypes rested on dubious assumptions, however. Very many fortune-tellers and magicians plied their trades in Britain and the West, too.

by magicians to save their families from the diverse effects of harmful witchcraft.

Witchcraft detection and exorcism, as performed by some community experts, can be disciplinary or abusive. People may be sent for exorcisms by their families because they are not yet married or do not conform to expectations in some way. Major human rights abuses occur when people are accused of being demonic or harmful witches. This is particularly the case in sub-Saharan Africa, and among the diaspora, because of the emergence since the late 20th century of 'the idea that children, even as toddlers or babies, may be witches', as British anthropologist Jean La Fontaine (b. 1931) notes. Refuges for probably tens of thousands of people accused of witchcraft are needed in Ghana, Malawi, the Democratic Republic of Congo and Nigeria (the problem goes beyond Africa, notably to rural India and Melanesia). Sometimes, healers or Pentecostal exorcists help to inspire accusations.

Some community experts sell magical revenge and control. On plantations in the American South in the early 1900s, hoodoo doctors made malignant

< **Binding female figurine, Roman-era Egypt, 200–399 CE**
The figure is depicted kneeling, hands bound behind her back, and pierced with thirteen needles in her ears, eyes, mouth, head and genitals. The figurine was intended to bind and disable, not kill – perhaps because the target was a spirit, demon or divinity who could not be killed.

> **Cursing bone, Scotland, 19th century**
This macabre item was used to 'ill-wish' people by pouring the blood of a newly-killed hen through the hole in the middle of the bone while speaking a curse. It is made from the thigh bone of a deer or sheep, fixed through a naturally formed piece of bog oak.

'conjure bags' to harm an enemy's health, sour their relationships or spoil their prospects. Ancient Greek magicians crafted *kolossoi* (effigies) from metal, wood and wax. The aim was often to bind (control or limit actions) rather than simply destroy, because their clients' antagonists were not only people but beings that could not be killed, such as troubling ghosts and dangerous gods. Figurines were crushed, had hands tied, mouths covered, heads cut off and specific limbs impaled. Binding formulas were then pronounced or inscribed on the individual kolossos: 'I hereby bind ___' or 'Let ___ be restrained.' Likewise, cursing tablets were widely used in ancient Greece and Rome and were always suspected during interpersonal quarrels, according to classicists such as Radcliffe G. Edmonds (b. 1970). Often, magicians inscribed curses on sheets of lead, punctured with nails, that were then given to the gods at temples or spirits in graves. Cursing tablets gorily specified what the target should suffer: may they spill blood, go mad, not sleep, have their limbs wasted and intestines eaten away. Sometimes, for added power, words were written backwards or in capitals. Magicians among some Aboriginal peoples of Australia seem also

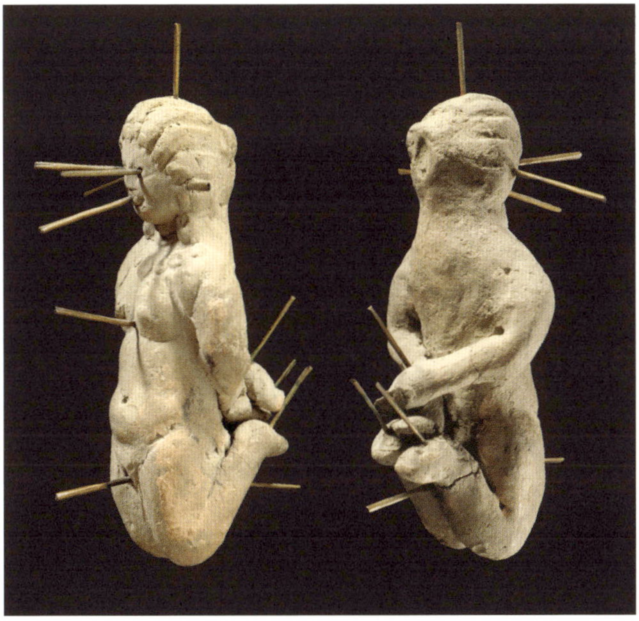

to have formerly used a technique known in English as 'pointing the bone' to dispense deadly magic justice. An instrument known as a *kundela,* which was usually made from a sharpened and resin-covered kangaroo or emu bone, was endowed with magical power then secretly pointed at the intended victim.

In certain contemporary societies, expert magicians play important and valuable roles in public life. In West Africa, the Zangbeto cult among Ògù peoples helps maintain peace and order, as reported by scholars such as George Olusola Ajibade. Zangbeto literally means 'night person', and it is a protective and night watchman-type spirit, who supervises the hours of dark while clad in leaves of the raffia palm tree. According to oral tradition, the original Zangbeto was a benevolent ocean spirit lured long ago from the sea. He is now worshipped by adherents who are believed to possess enhanced magic powers. Wearing raffia costumes, they carry out Zangbeto performances at annual festivals and governmental commemorations. When Zangbeto move through a market or street, magic powers threaten to expose evildoers and punish them with curses.

A few community experts have used their magical skills to become wealthy or powerful. The first leader of the Haitian Revolution in 1791 was a vodou houngan, Dutty Boukman (1767–91), a man who even hostile observers remembered as being intelligent, authoritative, charismatic, brave and also generous in saving white people with whom he had had a good relationship. According to historian Jeremy D. Popkin (b. 1948), after this inspiring leader was killed, his comrades cried in despair: 'Boukman is killed, what will become of us!' Another extremely impressive and successful service magician, from a similar background, was Graman Quassi (*c.* 1692–1787). Kidnapped from Ghana to Dutch Suriname in the early 1700s, he was a magician who became rich and free – and also a botanist who contributed much to our knowledge of plants. More generally, non-conformist women and men have quite often become community experts in magic. The work offers freedoms and possibilities not always found in wider society.

Zangbeto dance, Abomey, Benin, 2018

With spinning movements and intimidating costumes, Zangbeto dancers entertain their communities at festivals and celebrations. They are believed to be animated by guardian spirits who use their powers to dispense justice and expose evildoers – and sometimes to perform tricks such as swallowing glass without injury.

3 LOCAL MAGIC 3

'THERE BE MANY PLACES CALLED FAIRIE HILLS, WHICH THE MOUNTAIN PEOPLE THINK IMPIOUS AND DANGEROUS TO PEEL OR DISCOVER, BY TAKING EARTH OR WOOD FROM THEM.'

ROBERT KIRK, *THE SECRET COMMONWEALTH OF ELVES, FAUNS AND FAIRIES* (1691)

At many places, magic surges. Spells supposedly gain additional force from being cast at crossroads, graveyards, churches, ancient monuments and other symbolically significant human-made locations. Magical wells, stones and other sites for healing, blessing and cursing mark many landscapes. Mystical atmospheres cloak some regions, such as Southwest England, while certain towns and cities, including New Orleans and Glastonbury, are places of magical tourism. Beautiful and often harmful nature spirits are globally said to inhabit pools, rivers, woods, hills and mountains. Historically, local magic like this was generally cautionary, but today it is often positive.

3 LOCAL MAGIC 3

Experts are not the only source of enhanced magic. Heightened powers are also believed to stem from exceptional locations that fizz with supernatural forces. Many magical places were and are human creations: notably, the graveyard. Ancient Roman and Greek cursing tablets were sometimes buried in graves, to send magical messages to the gods and spirits of the underworld. Sites of execution were similarly locations of dire but powerful magic. The gibbet, where executed criminals were hanged in chains to rot and be eaten by birds, was a place where demonic witches conducted their rituals, according to accusations levelled during the period of the witch trials. Churches, too, were magical places. In English folklore, walk around a church anticlockwise to see the Devil, and through him gain the power to do supernatural evil. The Russian *banya* (bathhouse) was another major location where villagers went to say charms and cast spells.

Crossroads were widely seen as magical places and feature in historical spells. You should leave bundles of enchanted objects at the crossroads to set someone's heart ablaze, according to ancient Greek texts. Malignant witches allegedly worked their wicked magic at crossroads. One of them was Dame Alice Kyteler (1280–1325), a Flemish woman living in Ireland, and one of the first people in Europe to be convicted of committing demonic witchcraft. Alice and her fellow witches were accused of making animal sacrifices to a demon, calling himself Robin the son of Art, from the lesser levels of Hell, by cutting up animals and scattering them around the crossroads at night. Today, many people still know that the crossroads is where you meet the Devil if you want to sell your soul. It explains, according to legend, the sudden brilliance of the African American blues artist Robert Johnson (1911–38): 'I went down to the crossroads, fell down on my knees. Asked the Lord above, "Have mercy, now, save poor Bob if you please."'

Holy wells are common in regions such as Brittany and Cornwall. Ireland has the most holy wells, at slightly more than 3,000, although not all are used today. Holy wells generally cure or help specific ailments, especially

‹ *page 92*
Photograph of a fairy charm painted on a farm wall, County Kerry, Ireland, 1939
In historic Ireland, popular Christianity used various crosses for protection against potentially dangerous magical powers like witches and fairies. The Parshell and the St Brigid's crosses were strategically placed in households and barns to defend people and animals. A cross within a circle, rather like the Celtic Cross, was also painted or marked on walls for defence.

Stone depiction of an Aztec Cihuateotl demon, Mexico, *c.* 1400–1550

Among the Aztec people, crossroads were supposed to be haunted by Cihuateteo demons, who were vengeful spirits formed from the souls of women who died in childbirth. On five specific days of the Aztec calendar, the Cihuateteo were said to come to Earth to steal young children whom they had never possessed in life.

if you approach them silently and reverently. There are also a few wells where curses can be laid. The wells of St Elian, one on the Welsh isle of Anglesey and another at the village of Llanelian-yn-Rhos in North Wales, are two macabre examples. At Ffynnon Elian (St Elian's Well) at Llanelian-yn-Rhos, cursing became a big business between about the 1770s and 1850s, run and administered by the men renting the land on which the well stood. As Welsh historian Richard Suggett (b. 1959) describes, the theoretical possibility of laying a curse without cause 'was transformed into terrifying practice in the late eighteenth and early nineteenth century.' Ireland, meanwhile, possesses several ancient rocks with undulations where stones can be turned, while pronouncing a curse or blessing.

Enhanced places, where heightened magic can be practised, continue to emerge. Stone circles and other prehistoric remains have increasingly become sites of magic in Europe following the decline of Christianity and the rise of neo-paganism from the mid-20th century. At these charismatic locations, practitioners commune with ancient energies, recharge crystals,

St Elian's Well, Anglesey, Wales
Today, the holy well dedicated to an early medieval evangelist (b. c. 450) is marked by a plaque on the route of the Isle of Anglesey Coastal Path. During the 18th and early 19th centuries, it was known as a well where curses could be laid.

Bullaun stone, County Kilkenny, Ireland
Bullaun (derived from the Irish word for 'bowl') stones were rocks possessing natural or human-made hollows. Historically, they were locations for collecting beneficial water or turning other rocks in rituals of healing, blessing and cursing.

hold festivals and cast spells. The Rollright Stones, in Oxfordshire, England, form a slightly foreboding stone circle, near a village renowned for witchcraft (Long Compton). Legend tells that the Rollright Stones were created by a witch who turned a king and his army to stone. Yet, before the mid-1900s, the only evidence of magic there is travellers chipping off bits of the stones for luck. From the mid-1950s, however, the stone circle has become a place for practising various types of modern witchcraft and magic.

Worldwide, many towns and cities provide tourists with magical heritage, shops and services. In several cases, this builds on an older reputation for witchcraft or illicit magic, as in New Orleans, USA, Catemaco, Mexico, and Quedlinburg, Germany. Some mystical towns have a history of pilgrimage, healing and myth, such as Glastonbury in England. Others are linked with scandalous witch trials, including Salem, USA, and Triora, Italy. Although most connect with the past, these magical towns are modern creations, reflecting the growth of mass tourism and the increasing acceptance of magic in society at large. At a broader

PROFILE SITES OF FERTILITY MAGIC

Fertility is precious, precarious and risky. This fundamental aspect of human life naturally lends itself to magic, as worried and suffering people (especially women) look for aid from beyond the natural realm. One means of practising enhanced fertility magic is to travel to special locations to interact with potent objects, such as statues or stones. Often, the rites or objects are sexually graphic. To achieve its effects, fertility magic temporarily overthrows prevailing conventions of modesty.

FERTILITY STONE
Brittany, in Western France, is particularly notable for standing fertility stones (*pierre de fécondité*). Most of these magical rocks were solitary, phallic-looking menhirs. Women would rub their bellies against the stones in the hope of improving their chance of falling pregnant.

FERTILITY SLIDE
Throughout Italy and France, numerous elevated stones are known as 'fertility slides'. According to local folklore, they have been used since prehistoric times by women looking to improve their chance of a successful pregnancy. Invariably, fertility slides are smoothed from much use.

ROCK GAP
Passing through naturally occurring rock gaps was widely believed to help cure fertility problems. The Maiden's Stone in the Scottish region of East Lothian and St Levan's Stone in Cornwall both have a small gap in the middle. Women who passed through, ideally naked, were said to improve their fertility.

SHEELA-NA-GIG
These graphic medieval carvings show females, with skull-like heads, in exposing poses, holding open their labia to display enlarged and exaggerated vulvas. Sheela-na-gigs are found particularly in churches, castles, walls and stone houses (some having been removed from earlier buildings).

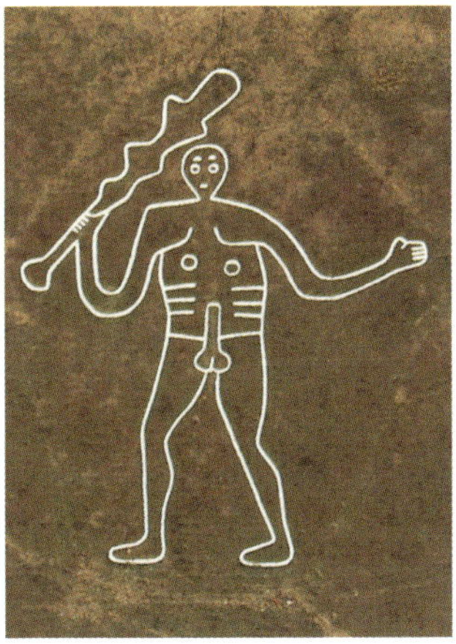

CERNE GIANT
The giant chalk man, with a conspicuously erect penis, is cut into a hillside in Dorset, England. Since at least the 19th century and probably for a lot longer, local folklore has held that women can increase their chances of conception by sitting, laying or having sex on the penis.

FERTILITY CAVE
Across the world, certain caves are established sites of fertility rituals. Phra Nang Cave in Krabi, Thailand, is a sacred place of such rituals. As part of the practice, a woman wanting to become pregnant must pray to the goddess-spirit Phra Nang and leave an offering or gift of a wooden phallus.

Feng shui wood in Hong Kong, 1985, and a Shigandang stone in Beijing, China, 2017

Across East Asia, villagers plant, cultivate and protect feng shui groves because the woods are believed to increase harmony, prosperity and protection. Shigandang stones are likewise found throughout East Asia. Large versions bring good fortune and reduce evil in public places, while small examples are kept in private residences.

level, magic is strongly connected with certain areas and regions, including the West Country of England, Germany's Harz Mountains, the Brittany region of France, Siquijor in the Philippines (which is also known as the Island of Healing) and Mayong, India. Partly because magic is an accepted piece of local identity, with deep roots in regional folklore and history, some magical believers travel to these places, to work, practise or seek treatment.

Magic can police borders. Viking runestones, for example, were sometimes placed at boundaries and enforced with a curse that threatened dreadful magical punishment on anyone who dared tamper with them. Local magic also directly protects landscapes, nature and communities. Feng shui woods, ancient forest groves that are preserved to ensure the proper flow of qi, surround many villages throughout East Asia. In China, Hong Kong alone has more than a hundred feng shui woods, mostly in the north-east of the region, which are supposed to 'maintain a prosperous future for nearby rural villages', as environmental researcher Paul G. Harris notes. Visited mostly by locals, feng shui woods are typically peaceful places that are valued for their positive impact on the future fate and destiny of the nearby community, including residents' offspring who may have moved elsewhere. In towns and suburbs across East Asia, Shigandang stones placed at intersections or within communal walls bring good fortune to the inhabitants. The ancient practice evokes holy Mount Tai, the grand mountain that is colloquially known to be so heavy that it could hold down any evil.

Historically, most local magic was cautionary and threatening. It vividly symbolized the perils of the world outside, through stories about dangerous spirits of air, earth, fire, water, night and nature. Beyond the bounds of home, village and town lived powerful magical beings. If not treated with sufficient respect, they may harm, kill or even carry a person away. Most of these dangerous nature spirits are humanoid. Some though are animals. Hundreds of ghostly and demonic black dogs haunt the folklore of Britain. They include Black Shuck, a beast with flaming eyes who stalks Eastern

A straunge.
and terrible Wunder wrought
very late in the parish Church
of Bongay, a Town of no great di-
stance from the citie of Norwich, name-
ly the fourth of this August, in ye yeere of
our Lord 1577. in a great tempest of vi-
olent raine, lightning, and thunder, the
like wherof hath been sel-
dome seene.
With the appearance of an horrible sha-
ped thing, sensibly perceived of the
people then and there
assembled.
Drawen into a plain method ac-
cording to the written copye.
by Abraham Fleming.

‹ **Cover of Abraham Fleming's *A Strange, and Terrible Wunder*, 1577**
Fleming's work recounts how a devilish black dog burst into two churches in Suffolk, England, during a storm and ran down the aisles, terrifying the worshippers and killing three people. Mysterious black dogs had been reported in Eastern England since at least the 12th century.

› **Kelpie water spirit, engraving in *The World Guide to Gnomes, Fairies, Elves and Other Little People*, 1880**
Literary references to Scotland's shapeshifting water spirits, known as kelpies, became notable during the 18th century, but the spirits likely have a much longer history in popular folklore.

England after dark. Black dogs are not all bad: some have helped lone female travellers get home safely. In 2014, an American woman living in Armenia wrote to British folklorist Mark Norman telling him of her encounters, in a public garden, with an enormous black dog who 'radiated this sense of peacefulness and tranquillity', such that she intuitively knew it was protecting her, as a sort of guardian spirit. Traditionally though, many animal spirits were threatening. Scotland's kelpies were shapeshifting water beings, who in horse form enticed and then drowned exhausted travellers. The fairy dog or Cù Sìth was a massive and silent hunter, with shaggy green fur, commanded by fairies to snatch human women and children.

Nature, in folklore, is the property of magical humanoid spirits. These spirits are called 'the supernatural owners of nature' in a classic study of Scandinavia local beings, published in 1961 with the same name. In Swedish tradition, the rå (meaning 'keeper' or 'warden') are custodians of forests, lakes and rivers. They take many forms, including the skogsrå: an erotic female forest spirit, who lures men away with

< **August Herman Neujd, *Skogsrå*, bronze statuette c. 1910–14**
In Swedish folklore, these spirits seduced men into the woods. In many tales, the men died or went insane. Skogsrå were not always harmful; some brought good fortune or assistance, if treated well.

> **Per Daniel Holm, 'A Skogsrå meeting a woodcutter', from *Svenska Folksägner*, 1882**
Although skogsrås looked like women from the front, on their back was supposed to be a tail, bark or a tree's hollow.

promises of sex. Across Scandinavia, trolls are strange spirits of mountain and forest. In art, they are lumbering giants, but in folk tales trolls play tricks and can become invisible. In Latvian and Baltic folklore, Vadātājs are sinister spirits who lead people astray to dangerous locations like bogs and watercourses, where they suffer unnatural deaths. Descriptions of their appearance are vague and inconsistent: devil, ghost, human, animal, wrapped in a cloud or connected with trees. Traditional solutions for escape include looking backwards through your legs, looking through crossed thumbs, saying 'The Lord's Prayer' three times backwards, turning clothes you are wearing inside out, and other reversals. Similar contortions are found elsewhere and perhaps served to keep travellers alert in dangerous environments.

Diminutive nature spirits exist worldwide. They can be found almost everywhere, but fairies seem to be slightly more common in landscapes whose human inhabitants possess some Celtic heritage. From pucks and pixies to pouques and the faiteaux, many varieties of these tricky and powerful spirits can be found across Ireland, Wales, England, parts of Scotland, the Isle of

PROFILE
NATURE SPIRITS ACROSS THE GLOBE

Across the world, spirits of nature often reside in or near bodies of water. Beautiful female vilas and dangerous female rusalki haunt the waterways of Slavic regions. Mermaids are reported throughout the world, including Melusine, a spirit with a female upper body and serpent or fish lower half, found in holy wells or rivers in Western France and the Low Countries. In Nordic folklore, male water spirits known as 'nixie' play enchanted songs to lure women and children to the waters. Some take horse form and entice travellers to climb on, before jumping into the water to drown them.

RUSALKI
In Slavic folklore, rusalki are the water-bound ghosts of young women who suffered a premature death. Pale, and with long flowing hair, they mislead travellers (usually male) to their deaths.

NÄCKEN
This shapeshifting male water spirit is found across Germanic and Scandinavian folklore. He plays enchanting music on a fiddle or harp to lure innocent people to a watery death.

KELPIE AND NIXIE
In both Scottish and Nordic folklore, certain shapeshifting spirits appear as horses. These dangerous spirits linger near lakes and rivers to entice passers-by to trust them.

MARIA MAKILING
This beautiful nature spirit is the benevolent guardian of Mount Makiling in the Philippines. She protects plants and animals and helps local people, but can be dangerous if angered.

TANIWHA
Māori legends tell of terrifying taniwha in lakes, caves, rivers and the sea. They are described as huge serpents, sharks, lizards, whales or logs, protecting people and places from misuse.

MAMI WATA
This West African and African American nature spirit is known for protecting mothers and babies. During the 19th century, imagery of Mami Wata began incorporating snake charming.

YARA-MA-YHA-WHO
Aboriginal Australians use tales of this frog-like creature to warn youngsters about the dangers of travelling alone into the Bush. It can devour children, suck blood and swallow people whole.

KAPPA
Japan's rivers, lakes and ponds are said to be home to this mischievous, sometimes malevolent, water spirit. The large depression in its head must remain wet to sustain its power.

MELUSINE
Folktales tell of men who marry a fairy-woman called Melusine. The union fails when the man breaks a pact never to see her on a specific day when her legs transform into the tail of a fish or serpent.

Man, the Channel Islands, Galicia in northern Spain and Brittany in north-west France. Fairies initially seem to have had limited impact on Irish immigrants to the USA, although historian Chris Woodyard (b. 1954) has found a handful of later 19th-century US newspaper articles describing local people who were apparently led away or abducted by fairies, as well as one disturbing report of a baby deliberately burned in New York by parents claiming it was a changeling. Fairies emigrated more successfully to the bleak seaboard of Newfoundland, in eastern Canada, as folklorist Barbara Rieti (b. 1952) shows in a study of strange fairy experiences in the area during the 20th century. Eventually, waves of globalization and colonization spread fairies very widely, including into the USA. By the 1950s, the Fairy Investigation Society (established in London in 1927) and fairy researcher Marjorie T. Johnson (1911–2011) had together collated hundreds of reports of fairies from sites as diverse as Africa, Australia, the USA and New Zealand. Britain and Ireland are the centre of fairy sightings recorded by the amazing The Fairy Census, a survey by folklore historian Simon Young (b. 1966) of late 20th- and 21st-century experiences. Many reports also come from the USA, Australia, Canada and New Zealand, as well as a few from other places such as Romania, Portugal and Germany.

Ireland, however, remains the great land of fairies. Until a century and a half ago or less, only the most confident disbelievers called the spirits by that offensive name. Fairies were the 'good people', the 'gentry', the 'good neighbours' and, in Irish, the 'daoine sidhe' (people of the mounds). They guarded hawthorn trees, great hills and little medieval defensive enclosures known as raths, ringforts and fairy forts. Tens of thousands of these structures still mark the Irish landscape, thanks primarily to the idea that anyone who interferes with them will be harmed. Hawthorn trees are similarly preserved. Fairies also provided excuses: if you came home late = 'I was fairy-led around the countryside'. They served as a coded language for crime and rebellion. They also explained misfortunes and were blamed for causing disabilities.

Fairy trees (top), fairy fort (bottom), Ireland

Historically, fairies were mainly seen as dangerous, but recently they have become gentler and more helpful. Some hawthorn trees on notorious fairy mountains or hills are now covered with ribbons and trinkets, each of which represents a wish. Damaging a 'fairy thorn' was thought to be unlucky, so some have protective walls.

Yan' Dargent, ***The Washerwomen of the Night* (*Les Lavandières de la Nuit*), 1861**
This masterpiece captures a chilling moment in Breton folklore. A lone traveller disturbs what were known locally as the 'night ducks' – spectral washerwomen scrubbing the shrouds of those destined to die. Ankou, the skeletal personification of death in Brittany, flies among the washerwomen.

Occasionally, fairies helped to demonize and inspire terrible violence against unwell people. For example, in 1895, a seamstress from rural Tipperary, Bridget Cleary, was burned and killed at home by her husband, while her family were also in the building. Sadly, it was not an isolated event. In the 19th-century Irish newspaper archive, there are reports of a dozen other examples of disabled or ill children and young women being labelled changelings or fairies, and then being beaten, burned, poisoned or drowned by mostly male family members.

In France, Bretons called the capricious spirits who marked the local landscape fées, fêtes and sometimes fions. As elsewhere, the fairies of Brittany were a varied tribe. Night dancers were wizened little men who, in the tales collected by 19th-century folklorists like F. M. Luzel (1821–95), danced beneath the full moon at eerie locations such as crossroads. Most terrifying of all were the washerwomen of the night, relatives of the Irish banshee who knew which people would soon die. The washerwomen, dressed in white, cleaned the shrouds of those who were soon to perish.

If you saw the washerwomen and ran, they would kill you. If you helped them but wrung the washing in the normal way, they would break your arm. However, if you did it contraways, you might get away.

The greatest account of magical beings is *The Secret Commonwealth of Elves, Fauns and Fairies* (1691) by Robert Kirk (1644–92), the minister of Aberfoyle in the Scottish Lowlands. Using his own gift of second sight and accounts from his parishioners, he described an intricate but melancholy fairy civilization. Fairies, the Reverend Kirk thought, were air spirits occupying a middle nature between humans and angels. They took many forms: men, women, young and old. Beneath hills and in rocks, they worked trades like smithing, baking, dyeing and sewing. They had classes, orders, a system of government and leaders. Fairies even fought battles with each other using magical weapons. They had many pleasures and plenty of books, including mysterious works of magic. Fairies were expert in charms and never got sick, although they did dwindle and decay eventually. Yet they were never happy. As Kirk put it,

the fairies were 'unusually silent and sullen' and lived in 'continual sadness'. This was why they resented human happiness and took opportunities to spoil it. Fairies did magical harm and stole the children, women and nurses of humans. In the place of these taken people, they left changelings: seemingly the same, but angry, sickly and insatiably hungry.

Many of our world's nature spirits look like members of the same family. Jinn, of Arab and Islamic tradition, are similar enough to fairies to seem like their cousins. Both are pseudo-humanoid spirits, made of magical elements. Fairies are formed of 'congealed air', according to Kirk. Jinn are made of a smokeless and 'subtle fire', wrote the orientalist and translator of *The Arabian Nights*, Richard F. Burton (1821–90). Like traditional fairies, jinn are generally but not always harmful to people. Both spirits steal betrothed women away, shortly before their wedding. Both punish selfish people who are careless about the environment. Like scary fairies, jinn also live in dangerous places: graveyards, ancient tombs, waterways and deserts. Belief in jinn varies widely among Muslims: a 2012 Pew survey showed 19 per cent believing in Central Asia, 30 per cent in Southern Eastern Europe, 77 per cent in South Asia and 86 per cent in Morocco.

Dangerous places continue to inspire cautionary supernatural beings. In the late 1700s and 1800s, the Pine Barrens in New Jersey, USA, became home to the Jersey Devil, a terrifying cryptid with wings and the head of a goat. Vanishing hitchhiker ghost stories spread worldwide during the 20th century, symbolizing the dangers of lonely highways. In conflict zones, people still use stories of ghosts and spirits to scare their children into staying safely inside. Yet, in recent decades, local magic has become less threatening. Fairies are now actively sought out, communed with and worshipped in some types of modern magic, such as Fairy Wicca. Fairy doors appear on trees, and fairy trails are popular family days out in places once avoided. As the natural and human world has becomes less perilous, the magical owners of nature seem to have become less dangerous.

Jinn album painting, India, 1590s

Here, several jinn are having a party. The blue jinn plays a rabab, a string instrument favoured by the Mughal court. The donkey-headed jinn dances, while the bird-headed figure beats a daire *(tambourine-style drum). In Islamic theology, jinn were and are beings of free will, some of whom were religious believers; others rejected God.*

II

1

CEREMONIAL MAGIC

2

POLITICAL MAGIC

3

PERFORMANCE MAGIC

HIGH MAGIC

'THERE ARE TWO THINGS, WHICH RULE EVERY OPERATION OF CEREMONIAL MAGIC, NAMELY RELIGION AND SUPERSTITION.'

CORNELIUS AGRIPPA, *THREE BOOKS OF OCCULT PHILOSOPHY*, TRANS. J. F. (1651)

Of all occult acts, ceremonial magic is the most demanding and powerful. Detailed instructions are provided by complex texts called grimoires. Since antiquity, these manuals of ceremonial magic have been repeatedly recombined and reproduced, mingling traditions from across Eurasia and beyond, often with false dates and authors. Grimoires primarily explain how to summon and command awesome spirits with powerful abilities. These acts require precise rituals, consecrated objects and elaborate magic circles, as well as a focused and faithful mind. Riches, influence, knowledge and more are promised by ceremonial magic, along perhaps with grand feelings of elation and ecstasy.

Ceremonial magic can induce magnificent convictions of power and insight. For a time, some practitioners feel almost divine. 'Let your mind be wholly absorbed in the act, until the veil of the world parts,' advises a god-summoning spell from the Greek magical papyri (100 BCE–400 CE). Elation can follow. Magicians should walk around the magic circle until 'wearied with a dizziness', then collapse and be 'wrapt up in an ecstasie', so advises a 1650s edition of the *Fourth Book of Occult Philosophy*. Some high magicians unfurl frenzied prophesies, rather like the Cumaean Sibyl in Virgil's *Aeneid* (*c.* 30–19 BCE). Others break down crying, in a huge emotional release after long and demanding rites.

This is the most demanding form of magic. It can bring great rewards, but in extreme cases ceremonial magic can also take over your life. Take Samuel Falk (*c.* 1708–82), known as the Ba'al Shem of London. ('Ba'al Shem' is a Hebrew term for a miracle worker, meaning literally 'master of [God's] name'.) He used his expertise in the Jewish Kabbalah tradition of ceremonial magic to become wealthy and famous. But Falk was not, to put it mildly, easy to live with. Nor was his life marked by much happy ease. He barely slept for days and nights on end while conjuring. He shouted at his assistants and cursed his wife, then locked himself away in a disturbing nocturnal lifestyle. A nine-hour stretch of continuous magic was not unusual. A ritual took weeks to prepare then had to be done at the correct time and executed perfectly. It required clean vestments, a carefully set-up altar, prepared amulets, precise texts, the right mindset and an unsoiled 'book of spirits' touched by only the magician. Extreme concentration and high emotion could go on for weeks. It was exhausting and the Ba'al Shem made himself ill. Yet the feelings of power and understanding were vast.

Since antiquity, controversial texts have explained how practitioners of ceremonial magic should conduct their complex and demanding art. During the 18th and 19th centuries, these magic books became known as grimoires, a name that historian Owen Davies (b. 1969) notes probably derives from the French word 'grammaire', meaning a Latin manuscript.

« *page 112*
'King and astrologer', from the *Tübinger Hausbuch*, 15th century
The Tübinger Hausbuch *is a renowned German astrological work that explains how celestial bodies influence health, medicine, the human body and daily life. The book is also celebrated for its coloured images of late medieval European life, high and low. In this image, a monarch points to astrological charts in a magician's book.*

‹ *page 114*
'Doctor Faust', from José Coroleu's *Las Supersticiones de la Humanidad*, 1881
Johann Georg Faust was a German travelling astrologer and magician. His life and name inspired the fictional legend of a scholar who makes a bargain with a demon named Mephistopheles, who provides twenty-four years of power in return for Faust's soul. The motif may also derive from older legends about clerics making demonic pacts.

Michelangelo, *The Cumaean Sibyl*, Sistine Chapel, Vatican City, *c.* 1511

In Virgil's Aeneid, *the Cumaean Sibyl is an oracle of Apollo, who prophesizes in a frenzied state from a mysterious hundred-mouthed cave. Michelangelo portrayed her as weathered but powerful (physically and intellectually). According to Christian tradition, she was one of several pagan prophets who foretold the birth of Christ.*

Greek magical papyrus, Egypt, 3rd or 4th century CE
This papyrus contains several complex and demanding rites. One love charm promises to act 'in the same hour' but requires holy names to be written on a donkey's back. Another love spell must be written using a copper nail from a shipwreck. A further 'strong' love spell invokes the goddess of the moon, Selene. All the spells are multistage rites, and many use special magic words that are otherwise unintelligible.

The extraordinary works originate in lists of demons and magical formulae, inscribed on cuneiform clay tablets by the ancient Mesopotamians. Later, selections from that body of work mingled with practices and ideas from many other traditions, including Egyptian temple magic, Jewish Merkabah mysticism and Greek magic. Among the earliest surviving grimoires are the Greek magical papyri, which detail many eclectic methods to summon various gods, spirits and daimons that were used around the ancient Mediterranean.

Most grimoires recombine older texts, with changes and additions, although in recent decades magical practitioners have used more original material. Unacknowledged copying and adaption are extremely common. So is false attribution: many grimoires assert grand authors and more ancient origins than they really possess. Since antiquity, many claimed to contain the discoveries of preeminent figures, from prophets like Moses to popes, princes and leaders such as Solomon and Alexander the Great. In reality though, the greatest genuine magician scholar was surely Heinrich Cornelius Agrippa von Nettesheim (1486–1535). He learned magic from cryptographer Johannes Trithemius (1462–1516) and was only twenty-three when he wrote *Three Books of Occult Philosophy*, with volumes on natural magic, celestial magic and ceremonial magic (1533: trans. 1651).

Today, this impressive work is a cornerstone of Western esotericism, a high magical tradition derived primarily from European and Middle Eastern sources.

Older grimoires naturally cater to historical problems. During the medieval era, lazy monks took shortcuts to learning via a popular 13th-century grimoire called the *Ars Notoria*, which promised to help people acquire whole disciplines and subjects in as little as a month. Grimoires from the 1700s have rites to guard sheep, stop hail, become invulnerable during a duel or enchant garters to ensure the wearer will not tire on the road. Today, short books detail ceremonial magic rituals that may help someone gain employment in a tough market, notably *The Magickal Job Seeker* (2014) by Damon Brand. In the same year, Brand published *Magickal Cashbook: Attract Money Fast With Ancient Secrets and Modern Wealth Magic*. Such works are highly attuned to 21st-century problems, but getting wealth has been an enduring preoccupation of ceremonial magic since antiquity.

Ancient or modern, the single biggest focus of ceremonial magic is other people. Reading minds, controlling thoughts and influencing actions are among the most persistent themes. American historians Dan Attrell (b. 1988) and David Porreca (b. 1974) have tabulated the 'ritual objectives' of spells and rites in

Illustration from an edition of the *Shams al-Ma'arif al-Kubra* (*The Sun of Knowledge*), 1868

An influential grimoire, The Sun of Knowledge *details the magical uses of the many names of God and describes the production of magical talismans based on Quranic verses. It outlines how magic squares and diagrams can be used to gain victory in battle, avert plague, stop fever, soothe crying children, prevent fits and more.*

a grimoire named the *Picatrix* (2019), a Christianized translation of an Arabic and Muslim grimoire written probably in the late 900s as *The Aim of the Sage* or *The Goal of the Wise*. The latter was prized in medieval Europe and remains popular among ceremonial magicians today because it provides an unusually detailed education in the production of talismans enhanced by astrological magic involving the 'mansions of the Moon'. The biggest single category of spells in the *Picatrix*, comprising around a third of the total, is interpersonal relations. After this comes health and healing (around one-sixth of the rituals), followed by knowledge, protection and wealth, and then many other categories such as travel, agriculture, war and more.

Theurgy is a branch of ceremonial magic with philosophical, psychological and spiritual aims. Drawing on works such as the 13th-century Arabic *Shams al-Ma'arif al-Kubra* (*The Sun of Knowledge*), it aspires to raise a magician's consciousness to the level of divinity, in an epic act of worshipful transformation called *henosis*, meaning 'union with the divine'. Thaumaturgy, by contrast, is a type of ceremonial magic that is supposed to change the physical world. Often, it involves summoning and commanding powerful supernatural beings. These awesome creatures then use their vast powers to enact uniquely potent spells. Ceremonial magicians in ancient Greece and Egypt summoned gods and also spirits known as daimons. Divinities such as Helios, Set, Aphrodite, Souriel, Adonai and many others were called upon to empower love spells, lay curses, heal illnesses, inflict enemies with nightmares or insomnia, and much more. This summoning of spirits and demons later became known as *goetia* and was often carried out using a bespoke spell book. Within this 'Book of Spirits', the *Fourth Book of Occult Philosophy* explains, the summoned beings' image must be drawn on the left-hand page, while its symbols should be inscribed on the right, with an oath above that specifies its name, rank, nature and power. Generally, the summoned spirits are extremely dangerous and unwilling assistants. To control them, a magus needs powerful help from gods and holy angels.

‹ **'Urieus Demon King of the East', from *Clavis Inferni* (*The Key of Hell*), a Latin and Hebrew grimoire, late 18th century**
Urieus was one of the four demon kings who ruled the cardinal directions. Possessed of great magic abilities, these middle managers of the spirit world helped to create magic circles and control lesser demons.

› **'Ashtaroth the Great Duke of Hell', from *Compendium Rarissimum Totius Artis Magicae* (*A Rare Summary of the Entire Magical Art*), c. 1775**
This archdemon was frequently depicted holding a snake (here, they burst from his body). He was known in grimoires as a demon with putrid breath who could magically provide answers, knowledge, invisibility, good will and power over serpents.

Many grimoires describe the various powerful spirits that can be called upon to empower spells. Each spirit has its own name, symbol, personality, abilities and active days. Fairies like Oberon feature occasionally. Good angels are common, particularly after Elizabethan magus John Dee developed angel-focused magic attributed to the Old Testament Prophet Enoch. With his crystal-gazing assistant Edward Kelley (1555–*c.* 1597), Dee developed a special Enochian language to call forth various angels. Elsewhere, lists of malevolent spirits occur in many grimoires. An early example is the *Testament of Solomon*, which may be among the first magical texts to be attributed to the legendary biblical king, although its date of composition could also be as late as the Middle Ages. The text takes the form of a narrative about a succession of demons, compelled by Solomon's magic ring to appear and truthfully answer questions about their powers and which archangel frustrates them. Obizuth (known elsewhere as Abyzou) comes forth in a woman's form but without limbs, explaining that she goes around the world at night attacking new mothers and babies. She can take many different forms, and her nemesis is the archangel Raphael and the number 640.

< **Julius Höppner, *Midsummer Night's Dream, Oberon, Titania and the Fairies*, 1888**
During the early modern era, fairies known as Oberon, Oberion or Oberyon featured in ceremonial magic as spirits to be summoned, bound and commanded. They seem particularly to have assisted in healing and treasure hunting.

> **'Angel presenting King Solomon with knowledge of the liberal, mechanical and forbidden sciences', from *Ars Notoria* (*Notary Art*), 15th century**
The Ars Notoria *informed practitioners how to use magic to infuse knowledge directly into their minds. Solomon was said to have received the divine revelation of knowledge from the angel Pamphilius.*

Many of the malevolent beings in grimoire lists ultimately descend from Middle Eastern and Near Eastern gods and demons, transmitted across cultures and ages by books such as the *Hygromanteia* or *Magical Treatise of Solomon*, another Greek magical instruction text purportedly written by Solomon. After the sack of Constantinople and the fall of the Byzantine Empire in 1453, scholars and refugees brought this book west into Europe, where it was translated into Latin and vernacular languages and survived as the inspiration for later demon-listing grimoires. Among the best known of these are the 16th-century *Pseudomonarchia Daemonum* (*False Monarchy of Demons*) by Dutch physician Johann Weyer (1515–88) and the *Ars Goetia* book of the *Lemegeton Clavicula Salomonis* or *Lesser Key of Solomon*, first compiled around the 1600s. Many of the same spirits are found in both texts. First is Bael, descended from the ancient Levantine god Baal. He, Weyer says, is the king and ruler of sixty-six legions of devils. He appears with three heads – a toad, a man and a cat – and has the power to make a magician go invisible or become wise. The second spirit is Agares,

DECODING
COMMONWEALTH OF DEMONS

Much ceremonial magic is based around summoning spirits, many of whom are demons. They possess distinctive physiognomies, personalities, ranks and most importantly powers. In the premodern period,

these demons were quite widely known. Several appear in this plate from *An Entire Body of Philosophy According to the Principles of the Famous Renate Des Cartes* by Antoine Le Grand and Richard Blome (1694).

1.

BELZEBUB
King of Flies and ruler of the rest, Belzebub belongs to the first demonic order, who usurp the name of God and aspire to be worshipped like him.

2.

PYTHON
From the second order of Lying Spirits, these serpentine demons make it their business to delude, deceive and spread false truths.

3.

BELIAL
Associated with the third order of demons, Belial is the prince of the Vessels of Iniquity, who invent and propagate wicked arts.

4.

ASMODEUS
Known as the Executioner of Justice, Asmodeus is part of the fourth order of demons, who are the Avengers of Wickedness.

5.

SATAN
In this image, Satan is linked with the fifth order of Devils, known as the Jugglers. They imitate miracles, often by assisting wizards or witches in spells.

6.

MERIRIM
The sixth order of devils are the Powers of the Air. They make thunder and lightning, corrupt the air and cause plagues. Their prince is Meririm, or Meresin.

7.

APOLLYON
The seventh order are Furies, who sow mischief and dissent, causing wars and devastation. Their prince, in the Book of Revelation, is Apollyon.

8.

ASTAROTH
The eighth order of demons are the Accusers and Inquisitors. Their prince is Astaroth, or Diabolus in Greek, a spy and a slanderer.

9.

MAMMON
The ninth and final order are Tempters and Liars. These bad angels follow people around, constantly tempting them to do evil.

a duke notable for appearing more willingly, in the form of an old man riding a crocodile and carrying a hawk on his fist. He can teach all languages, bring back or halt runaways and make earthquakes. Agares's mildness should not be mistaken for weakness: he can overthrow all great powers and dignities, in earthly and supernatural realms.

Before summoning supernatural beings, ceremonial magicians should be cleansed. Traces of unholiness and corruption must be removed, lest they interfere with the ceremonies or make God and his angels less likely to assist. Most grimoires stipulate that magicians ought to spend several days in a pious state, preceding the summoning. According to a 1655 edition of the *The Heptameron,* attributed to Peter of Abano (*c.* 1257–*c.* 1315): 'The Operator ought to be clean and purified by the space of nine daies before the beginning of the work.' Fasting, chastity and abstinence from luxury were required for three days before the magical operation. On the day itself, the summoner should wear clean garments and be washed and perfumed. All their materials must be consecrated – gown, pen, ink, paper, candles and ritual knife – and an altar must be carefully arranged, in a quiet and clean place.

Magic circles are among the most vital spaces and symbols for ceremonial practitioners. Circles with supernatural powers can be found throughout the cultures and faiths of our world, from yantras in Hinduism, to mandalas in Buddhism and *vèvès* in vodou. Circles specifically for ceremonial magic have been used since antiquity: as with so much magic, the ancient Mesopotamians drew the first circle, which they called the *zisurrû,* using flour. Later grimoires included intricate, beautiful and complex circles, to create a powerful but bound location onto which spirits could be summoned, and also to provide a potent and protective place for the magician to conduct their ritual. In his *Second Book of Occult Philosophy*, Agrippa explains that the circle was judged the 'most fit' shape for 'bindings and conjurations' because it was first a most perfect geometrical figure, characterized by unity and one infinite line, with no beginning or end.

Aleister Crowley bathing in a glacial spring during an expedition to the Himalayas, Pakistan, 1902

For Crowley, mastering physical discomfort in a spiritual environment served to 'inflame' the psychological 'will' that was so essential for magic. His Himalayan expedition lasted a brutal sixty-eight days and served as spiritual preparation for the founding of his magical religion Thelema in Egypt in 1904.

PROFILE
GRIMOIRE SPELLS

Grimoires help magicians work complex and powerful magic. However, before any spells are cast, the 'karcist' (magician or sorcerer) must be orderly, clean, abstinent and pious. For a quarter of a month before the conjurations, *The Grand Grimoire* (created in early 18th-century France) recommends sleeping as little as possible, eating two meals a day at precisely twelve hours apart and putting 'all of your faith' in the Great Adonay 'who is the leader of all the spirits'. When these and other grand preparations are complete, the spells may begin.

LOVE MAGIC
Johann Erdmann Hummel depicts love magic in *A Roman Love Charm* (1848). According to the 18th-century *Grimorium Verum*, you can make someone love you by being chaste for three days then swallowing a nutmeg to which is attached paper bearing certain magic words.

SPIRIT INVOCATION
Most grimoire spells begin by summoning a powerful spirit, as seen here in this detail from *The Shade of Samuel Invoked by Saul* (1857) by Nikiforovich Dmitry Martynov. Within a magic circle, the purified magus utters awakening, prayerful words to conjure up the apparition.

NECROMANCY
Grimoires suggested that necromancy should occur in churchyards, or better still at places of criminal execution, violent death and slaughter in war. This aquatint from *c.* 1825 depicts Edward Kelley, a 16th-century magician, summoning a person recently deceased.

DEMONIC PACT
This woodcut from *The Grand Grimoire* depicts Lucifuge Rofocale, described as the Prime Minister of demons. The text explains through a long dialogue how to make a deal with Lucifuge Rofocale, who controls worldly wealth and has the ability to make people rich – as long as they follow his rules.

HAND OF GLORY
This macabre burglar's tool renders the user invisible. Some editions of the *Petit Albert* (*c.* 1702) specify that the hand must be cut from a hanged man, squeezed of blood, prepared with herbs and salts, then dried and baked. To work, it must hold a burning candle made of the hanged man's fat, as here.

ABRAMELIN OPERATION
The Abramelin Operation is a powerful spell to commune with one's Holy Guardian Angel (HGA). It takes at least six months of prayer, fasting, rituals and purification before the HGA bestows powerful knowledge. In Rembrandt's *A Scholar in His Study ('Faust')* (*c.* 1652), an old man is transfixed by an apparition.

LICENCE TO DEPART
Almost every grimoire emphasizes the importance of permitting invoked spirits to return to their realm. This 18th-century watercolour shows that the method is often simple. Spirits must be clearly and courteously told that they can, for the present, return to their destined place.

TREASURE DISCOVERY
To find buried treasure, the *Grimorium Verum* details how a magician can ask for the help of Lucifer and the mystical guard-dog Cerberus, then magically subdue the spirit of the person who buried the riches. This 14th-century illuminated manuscript portrays demons bringing treasure to a magician.

SPIRIT CURSE
Spirits who rebel or refuse to appear can be threatened (in this 18th-century watercolour, engulfed in flames) into obedience with a curse. 'O thou wicked and disobedient spirit', begins the first curse of the *Lesser Key of Solomon*, an immensely influential compilation made in the 1600s.

Maxine Sanders demonstrating ceremonial magic for the producers of the horror movie *The Eye of the Devil*, London, 1966
Maxine sits in a magic circle, with consecrated wine, Solomonic symbols, holy words and a black-handled knife (athame). Together with her husband Alex, she was an influential early proponent of a style of modern witchcraft or Wicca that from the 1970s was known as Alexandrian.

The Heptameron likewise explains that the unadorned circle is an exceptionally protective symbol, then offers precise instructions on how to draw complex circles. Today, many ceremonial magicians use static circles, with consistent shapes and details. But *The Heptameron* insists that magical circles must be dynamic, changing according to the spirits called, planetary positions and the precise timing of the ritual. Sometimes, these circles are drawn on paper, or even in the mind, but conventionally magic circles are drawn on the floor using chalk or charcoal. A knife (preferably black handled), sword, staff or wand may be used to draw circles outdoors, in dirt or sand.

Ceremonial magicians need a special pentacle or talisman to protect and empower them during spirit summoning. Ancient texts such as the Greek magical papyri call this talisman a magician's phylactery. From medieval times, the magical breastplate was known as a lamen or lamella. The form can be metal or wax, but most are parchment or paper. The front bears the symbol of the spirit being invoked, and the reverse contains the sigil, star or angel who thwarts and

Paranormal investigator Harry Price (right) and philosopher C. E. M. Joad, Brocken Mountain, Germany, 1932
The pair's well-publicized experiment was intended to recreate a scene in Goethe's Faust, *in which a goat turns into a young man. Price followed instructions from a 19th-century manuscript, which he claimed had been copied from a 15th-century text, but the goat remained a beast.*

controls the spirit. The lamen protects the magician and increases the chances of successful summoning. It should be made, says the *Fourth Book of Occult Philosophy*, when the moon waxes (increases in size).

Powerful belief is key for a ceremonial magician. Ancient magical papyri demanded fear of the gods. Lively religious faith, Agrippa stipulates in his *Third Book of Occult Philosophy*, provides 'firmness of mind' and protects against evil spirits. Unbelief is dangerous. It hinders magical work 'in every operation', occultist Francis Barrett warns in *The Magus* (1801). Belief, however, must be hidden from outsiders, along with other details of ceremonial work: 'Let silence hide these things within the secret closets of thy religious breast, and conceal them with constant taciturnity,' commands the *Fourth Book of Occult Philosophy*.

Elite fraternities and private societies have long taught varieties of ceremonial and ritual magic. These teachings seem to have increased, however, during the period when magic began leaving mainstream culture. Beginning around the 1610s in Germany, Rosicrucian societies sought spiritual enlightenment

DECODING
MAGIC CIRCLE

Books of ceremonial magic such as the *Key of Solomon* (mid-18th-century edition, below) explain how to draw magic circles, which serve two key purposes. First, they increase the authority and power of the magician, with sacred names and symbols enabling them to summon and command a spirit. Second, magic circles provide protection, establishing a space where spirits can appear but not go beyond, while enclosing a magical safe zone for the magus.

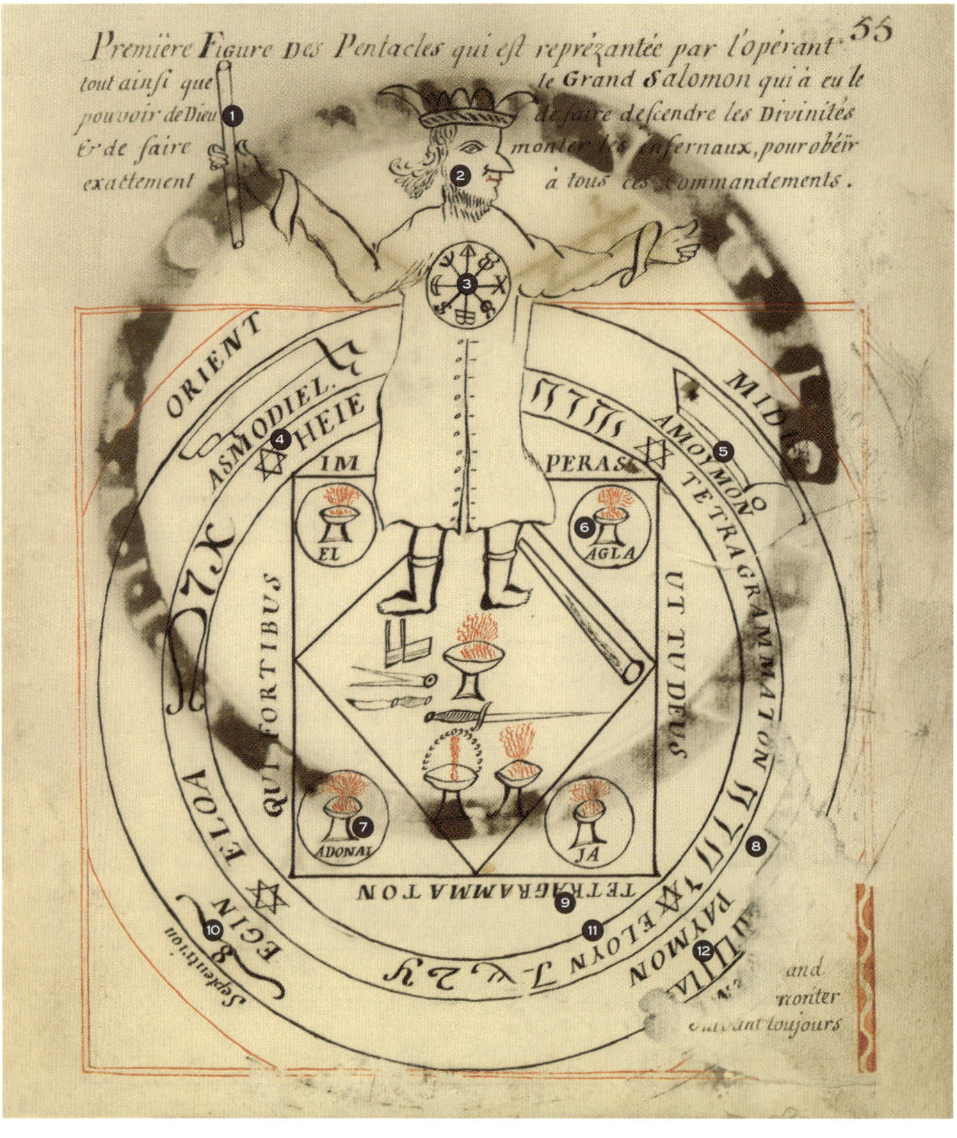

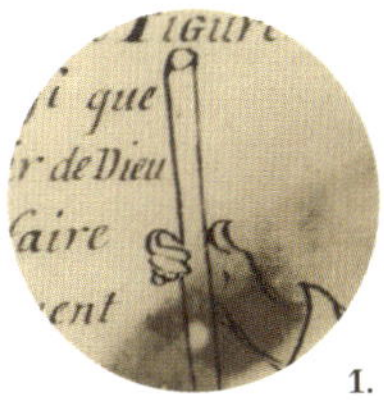

1.

MAGIC WAND
A magic wand was not only used to direct magical energy, but also to summon or smite disobedient spirits.

2.

CROWN
The crown symbolizes authority over the spirits. Often, it is inscribed with divine names to protect against harm.

3.

LAMEN
This breastplate has the symbol of the summoned spirit on the front, and the sigil of the angel or star who controls it on the back.

4.

ASMODIEL
This angel is associated with love magic and romance as well as the astrological sign of Taurus.

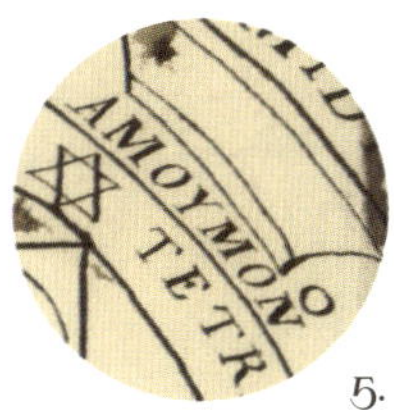

5.

AMOYMON
A chief among evil spirits, Amoymon can divine, protect, enable flight, raise the dead and cause visions.

6.

AGLA
AGLA is a kabbalistic acronym for the Hebrew phrase *Atā gībōr lə'ōlām 'Ădōnāy*. It means 'Thou, O Lord, art mighty forever'.

7.

ADONAI
Adonai is a Hebrew name for God, also meaning 'My Lord'. Holy names are written to empower and enable the rite.

8.

HEBREW CHARACTERS
These Hebrew characters יהוה denote a Hebrew theonym (proper name of a deity) meaning YHWH (Yahweh).

9.

TETRAGRAMMATON
This refers to '*Quis in fortibus ut tu Deus Tetragrammaton*', meaning 'Who is as strong as You, God Tetragrammaton'.

10.

EGIN
This demonic spirit king of the North is sometimes identified as king of the fairies, wearing royal or superior clothes.

11.

ELOYN
This name is an alternative spelling of Elyon, which in the Hebrew Bible means 'Most High'.

12.

PAYMON
This demon king of the West commands 200 legions of spirits. He is often depicted riding a camel, wearing a crown.

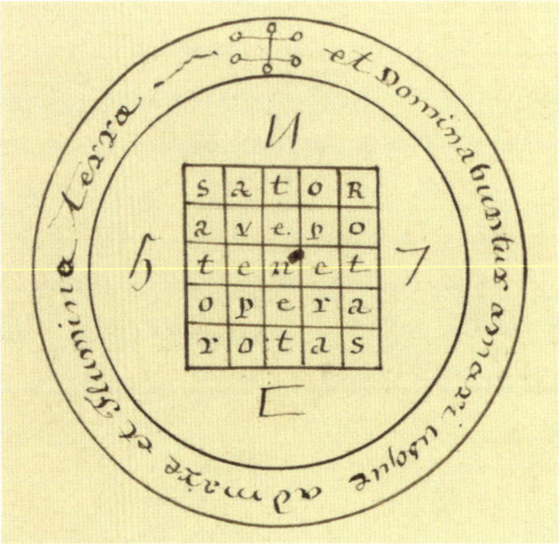

Sator Rotas squares
The earliest known example of a Sator Rotas square comes from Pompeii before 79 CE. By the medieval and early modern periods, the squares functioned as a form of magical protection against the likes of fire, fits and scabies across Europe, West Asia, North Africa and later the Americas. The translation of the Latin is uncertain, but it may be a maxim meaning something like 'Reap what you sow'.

from secret doctrines that blended Christian mysticism with alchemy, hermeticism, exotic traditions and various types of magic. Ceremonial magic is particularly guarded and hidden in Kabbalah. This iconic Jewish mystical tradition, which emerged during the late Middle Ages, includes a style of ritual magic that makes great use of the secret Hebrew names of God and angels, which could be found in texts such as the *Sha'arei Kedusha* (*Gates of Holiness*, 1734), on amulets and in spells. The true name of God is a 'secret of secrets' that can cause 'heaven and earth to tremble' – so advised the *Zohar*, a foundational text compiled and written in Spain in the 13th century. The allure of secrecy has helped make kabbalistic ceremonial magic highly influential. During the Renaissance, Kabbalah inspired a Christianized form called Cabbalah, using ceremonial magic to spiritually regenerate participants and build relationships with angels and God. From the 19th century, Kabbalah and Cabbalah were key ingredients in a Mystical Qabalah tradition of occultism. Still today, secrecy shrouds Kabbalah's highest mysteries. In 1993, Israel's oldest and most respected Kabbalist, Rabbi Yitzhak Kadouri (1898–2006), told booksellers to interview potential customers to ensure piety before selling certain books on the topic.

During the 19th century, industrial publishing made learning about ceremonial magic more accessible and

Temple of the Societas Rosicruciana in America, New York City, USA, *c.* 1913
The Masonic-style order taught Rosicrucian mysteries and ceremonial magic based on rituals from the Hermetic Order of the Golden Dawn. Founded in 1878, the Societas Rosicruciana in America was led from 1909 by Supreme Magus and Imperator Dr George Winslow Plummer. He opened the society to women in 1916.

appealing. No longer did you have to source a hard-to-decipher manuscript or grimoire, or rely on a plain printed copy for details of rituals, ideas for rites or lists of holy names or magic numbers. Barrett's *The Magus* is an elegant printed grimoire, which draws heavily on the work of Agrippa, with plates beautifully depicting the spirits in vivid detail and colour. In Paris, Jacques Albin Simon Collin de Plancy iconically represents the spirits of the grimoire tradition in his *Dictionnaire Infernal* (1818). From the 1850s, Alphonse Louis Constant (1810–75), also known as Éliphas Lévi, wrote extensively on the Kabbalah and ceremonial magic. Drawing on Renaissance occultist Paracelsus (1493–1541), he developed the concept of astral power, which is similar to psychic power but rooted less in the human mind and more in cosmic energies. Constant also reinterpreted Baphomet, taking the name of an idol whom the Knights Templar were falsely accused of worshipping and making him into an androgynous goat representing balance. This Pan-like figure later became the Horned God of Wicca and modern pagan witchcraft.

Ceremonial magic was further reenergized, but also adapted, during the late 19th century and early 20th

DECODING THE ROSE CROSS LAMEN

The Rose Cross Lamen symbolizes the immensely complex magical system of the Hermetic Order of the Golden Dawn. It is a Hermetic version of the Rosicrucian Rose Cross, a symbol that since the early modern period has been associated with esoteric Christianity and theurgic magic (aimed at spiritual

perfection and union with the divine). The Rose Cross Lamen is hung around the neck from yellow silk and worn by adepts who have progressed from studying Golden Dawn magic to practising it. Ideally, the lamen should be self-constructed, consecrated, then stored in white cloth when not being used.

1. *MERCURY*
Mercury represents the connection between divine and natural forces. It is the mediating or balancing symbol of alchemy.

2. *SULPHUR*
The active and masculine symbol of alchemy, sulphur represents the will, soul and inner fire that fuel transformation.

3. *SALT*
The passive and feminine symbol of alchemy. Represents the manifestation of spiritual forces in nature and humans.

4. *YELLOW ARM*
Yellow signifies the magical element air. Symbols are written in violet, as the 'positive' and complementary hue.

5. *LARGE RAYS*
In Christianity, INRI denotes Jesus of Nazareth, King of the Jews. In the Golden Dawn, it is the key to a magical formula.

6. *SMALL RAYS*
LVX is Latin for 'light' and IAO denotes the Egyptian gods Isis, Apophis and Osiris, signifying birth, death and resurrection.

7. *RED ARM*
Red represents the magical element fire. Symbols, here written in green, are repeated on each arm of the cross.

8. *FLASHING EFFECT*
Adjacent vibrant and complementary colours make the cross seem to pulse, shimmer or flash with power.

9. *OUTER RING*
Twelve petals with Hebrew letters symbolize the twelve constellations of the Western astrological zodiac.

10. *MIDDLE RING*
Seven coloured petals signify the seven planets of our solar system, and the metals associated with them.

11. *INNER RING*
There are three 'mother' letters in the inner ring that represent the mothers of alchemy: water, air and fire.

12. *ROSE PETALS*
The unfolding of the human soul is symbolized by rose petals, flowering from nature's receptiveness to the divine light.

13. *GREEN BARBS*
The green barbs, or sepals, point in four cardinal directions. Green represents the receiving force of nature.

14. *KING SCALE*
The petals run anticlockwise from red to violet in a magical colour scheme that symbolizes active, direct and masculine forces.

15. *BLUE ARM*
The magical element water is represented by the blue arm. On the edge, the salt symbol is chief (central), linking to the ocean.

16. *WHEEL OF SPIRIT*
Located above the pentagram, the wheel symbolizes the rule of spirit over the other four magical elements.

17. *PENTAGRAM*
The star signifies the microcosm, the blend of spiritual and material forces in the individual human or magician.

18. *THE FOUR KERUBIN*
The astrological symbols around the pentacles represent the alchemical elements of water, fire, earth and air.

19. *WHITE*
White symbolizes divine light. In the Golden Dawn, white also represents purity and kether, the highest point of the Tree of Life.

20. *HEXAGRAM*
This symbol represents the Supreme Ritual of the Hexagram, a ceremonial rite uses hexagrams to balance planetary energies.

21. *FOUR-COLOUR ARM*
This arm symbolizes the element Earth through four sub-elements. Citrine is airy, olive is watery, russet is fiery, and black is earthy.

century, by the Hermetic Order of the Golden Dawn. This elite society taught its adepts how to use magic to undergo psychological and spiritual transformation. The aim, ultimately, was to communicate with transcendent beings called the Secret Chiefs (similar creatures were the focus of other occult groups). Some Golden Dawn adherents believed that the Secret Chiefs literally existed, and were outraged when disputes within the society later revealed that these sacred entities may be symbolic. For others, this innovative form of ceremonial magic was a non-literal, consciousness-raising exercise. Either way, within the Golden Dawn, many potent traditions combined. Its doctrine was a version of Hermetic Qabalah. It began with Jewish Kabbalah and Christian Cabbalah. To this was added magic from Egypt and Greece, incorporating pagan deities and Neo-Platonism. The grimoire tradition was mixed in, along with the Enochian system of angel magic devised by Dee. Finally, Eastern mystical practices, particularly from Hinduism and Buddhism, were sprinkled on top. All this was collated and taught through rank structures that were inspired by Rosicrucianism and Freemasonry. It was a huge and heady range of influences. They were summed up in an iconic item of the Golden Dawn, worn on adepts' chests during rituals: the Rose Cross Lamen.

The Golden Dawn was numerically small but extremely influential. At most, the order had only a few hundred members, with temples in London, Edinburgh, Bradford, Weston-super-Mare and Paris. However, some of the adherents edited the grimoires that made ceremonial magic more widely available. They also helped make tarot cards indispensable magical items. Golden Dawn members Pamela Colman Smith (1878–1951) and A. E. Waite (1857–1942) worked with publisher William Rider & Son to produce an iconic deck in 1909. Waite provided ideas and Colman Smith created captivating illustrations for all seventy-eight cards. Previous decks only pictured the twenty-two trump cards, or Major Arcana, but Colman Smith illustrated the Minor Arcana, too, setting a new standard for magical tarot.

Rider-Waite-Smith tarot deck, 1909

This iconic tarot deck was unusual for its rich symbolism and entirely illustrated deck, both of which made it extremely popular for divination. Some readers consider that the cards represent positive qualities if upright, but more negative states if reversed or upside down.

ntellect' ipi dd cu uenit doech idume'
aul· et dix' illi· uenit dd in domu abim
in iniquitate·
ota die iniusticiam cogitauit

'BULLETS AND MACHINE GUNS CAPABLE OF DAUNTING DUVALIER DO NOT EXIST .... I AM ALREADY AN IMMATERIAL BEING.'

FRANÇOIS DUVALIER (1963)

Politics is prone to magic. Candidates facing elections may reassure themselves with lucky charms. In sub-Saharan Africa, politicians occasionally accuse opponents of witchcraft, or use magic themselves. Historically, rulers projected power using magical rituals and objects, then made difficult decisions by consulting astrologers. Family tragedy made Russia's last Tsar Nicholas II and his wife Tsarina Alexandra scandalously over-reliant on the supernatural healing of Rasputin. Elsewhere though, soldiers and revolutionaries have taken courage from talismans and oaths, while painting their political enemies as satanists or demons.

'Magic and politics are closely linked in history,' notes historian Francis Young in a recent study of the relationship between the occult and governments in Britain. Today, however, political magic is mostly subtle and low key. Politics is stressful and uncertain. Conflicts are constant. Sense of personal control is low. No wonder even the toughest politicians can appreciate a little magical comfort. In 2002, the British media reported that Cherie Blair (wife of then Prime Minister Tony Blair) had been gifted a healing crystal necklace by Hillary Clinton. British Prime Minister Margaret Thatcher appreciated a few lucky charms, as recorded in her autobiography and letters. Before elections, the Iron Lady was known to wear a pearl necklace. In nervy 1989, facing a leadership challenge and mass opposition to her proposed poll tax, Thatcher found comfort in a beautiful and personal lucky charm – a golden acorn, gifted to her by romance novelist Dame Barbara Cartland.

In parts of Africa, however, magic courses through politics. Witchcraft, known locally as *djambe* and supposedly rooted in a specific physical organ located near the gallbladder, had an omnipresence among the Maka people of Cameroon, Dutch anthropologist Peter Geschiere (b. 1941) noted in the 1990s. Australian anthropologist Adam Ashforth (b. 1957) agreed, on the basis of living and conducting fieldwork in South Africa, that 'no one can understand life in Africa without understanding witchcraft'. In some nations, witchcraft and powers such as juju are quite often suspected and sometimes used in political struggles. Examples noted in the media or US diplomatic cables include a potential presidential candidate in Malawi (Sam Mpasu) who was accused in 2006 of doing harmful witchcraft after being arrested in a graveyard. In 2009, Gambia's president employed magicians to accuse opponents and non-supporters of witchcraft, then force them to relent while pledging loyalty to the regime. The king of Swaziland used and feared magic, particularly *muti* spells and curses, leaked diplomatic cables revealed in 2010. Libya's Colonel Gaddafi used 'African magic' to prolong his

< *page 140*
David and King Saul with a demon, illuminated psalter, France, *c.* 1205
Envious of David's popularity after he slew Goliath, King Saul menacingly draws his sword. A demon whispers into the king's ear, while pointing at the young hero. According to the Old Testament, God sent a harmful spirit to torment Saul, leading eventually to his downfall.

Horseback armour (*yoroi*) belonging to the founder of the Ashikaga shogunate, Japan, early 14th century

Saturated with symbolic meaning, the armour originally featured multicoloured lacing that evoked good fortune. The fierce yet calm Buddhist deity Fudō Myō-ō, stencilled on the breastplate leather, enhanced the samurai wearer's powers while protecting him from spiritual and psychological harm.

DECODING ANCIENT EGYPTIAN DEATH MASK

In ancient Egypt, magic was unusually focused on the dead, helping Egyptians journey through grim death to be reborn in the glorious afterlife. Mummification, reserved for royalty and elites in the Old Kingdom though more widespread after, fizzed with magic at every stage. Funerary masks, including this one from the 1st century BCE, were used to protect the head and chest of the mummified body. They presented an idealized version of the dead, ensuring their success in the next life.

1.

EYE OF HORUS
The god Horus had his eye destroyed by his uncle, Seth. Eventually, though, it was miraculously restored. The Eye of Horus, or *wedjat*, symbolizes miraculous restoration, health, healing, protection and wholeness. Here, it is featured at the centre of the headdress.

2.

GOLD SKIN
The skin of this mask is embellished with gold leaf. In ancient Egyptian cosmology, gold was the flesh of the gods, a sacred material. The gilding of this mask, therefore, confirms the intention that the wearer would be reborn as a divine being in the next life.

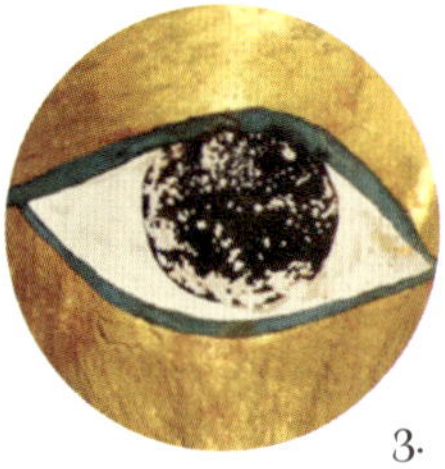

3.

ENLARGED FACIAL FEATURES
Big and beautiful eyes, ears, nose and mouth ensured that the deceased could see, hear, smell, breathe, eat and speak in the next life. The idealized form of these features also shows the deceased's desire to be reborn as a divine being.

4.

HEART-SHAPED AMULET
Ancient Egyptians believed the human soul resided in the heart, not the brain. After death, their soul would be judged worthy, or not, by weighing the heart against Maat's feather of truth. The heart became a key amulet and can be seen on this necklace.

5.

BLUE HAIR AND LOTUS FLOWERS
The colour blue is associated with water, and hence the River Nile and the primeval waters of chaos. It therefore symbolizes life, creation and regeneration. Similarly, the daily blooming of the lotus flower links the motif to rebirth.

6.

OSIRIS PREPARES FOR THE AFTERLIFE
Along the base of the mask, Osiris (identifiable by his crook and flail) sits flanked by other gods. Many of the gods hold strips of linen, to be used as mummy wrappings to help prepare the deceased for the afterlife.

1
2
3
4
5
6

< **Gold coin and medallion necklace, Byzantium, late 6th century**
In the Eastern Roman Empire, elites wore lavish pendants that signified wealth and loyalty and also provided religious and magical protection. The medallion depicts the Annunciation to Mary and the Marriage at Cana. The reverse bears the inscription 'Lord Protect the Wearer'.

> **Bioelectric shield worn by Cherie Blair, wife of the then British Prime Minister Tony Blair, 1998**
The amulet reportedly protected against harmful electronic rays from computers and mobile phones and also harmful energies from people.

rule, insiders reported in 2013, while service magicians from Zambia were arrested in 2024 for bewitching the country's president.

Across the world, political magic was once open and conspicuous. It symbolized power and took magnificent forms. Elites poured great resources into magical objects. Beautiful magic rings became family heirlooms. Lavish magical necklaces were worn at ceremonies, along with gem-encrusted magical knives, or swords engraved with supernatural markings. In battle, elites wore magical armour that was empowered by scriptures, symbols and gods. Japan's aristocratic samurai, for example, had intimidating Buddhist deities depicted on their shields and breastplates, to slow or immobilize enemies while improving the samurai's fighting skills. Great rulers sometimes employed vast magical protection, because the survival of a kingdom or dynasty was at stake. Ancient Mesopotamian and Assyrian royalty covered the interior rooms of their palaces with huge reliefs of magical figures. Gods, demons and lyrical inscriptions were chiselled in imposing detail, to magically protect and empower the king.

***Raja Sidh Sen of Mandi as Vasudeva Carrying Baby Krishna across the Yamuna River*, India, late 18th century**
This miniature depicts the ruler of the Mandi Himalayan state as Vasudeva, carrying the newborn Krishna to safety. Raja Sidh Sen was a highly religious tantric practitioner known for his supernatural powers.

Many elites used magic to appear special. Emperor Qin Shi Huang (259–210 BCE), first ruler of unified China, built an image of supernatural invincibility by openly consulting alchemists and sorcerers. When he died, he was guarded in the afterlife by the vast Terracotta Army. Raja Sidh Sen (1684–1727), a prolific war leader from the Indian state of Mandi, was said to have a book of spells and to possess various supernatural abilities, including the power to fly. Until the 1700s, the monarchs of England and France held regular ceremonies to administer the magical royal touch, which was supposed to cure the disfiguring illness of scrofula (non-bacterial tuberculosis). English rulers between Edward III (crowned in 1308) and Mary Tudor (crowned in 1553) also blessed rings that magically protected against cramp and epilepsy. Yet magical rulers do not belong exclusively to the deep past. Fascist and communist personality cults were 'tinged with superstition and magic', notes historian Frank Dikötter (b. 1961). In Italy, Mussolini (1883–1945) inspired pilgrimages, holy pictures, holy locations and even belief in the healing

François Duvalier, dictator of Haiti, *c.* 1970
Duvalier enhanced his fearsome reputation by imitating the vodou lao Baron Samedi. Here, he holds a smiling yet intimidating gaze.

touch of the leader. Some carried his photograph as a lucky talisman.

The modern leader who used magic most was Haiti's notorious dictator François Duvalier (1907–71). He was long fascinated by the highly magical religion of vodou. In power, he used it to terrify opponents. He dressed like the vodou *loa* of death Baron Samedi: bespectacled, in a black hat, white shirt and black funeral suit. Duvalier's feared militia was called the Tonton Macoutes, meaning 'bogeymen'. The message, as Canadian biographer Elizabeth Abbott (b. 1946) puts it, was that 'through magic and sacrifice, the President had harnessed great forces of evil to assist him in his quest for absolute power.' Duvalier's vodou was not just cynical; he really believed. In 1963, Tonton Macoutes leader Clément Barbot (1914–63) tried to oust Duvalier. The plot failed, then rumours circulated that Barbot had escaped by shapeshifting into a black dog. Duvalier ordered that every animal of that description in Haiti was to be shot. On another occasion, he ordered an enemy's decapitated head to be packed in ice then carried to his palace.

'Kings consulting their astrologers', from *De Secretis Secretorum* (*The Secret of Secrets*), 14th-century Latin translation
The Secret of Secrets *was an Arabic 'mirror for princes' text, advising rulers on many topics of state, including the occult sciences. The manuscript containing these two images was made for the future Edward III of England.*

His intention was to summon and converse with the deceased's spirit.

The link between magic and politics is represented in images of rulers being assisted by diviners, wizards and astrologers. The iconic scene usually occurs during a crisis. A leader will 'seek out the oracle's response in hours of doubt', as Virgil puts it in the *Aeneid*. Pondering war, rebellion, alliances or important acts of state, the ruler asks the magicians to interpret dreams, stars or other omens. This extends important decision making, giving time for reflection and opportunity to change strategy. For leaders, divination can be useful.

Virtually all ancient rulers used divination. When danger beset the Roman Republic and Empire, the call went out to consult the Sibylline books. These originated with three books of prophecy, sold by an old woman to Lucius Tarquinius Superbus, the last Roman king, who ruled from 534 to 509 BCE. From their capital of Anyang, in Henan Province, ancient China's Shang dynasty (*c.* 1250–*c.* 1046 BCE) used oracle bones to divine the wishes of ancestor spirits. Turtle underbellies and ox shoulder blades were etched with questions then heated over fire. Small cracks would slowly appear, helping diviners establish which

Astrologer working in Friedrichstrasse, Berlin, Germany, 1923

Passers-by are curious about an astrologer in the street. Occult interests surged amid the political and economic instability of interwar Germany, especially during the hyperinflation of 1923. By the 1930s, Berlin was estimated to be home to around 20,000 magical and mystical practitioners such as astrologers and faith healers.

ancestor spirit to propitiate, and how. Although oracle bone divination ended when the Shang dynasty was overthrown, more than 130,000 bone fragments have since been found.

Astrology was closely linked with European politics until the late 17th century. Elites cherished personal nativities, drawn up for special birthdays. Among the public, horoscopes of great people and nations formed a popular genre of literature. This political focus made astrology potentially dangerous. Italian scholar and astrologer Gerolamo Cardano (1501–76) had his worked banned in France and Spain, and was investigated by the Roman Inquisition for suggesting that religious heresy had its origin in astrological influences. Astrology lost prestige in Western societies around 1700, yet remained widely intriguing. Coloured lithographs, linking horoscopes with political events, were very popular during the 19th century. In times of anxiety and turmoil, such as World War I, the appeal of astrology exploded.

Obsession with magic, or excessive interest in the occult, makes political leaders vulnerable. The rule of Russia's tsars collapsed in 1917, partly because the emperor and his family became dangerously over-reliant on the mystic Rasputin (1869–1916). This was part of a much deeper interest in supernatural powers among the Romanovs. Tsarina Alexandra (1872–1918) had for decades been fascinated by strange powers. From the early 20th century, she made talismanic use of the swastika, a mystical symbol brought to Russia from South Asia, probably by the Eastern magic of theosophy. Alexandra drew the swastika for good fortune in diaries, correspondence and prayer cards. Her enthusiasm for mysticism increased when she experienced difficulties conceiving a male heir. It exploded when that heir, Alexi, was revealed to be dangerously and chronically ill with haemophilia. A single fall could cause his death. There was nothing the doctors could do.

Enter Rasputin. Like many great magicians, he mingled religion with practical mystical powers. His style was of a Russian stranniki (wandering holy man).

Rasputin, St Petersburg, Russia, 1914
Rasputin is surrounded by his admirers, mostly socially elite women. His father, Efim, is the bearded man in black. Both Rasputin's supporters and critics attested to the extraordinary power of his gaze.

His doctrine included erotic Christianity, inspired by the free-loving and heretical Khlysty Christian sects. But mystical powers were at the core of Rasputin's life and work. His magic-like abilities emerged first, and, according to the disturbingly pornographic memoirs of his daughter, Rasputin developed mystical gifts long before an association with God. As a child he could apparently tell who was lying, see who was going to die, and heal both animals and people. Rasputin could transfix with his eyes. Some said he could contract and expand his pupils at will and had been trained in the art of hypnotism. Rasputin once told his secretary he used Tibetan drugs or whatever drugs were at hand, before inventing and mumbling prayers. He could electrify with his touch. 'I can do anything' was his magical-sounding catchphrase.

Rasputin became indispensable to the Romanovs after he seemed several times to save Alexi, the Romanov heir, from death. In the Spala miracle of 1912, Rasputin healed Alexi remotely after being notified by telegram. Probably, he exercised a calming influence and a placebo effect. Whatever the case,

Bowl for destructive political magic, Egypt, 2150–1991 BCE
Magically attacking neighbouring rulers was a regular part of Egyptian statecraft. Bowls like this one used a standard text, written in Hieratic, and they were ritually broken then deposited to bind and destroy Egypt's enemies.

Rasputin abused his position for money, sex and the primal feeling of power. He made an already unpopular monarchy scandalous. Amid Rasputin's exploits, the Romanovs lost the crucial support of previously loyal elites. They killed Rasputin in 1916, but the damage could not be undone. And the Romanovs' connection with magic did not end with Rasputin's death. Desperate for help, Alexandra drew a left-handed swastika on the walls of the house in Ekaterinburg, where in 1918 her family would be murdered. Rasputin's magic also survived his death. Seances to communicate with his spirit were later conducted by his followers and daughter.

War is the continuation of politics by other means. And war is saturated with magic. Sometimes it is aggressive: four thousand years ago, ancient Egyptians ritualistically smashed bowls inscribed with the names of foreign rulers and administrators. Few go into battle without some sort of supernatural protection, even if it is only a lucky charm. 'The combat Infantryman is the most superstitious person in the world,' observed Captain Harry G. Summers (1932–99), an American veteran of the Korean War, in a 1963 article for the journal *Infantry*. Elite Muslim warriors, from the Mediterranean to Africa, adorned their weapons and armour with protective words and symbols. Most were verses from the Quran and Hadith. Some mysterious markings, however, invoked the assistance of powerful but dangerous spirits: jinn.

Time and again, magic inflames rebellion and revolution. Rebels worldwide use oaths promising supernatural punishment for betrayers to bind people to their cause. Many credit their leaders with supernatural powers and use amulets or rituals to protect against harm. This sort of magic pulsed through anti-slavery revolts against white rule in the 18th- and 19th-century Caribbean, as well as anti-colonial movements in 20th-century Africa. The binding oath was a central strategy of the Mau Mau during the Mau Mau war (1952–60) against British rule in Kenya, for example. Participants would swear to become a soldier, to fight, to never inform the enemy or give away secrets, to never leave a comrade who needed help, to never sell land to a white person, and to never retreat. If they broke their oath, swearers asked: 'May this soil and all its products be a curse upon me,' according to chroniclers of the movement Donald L. Barnett (1930–75) and Karari Njama (b. 1926).

In recent years, revolutionary magic seems to have grown in the West, notably with the QAnon conspiracy. This holds that the West is ruled by vile elites, who stay youthful and prolong their lives by consuming the hormone adrenochrome. They get that elixir of youth, according to the magical theory, by harvesting it from children during terrifying satanic rituals. QAnon was created on the messenger application Telegram, possibly in part by influencer and former military intelligence officer Ron Watkins (b. 1987), although he denies this. The theory has energized participants in revolutionary activity in the USA, and is also responsible for several deaths. Jake Angeli (b. 1988), known as the QAnon Shaman, led the storming of the US Capitol Building in January 2021. Ashli Babbitt (1985–2021), the woman fatally shot during the attempted insurrection, also believed in the QAnon magical conspiracy. It speaks to the depth of alienation and radicalization felt by some people that they have begun seeing demons in our leaders and public figures.

› *pages 156–57*
Remedios Varo, *The Juggler (The Magician)*, 1956
A pentagram-headed magician mesmerizes his audience, a near-identical group of women dressed in grey robes. He stands on the platform of his wagon, which contains mysterious items, mystical animals and a melancholy woman.

QAnon 'Save The Children' march, St Paul, Minnesota, USA, 2020

QAnon holds that our world's leaders are child-abusing satanists. The theory gained particular ground among some of the most radicalized on the political right, as well as among some Christians and others with broadly New Age interests. In the early 2020s, around 15 to 20 per cent of Americans believed some of QAnon's major claims.

YONS & C

'LIKE EVERYTHING ELSE TO WHICH THE TERM MAGIC HAS BEEN APPLIED AND IS APPLIED, THE WONDERFUL AND MYSTERIOUS ARE ONLY THE SIMPLE AND THE COMMONPLACE.'

PROFESSOR HOFFMANN,
MODERN MAGIC (1876)

Performance magic seems to defy natural laws. Conjurors employ a slick mix of confidence, misdirection, sleight-of-hand, costume, storytelling and special effects. Tricks such as the cup and balls have entertained spectators since antiquity. Many performance magicians guard their secrets, yet guides to the art have been published since at least 1584. Elaborate illusions became increasingly sophisticated with the development of technologies like engines, electricity and film. Performance magic is not simply entertaining. The US Central Intelligence Agency commissioned espionage guides based on performance magic. Learning and performing magic is also good for your confidence, cognition and coordination.

Performance magic is a remarkable art. Young or old, rich or poor, its charm is universal, like storytelling, music and dance. Stage magicians create delightful surprises by seeming to defy the normal workings of physical reality. Neuroscientists now study the feelings inspired by performance magic, but conjurors have always known what it feels like.

Conjuring tricks are extraordinarily effective forms of deception. Although most are quite simple, they are almost never spotted. Occasionally, a mistake, or some insider knowledge, can reveal what is really going on. Even then, onlookers seldom realize. We are not just oblivious; it is not that we lack sharp eyes to see quick movements. Our brains work against us. Concentrating on one point only makes it worse, by raising inattentional blindness elsewhere. Hints and misdirection, from the conjuror, make us fool ourselves. That is where the real magic happens. Magicians induce sensory overload. We cannot keep track of what is happening.

What was the first performance magic? The cup and balls trick, probably. Some claim the earliest reference is ancient Egyptian, in a tomb wall painting of Baqet III (21st century BCE). Two men kneel, with what could be four upside-down bowls between them. But these 'bowls' may actually be bread, because there is no ball, and both men are touching the items (audience participation is not part of the cup and balls trick). The first certain reference to the illusion occurs millennia later. From the 60s CE, Roman Seneca the Younger noted the 'harmlessly deceptive' trickery of the 'juggler's cup and dice'. The Greek sophist Alciphron, who may have lived during the period 400 BCE to 350 CE, watched pebbles seemingly disappear from under cups only to reappear from the conjuror's mouth. It 'struck me dumb with astonishment,' he wrote in a letter.

Hundreds, perhaps thousands, of guides to performance magic have been written since the early modern period. American illusionist Harry Houdini (1874–1926) claimed in *The Unmasking of Robert-Houdin* (1908) to own a 1489 manuscript on 'Natural and Unnatural Magic' that detailed old conjuring

< *page 158*
Canadian stage magician James Randi performing a levitation trick on a rooftop in Eastbourne, England, 1958
Randi began his career as 'The Amazing Randi', an escape artist and mentalist. In 1986, he became the first magician to receive a MacArthur fellowship to expose fraudulent psychics and faith healers.

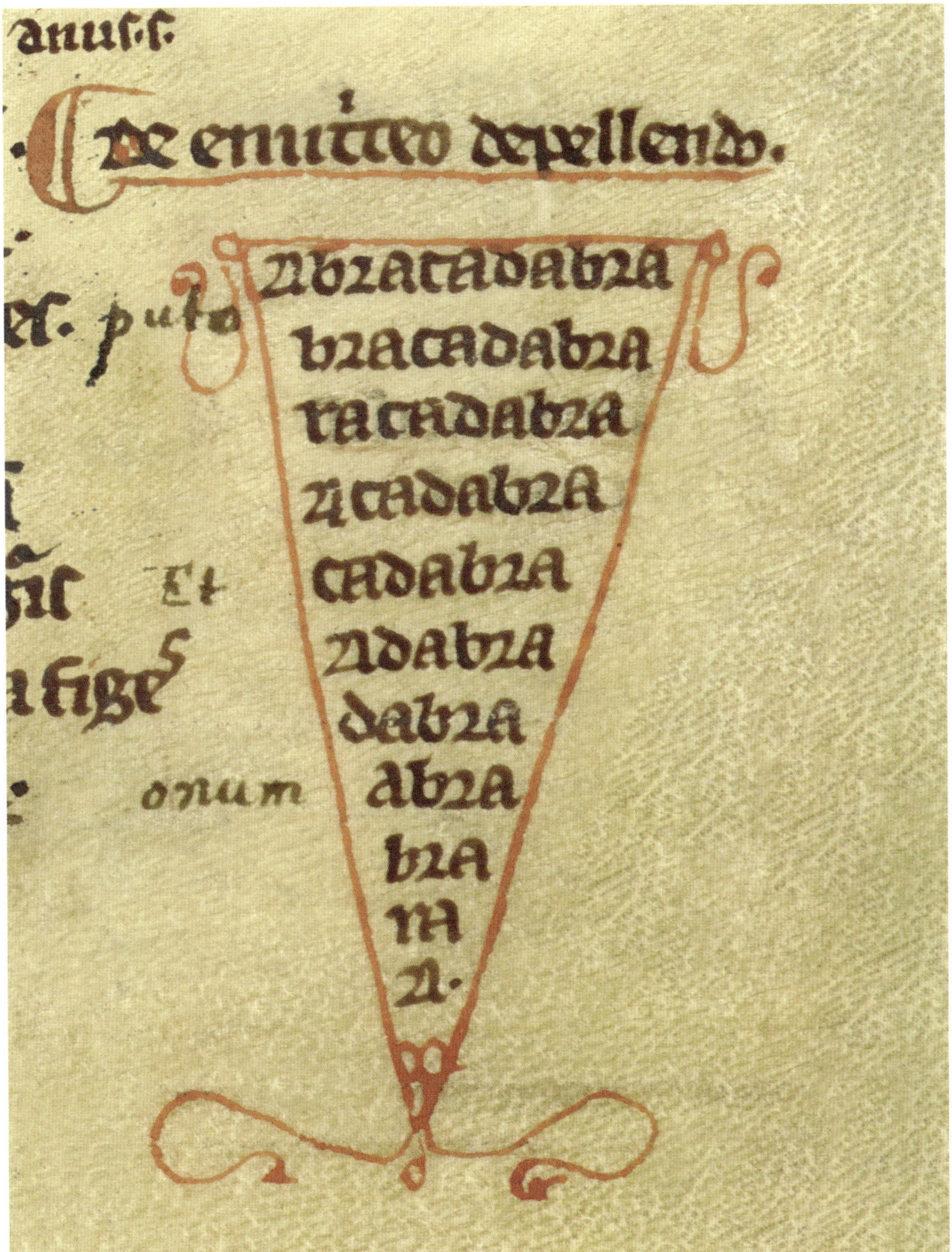

'Abracadabra triangle', from Quintus Serenus Sammonicus's *Liber Medicinalis* (*Book of Medicine*), 13th-century copy

If worn as an amulet, an abracadabra triangle was supposed to make fever 'little and little decline and pass away', as Cornelius Agrippa put it in his Three Books of Occult Philosophy *(1533). Like many other magical terms, the origin of the word 'abracadabra' is obscure.*

Diagrams of palming and passes, from Professor Hoffmann's *Modern Magic*, 1876
This book was the first English work to comprehensively and systematically categorize, illustrate and explain various passes and forms of palming. A sequel, More Magic *(1890), introduced further techniques such as the Charlier Pass.*

tricks. It is plausible, but a work of that description has not yet been tracked down in Houdini's book archive at the Library of Congress. The first widely published and comprehensive description of performance magic comes from *The Discoverie of Witchcraft* (1584) by Reginald Scot. It explains how to do the cup and balls trick and illustrates an early version of the decapitation illusion. It was followed, from the early 17th century, by dedicated guides to conjuring.

The chief skill of performance magicians, according to the guidebooks, is confidence. Conjurors require 'a bold, and audacious spirit', notes *Hocus Pocus Junior* (1635). With voice and intonation, the magician controls and beguiles. Gestures guide spectators' eyes. Shame and timidity, along with lack of practice, invite failure. What a performance magician needs most is 'a large amount of self-possession and impudence', advises Angelo John Lewis (1839–1919), also known as Professor Hoffmann, in his classic *Modern Magic* (1876).

'Forcing a card' is an evergreen trick for budding magicians. It involves giving the dupe the illusion they are choosing a card, when in fact the magician is guiding or controlling the choice. There are many methods. Careful hand movements can spread the cards then force the desired one towards the finger

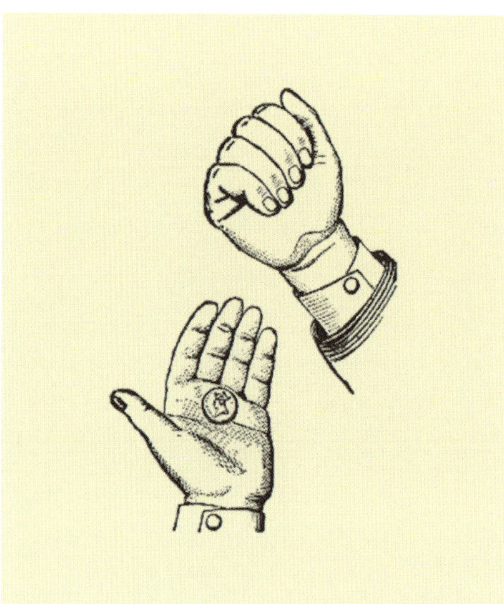

< **Harry Houdini stunt, Dayton, Ohio, USA, 1916**
The trick involved Houdini freeing himself from a straightjacket while suspended upside-down in mid-air. By this period, he had moved his escape stunts from the theatre to the open air for greater publicity.

> **David Copperfield illusion, 1985**
Copperfield performs a levitation illusion with his assistant Catherine Bach. His television specials were lavishly produced and culminated in grand illusions, including making a jet plane disappear.

the mark is choosing with. A 'riffle force' tells the mark to say 'stop', although really the magician controls where the break is made. A 'slip force' relocates a touched card, through quick and subtle finger work.

Making coins or small objects appear, disappear or move 'by magic' requires other forms of dexterity. Among the most useful is palming. It is the act of secretly holding something in the open hand, through slight contractions of the palm edges. To avoid detection, the palm must always face away from the audience. Magicians must practise moving their hand and fingers normally, and then learn the more advanced skill of passes, to move the hidden object from one hand to the other. Many styles exist. Confidence and misdirection are always necessary. The magician's eyes are crucial: they should be fixed on where the object is supposed to be, to lead the audience's eyes in that direction. When it is time to produce the object, the conjuror moves it to their fingers then feigns to take it from a mouth or ear (their own or a mark's).

Professional performance magicians can dazzle. The greatest are obsessives, and some began extremely early. David Seth Kotkin (b. 1956), also known as David Copperfield, was prolific from childhood. He adopted a stage name at the age of ten, became the youngest

DECODING THE CONJURER

This is one of several copies of a missing original, *The Conjurer*, created after Hieronymus Bosch in 1475 and kept in the collection of Musée Municipal in Saint-Germain-en-Laye, France. The painting is seldom displayed after it was stolen by a faction of the far-left group Action Directe in 1978, although it

was returned a year later. Bosch depicts a conjurer, equipped with magic paraphernalia including a wand, performing the classic cup and ball trick to a captivated crowd. The conjurer, audience and collaborators are vividly portrayed. The bleak background highlights the fascinating and complex foreground scene.

1.

2.

3.

4.

5.

6.

1. Spectators: the crowd of spectators includes a nun, a monk and a wealthy woman, showing how everyone can be easily taken in, and fooled, by performance magic. Some critics suggest that the presence of the monk and nun is an attack on the blindness of the Church.
2. Dupe: the dupe has a frog or toad coming out of their mouth. Another sits on the table. To vomit frogs/toads (animals associated with witchcraft) was a symptom of bewitchment. Bosch may be using this figuratively to suggest the dupe is under the conjurer's spell of deception.
3. Misdirection: a spectacled man steals the dupe's purse. He uses misdirection, looking up at the sky. He is also dressed like a Dominican monk, perhaps to appear less like a thief. Some critics suggest this depiction is a coded attack on the Church's financial exploitation of ordinary laypeople.
4. Foolishness: a child looks up, smiling at the dupe's foolishness. He seems to embody the Flemish proverb 'He who lets himself be fooled by conjuring tricks loses his money and becomes the laughing stock of children'.
5. Palming: the conjurer practises the key technique of 'palming' by secretly holding an additional ball in his left hand. Beside the conjurer's hand, an owl, which symbolizes darkness and superstition, peeps out from a basket attached to his belt.
6. Dog: animals often play a role in stage magic. This dog wears a devil-like joker's outfit, hinting at ideas of deceit and ridiculousness.

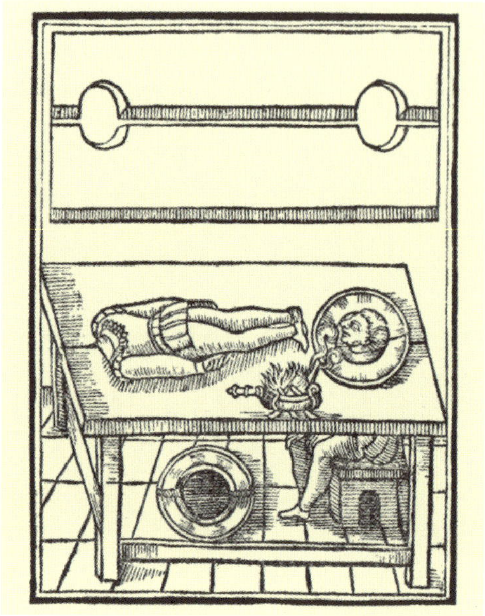

‹ **John Gaughan and Associates, *The Fantastic Orange Tree Automaton*, *c.* 1989**
Based on a 19th-century mechanical illusion of Robert-Houdin, this orange tree featured in British magician Paul Daniels' televised show.

› **John the Baptist illusion, from Reginald Scot's *The Discoverie of Witchcraft*, 1584**
This illustration shows the mechanics of a trick, in which a decapitated head appears on a platter. Scot's book was both a radically sceptical treatise about the practice of harmful witchcraft and a detailed manual of supernatural and performance magic.

member of the Society of American Magicians at twelve, invented new tricks from that age and taught magic at New York University from age sixteen. Great conjurors like him know that powerful stage magic goes far beyond the trick. Magicians must convincingly act the part. 'A magician is only an actor, an actor pretending to be a magician,' noted Houdini.

Symbolism and storytelling heighten emotion and build engagement. In 16th- and 17th-century England, decapitation illusions depicted the heartbreaking religious story of John the Baptist, who was beheaded by King Herod. Magical animal acts emerged during the 18th century, as urbanites became more interested in nature. Learned pigs were trained to choose cards of letters and numbers, as if they could do maths or spell. During the mid-19th century, Jean-Eugène Robert-Houdin (1805–71) thrilled Parisians with ornate illusions like The Marvellous Orange Tree. An audience member's ring and handkerchief were made to vanish then reappear in a beautiful mechanical tree, which blossomed and revealed butterflies. It captivatingly evoked ideas of beauty and societal rebirth, during an otherwise disturbing age of revolution and change.

Elaborate and technical illusions stretch deep into history. The 16th-century 'John the Baptist' decapitation illusion used a cloth-covered table that had concealed joints and holes. Beneath it lay two boys, ready as needed to put a plate around their head, or bring the decapitated head out of the correct hole. The head was presented on a platter, with bits of thread on the neck simulating blood vessels, and offal and blood dished around it. Burning brimstone cast the spectacle in a pale light. A suitably timed groan would shock the audience. Stage magic became bigger and better during the 19th century, brought about by artificial lights, mechanical tricks, music, acoustics, abundant materials (robes, smoke, crystal balls) and better venues. Robert-Houdin's Paris theatre, which opened in 1845, had an elegant atmosphere like a salon. Sensation increased in the early 20th century, when Houdini's death-defying escape tricks thrilled newspapers and audiences across the world.

Conjurors pioneered new technologies, such as film and cinema. Georges Méliès (1861–1938) created dozens of short silent 'trick films', with techniques like multiple exposures to give the impression of ghostly presences. Storytelling became a massive

Georges Méliès performing *Le Nain Jaune* (*The Yellow Dwarf*), Théâtre Robert-Houdin, Paris, *c.* 1890s
Méliès purchased the theatre in 1888. This cabinet illusion, inspired by a French card game, used trapdoors and hidden compartments to seemingly make an assistant appear by magic.

part of performance magic during the television age. In the 1980s, millions watched David Copperfield walk through the Great Wall of China, escape Alcatraz and make the Statue of Liberty disappear. His spectacular illusions made for compelling television shows, partly because they evoked powerful symbols, narratives and places. Emotive ideas like freedom, imprisonment and borders mingled with the curiosity and surprise of classic stage magic.

Conjurors, of course, imitate supernatural magic. Audiences expect a wand, a mystical stage name, magic words and a lucky tap or rub. Ceremonial robes became dispensable props centuries ago, although some conjurors still wear them today. Robert-Houdin is sometimes called the first stage magician to perform in eveningwear. However, images from the 17th and 18th centuries show his forebears wearing smart clothes. Other stage magicians followed the trends of supernatural magic. During the mid-19th century, some imitated spiritualism, including the Davenport Brothers. In the late 19th-century era of globalization and occult revival, stereotypes of exotic magic became prominent. These were replaced, during the 20th

Georges Méliès in *Un Homme de Têtes* (*The Four Troublesome Heads*), 1898
In this pathbreaking silent film, the French magician used double exposure techniques to enable him to remove his head three times and place the heads on a table. The decapitated heads then accompany the magician as he sings and plays the banjo.

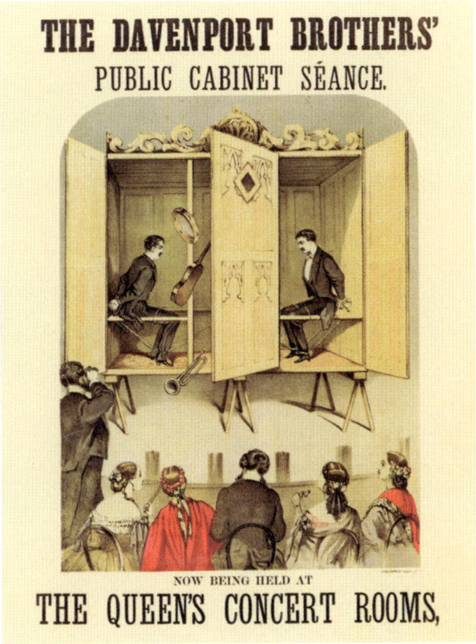

< **Poster for *Les Spectres et le Manoir du Diable* (*The Devil's Manor*), France, 1896**
The world's first horror movie was created by Georges Méliès and it was shown as part of a longer stage magic performance at Paris's Théâtre Robert-Houdin.

> **Advertisement for the Davenport Brothers' Cabinet Séance show, London, 1865**
Before these spiritualist-style stage magicians came to town, they would place notices in local newspapers, challenging potential customers to see if they could work out how the American showmen produced their phenomena.

century, by notions of psychic powers and mediumship. Conjurors such as Uri Geller (b. 1946), the spoon-bender, began displaying psychic-style mind abilities as well as energy control through their hands.

Because they know the power of tricks, performance magicians have always been among the sharpest critics of supernatural magicians. Recent campaigners for scepticism include the American duo Penn & Teller, British illusionist Derren Brown (b. 1971) and Canadian-American James Randi (1928–2020). They stand near the end of a very long line of debunking conjurors, going back to the guidebooks of the early 17th century.

Magic tricks have many applications beyond entertainment. During World War I, conjuror and artist Charles Folkard (1878–1963) created two pamphlets of *Tricks for the Trenches & Wards* (1915) to amuse convalescing soldiers. Today, performance magic programmes and therapies are used quite widely in physical and psychological care. Learning and performing conjuring tricks, it seems, does good for people, including those with anxiety, cerebral palsy, learning difficulties and cognitive decline.

DECODING MAGICIAN'S POSTER

For performance magicians, the start of the 20th century was a golden age. Harry Kellar, the so-called 'Dean of American Magicians', became the first American conjurer to attain worldwide celebrity. His tricks made great use of custom mechanical equipment manufactured by Martinka & Company (est. 1877). Kellar's success owed much to his thrilling lithograph advertisements, including this example from 1894, which mingled classic magical imagery with enticing contemporary trends. The iconic images were mostly produced by Strobridge Lithographing Company of Ohio and New York.

1. Ruins: an atmospheric and seemingly historic setting, suggests all kinds of ancient and mysterious powers.
2. Moon: the full moon is a special time, in low and high magic, when powerful spells are cast.
3. Floating instruments: inspired by the séance phenomenon of late 1800s spiritualism, musical instruments mysteriously float then start to play.
4. Imps and demons: they whisper secrets into Kellar's ear, evoking the tradition that a magician's powers come from spirits and demons.
5. Evening wear: Kellar's attire signifies that his magic is a respectable form of entertainment.
6. Grimoires: Kellar and his demons read from arcane tomes to suggest they are experts in secret and complex magic.
7. Wand: rival magicians criticized Kellar for not employing sleight-of-hand techniques. However, Kellar made up for this by being an absolute master of misdirection, using props like his wand.
8. Ghosts: to materialize ethereal spirits, Kellar used angled sheets of glass to reflect images of performers positioned off-stage.
9. Brazier: the burning container evokes ceremonial magic.
10. Princess Karnac: the celebrated levitation trick was achieved using a specially manufactured elevating platform, hidden inside the 'princess's' clothes.
11. Owl: a classic symbol of superstition and magic, the owl appears in many paintings on the topic from the early modern period onwards.
12. Cards: Kellar seemed to demonstrate psychic powers by predicting cards drawn by his assistant.

In a few instances, performance magic has also been successfully incorporated into programmes to assist with gang prevention, and drug and prison rehabilitation.

The trickery of performance magic once enticed spies. During the early 1950s, the US CIA commissioned stage magician John Mulholland (1898–1970) to write two espionage manuals based on conjuring techniques of stealth and misdirection, in a top-secret project codenamed MK-ULTRA. One manual used sleight-of-hand techniques for poisoning food and drinks and also stealing documents. The other explained covert signalling and secret communication. Although the manuals were ordered to be destroyed in 1973, both texts survived and have been published by historians H. Keith Melton (b. 1944) and Robert Wallace (b. 1944).

Some supernatural magicians use conjuring tricks. Service magicians from sub-Saharan Africa, for example, may seem to extract harmful objects (nails) from bewitched patients. Anthropologist E. E. Evans-Pritchard (1902–73) was unable to discover how magicians produced these objects during fieldwork among the Azande of Central Africa in the 1920s, because the trick was a carefully guarded secret. Broadly similar illusions have been used by service magicians worldwide. You could call it fraud. Yet there is also a therapeutic explanation. Such illusions help sceptical clients believe, and because belief is essential, tricks that foster it are justified – some magicians say.

The close relationship between supernatural magic and performance magic is depicted by the first trump or Major Arcana card of the tarot. The Magician, in Colman Smith's illustration (1909), wields supernatural powers. He represents balance and the union of spiritual and earthly forces, holding a wand to the sky in one hand, pointing to the ground with the other. In early tarot decks, developed for gaming in Italy and elsewhere, the Magician is a performance conjuror. He is a mountebank (charlatan), behind his desk, ready to practise the cup and balls trick. This duality of the tarot Magician, as either supernatural expert or performance illusionist trickster, symbolizes how real magic and performance magic have often been intertwined.

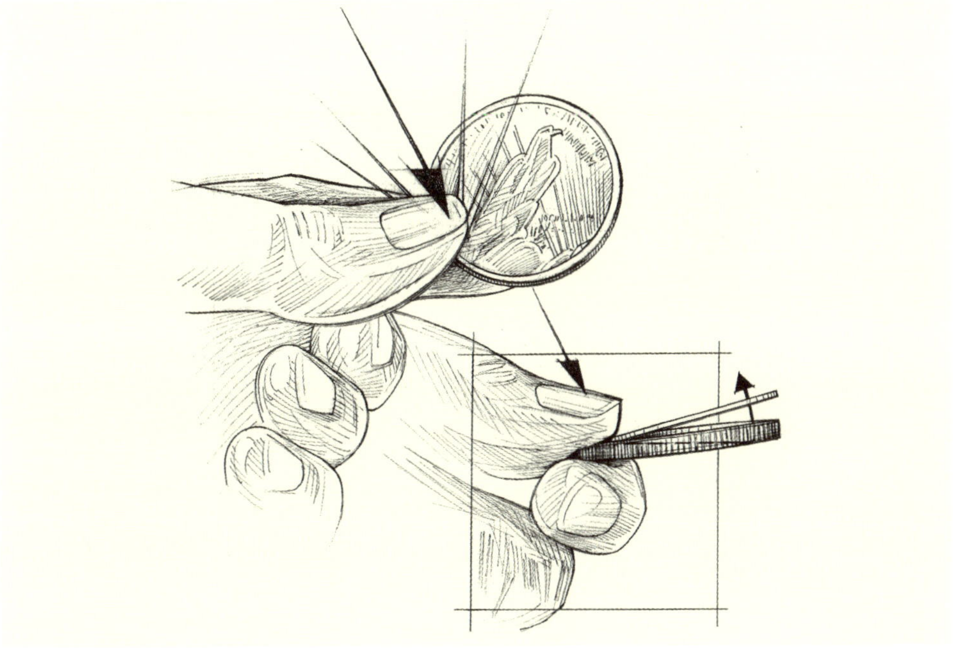

Phil Franke, illustrations for *The Official CIA Manual of Trickery and Deception*, 2009 reprint of John Mulholland's 1953 guide

The top image shows how an object could be passed under the cover of another. Below is a depiction of a concealment or 'dope' coin, with a secret cavity that could contain microfilm or cypher information. Mulholland had worked on the design of the coin for three decades.

III

1

MESMERISM & SPIRITUALISM

2

PSYCHIC POWERS

3

WITCHCRAFT, MAGICK & CRYSTALS

ALTERNATIVE MAGIC

1 # MESMERISM & SPIRITUALISM 1

'NOTHING CAN BE MORE ASTONISHING THAN THE SIGHT OF THESE CONVULSIONS.'

ANIMAL MAGNETISM: REPORT OF DR FRANKLIN AND OTHER COMMISSIONERS (1785)

In the West, mainstream culture rejected magic during the Enlightenment, around the early 18th century. Universities, courts and governments denied magic's reality. Writers mocked and artists satirized seekers of supernatural powers. Yet magic did not die. It developed more plausible forms that were pseudoscientific, countercultural and alternative. Mesmerism, unveiled by Austrian physician Anton Mesmer from the 1770s, healed with an invisible force named animal magnetism. Spiritualist mediums, from the 1840s onwards, not only communicated with spirits but also healed and divined, and even materialized spiritual forces called ectoplasm.

1 MESMERISM & SPIRITUALISM 1

When did magic decline and move to the margins? Why has it lost its formerly central place in mainstream culture? Despite this, why do forms of magic and mysticism often seem to be reviving?

Questions such as these have been debated for centuries, both in the public arena and also among scholars. In these debates, visual sources have received surprisingly little attention. Artistic depictions suggest that, in the West at least, magic first began losing prestige and was being made fun of longer ago than is often thought. From the 16th century, woodcuts, engravings and paintings started mocking various sorts of magic. Fairies became silly figures. Alchemy, above all, was lampooned. Alchemy was a rich branch of high magic, aiming at spiritual elevation, the creation of various health-improving substances and the transmutation of base materials into precious artefacts. Yet both the low and high visual arts depicted alchemy with disdain, disapproval, disgust and sometimes riotous laughter. Deluded or crazed alchemists are shown working perilously close to flames, spellbound by their bizarre experiments. Around them is domestic chaos, poverty, danger and misbehaviour. The subtext is clear: magical obsession is not a worthy life. By the early 18th century, alchemy symbolized outright madness in the series *A Rake's Progress* (1734) by English artist William Hogarth (1697–1764).

In the West, the status of magic shifted markedly in the decades around 1700. Astrology was removed from university curriculums. Courts stopped prosecuting witchcraft, believing the evidence too flimsy. Legislatures and parliaments repealed laws that recognized witchcraft as a supernatural reality and crime that deserved death. Encyclopaedic works about natural philosophy still accepted the reality of awesome powers such as devils and guardian angels, but magic like judicial astrology was judged 'vain and false' for not being able to answer questions such as: why is a horoscope cast at the time of birth, rather than conception? In public discourse and imagery, magic was increasingly portrayed as wild, silly and ridiculous. It was mocked and scorned, not disproved through

« *page 174*
***Two Women With a Cup*, Italian, 18th century**
A fortune-teller and her client are reading tea leaves or coffee grounds (known as tasseography). During the 18th and 19th centuries, fortune-telling remained common and was a well-established subject of European paintings.

‹ *page 176*
Richard Bergh, *Hypnotic Séance*, 1887
This detail from a Swedish painting captures the precise moment the psychic state shifts in hypnosis. The scene is tender but invasive, as the woman, in white, leans back and the man, in black, leans in.

William Hogarth, 'Tom Rakewell in prison', Plate 7 from *A Rake's Progress*, 1734

Tom goes mad in prison after his proposal for a play is rejected. His insanity is symbolized by the alchemist working in the background. Alchemy had once been a revered art, but by the 18th century it was often depicted as crazy and ridiculous.

DECODING HOGARTH'S CREDULITY, SUPERSTITION, AND FANATICISM

English artist William Hogarth's iconic engraving *Credulity, Superstition, and Fanaticism. A Medley* (1762) expresses the growing tendency, in the 18th-century West, to mock magic. The scene brims with contemporary references and tropes, showcasing different examples of misplaced beliefs.

1.

PREACHER
The fanatical preacher dangles a witch and devil. He represents George Whitefield, a Methodist believer in the 'invisible world'.

2.

GLOBE OF HELL
The grotesque chandelier is inscribed with labels that mock Roman Catholic and Methodist superstitions.

3.

TURKISH MAN
A Turkish Muslim man looks in from the window, smiling at the foolishness of the Christians gathered inside.

4.

PHANTOM FIGURES
Three ghostly figures decorate the pulpit, each holding a candle. They represent well-known appearances of phantoms.

5.

DRUMMER
The Tedworth Drummer refers to a much investigated and debated noisy haunting in Wiltshire, England, in the 1660s.

6.

COCK LANE GHOSTS
These icons represent the Cock Lane ghosts, from a notorious London haunting in 1762–63 that ultimately was exposed as a hoax.

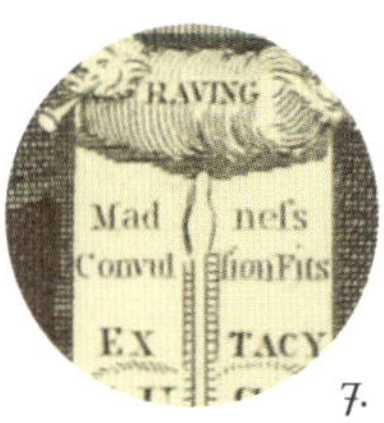

7.

THERMOMETER
The thermometer represents the immoderate, deluded and dangerous states of mind of the priest and congregation.

8.

VOMITING BOY
Sicking up pins and metal objects was a classic symptom of witchcraft across early modern Europe and beyond.

9.

JOURNAL
Methodist George Whitefield's journal recorded evil spirits and supernatural powers, which he combatted with faith and prayer.

10.

DEMONOLOGY
In the foreground is *Demonology* (1597), a well-known book by King James I affirming the reality of witchcraft and magic.

11.

WOMAN BIRTHING RABBITS
This is a reference to Mary Toft, who in 1726 tricked the royal physician into thinking she had given birth to a rabbit.

12.

NOTORIOUS BOOKS
Beneath a 'Methodist's brain' are copies of John Wesley's sermons and the philosopher Joseph Glanvill's *On Witches* (1681).

Pieter van der Borcht, *Monkey Alchemist Family*, late 1500s
In the 16th century, images often mocked alchemy and this Dutch engraving shows a group of monkey alchemists (on the right) begging at the poorhouse. While alchemists obsessed over worthless experiments, chaos and poverty beset their neglected homes.

rational argument. Laughter and ridicule dowsed a range of once respected or feared magical characters: the alchemist, the witch, the magus and the village specialist who knew many charms and cures.

In response to this criticism, esoteric practitioners and theoreticians created more plausible versions of practical mysticism. New technologies and scientific ideas were mingled with rhetoric that rejected the superstitious dimensions of magic. Under the surface, however, many of these novel therapies continued to employ traditional magical techniques and ideas, such as ritual, intuition, mystery, belief, storytelling, personal charisma and touch, as well as an intense focus on the mood and mindset of the client. The first great example of this modernization of magic was the occult force of animal magnetism, known mockingly as 'mesmerism' after its founder Austrian physician Franz Anton Mesmer (1734–1815).

Therapies and performances associated with animal magnetism surged in Europe during the 1770s and 1780s, and then again around the 1830s and 1840s when they also spread to the USA. To doubters, the

< **'Animal magnetism: The operator putting his patient into a crisis', from Ebenezer Sibley's *A Key to Physic, and the Occult Sciences*, 1794**
A magnetizer directs magnetic fluid towards his client. Crises induced by 18th-century animal magnetism often involved dramatic alterations in consciousness.

> ***Le Magnetisme*, after a lithograph by L. Boilly, 1826**
By the 19th century, animal magnetism was generally gentler, sleepier and less dramatic, as depicted in this French illustration.

ideas and effects seemed beyond belief, contrary to all known laws of nature, and reminiscent of discredited supernatural and magical notions. Not so, insisted the magnetizer Charles Poyen (d. 1844), a Caribbean slaveholder and student of animal magnetism in Paris, who first brought the concept to the USA. Animal magnetism, he argued, was not magic but 'a science of observation', grounded in facts not belief. Formally, he rejected 'ignorance and superstition'. And yet, magnetizers like Poyen often hinted that the strange powers they wielded were related to forces seen throughout the history of magic and the supernatural, from the miracles of Jesus to marvels from the period of the witch trials. Animal magnetism encompassed a discourse of science blended with references to intuition (the mind's eye) and traditional magical terminology, including great use of the word 'subtle'.

Since antiquity, many diverse cultures have maintained that mystical energies influence human fortunes and also the fate of the wider world. *Prana*, in Hinduism and yoga, is the breath of life. *Mana*, in Polynesia, is a spiritual power that flows into people, objects and nature. Qi, in East Asia, is a force whose flow can bring good or bad fortune, depending on

whether the direction is correct. In Europe, however, ideas about mystical energies developed later. During the Renaissance, Swiss physician and magician Paracelsus healed with what he said was magnet-directed healing fluid. Others, such as Scotland's William Maxwell (*c.* 1581–1641), continued his work, but it was not until Mesmer that the idea of mystical magnetism made a big cultural impact.

Mesmer had a long-standing interest in occult influences and practices such as astrology. His attention turned to mystical magnetism after he learned of the experiments of a Jesuit astronomer named Father Maximilian Hell (1720–92). Father Hell used steel magnets in healing, by applying plates that looked like bodily organs to his patients. Mesmer developed these methods, making them more magic-like by moving the focus from metal magnets to other substances and the practitioner themself. He explained this different, non-metallic magnetism in a letter to a follower: 'Iron is not the only substance containing it. I have rendered paper, bread, wool, silk, leather, stone, glass, water, wood, dogs and men, all magnetic.' Mesmer himself was the greatest magnet of all: 'All I touched became endowed with this fluid,' he added. This concept supposedly came to him during his medical rounds, when he noticed that patients' blood seemed to flow faster as he approached. This, he theorized, was because the human body was a potent instrument of a special kind of magnetism. This animal magnetism was an invisible but powerful medium that connected all things, living and inanimate. Illnesses, mental and physical, were supposedly caused by blockages in its movement.

Mesmer's therapy became so popular that he took on assistants. These followers and other imitators soon set up their own salons. Like Mesmer, many of these magnetizers removed blockages and restored the proper flow of animal magnetism with so-called magnetized machines: vats or tubs containing 'magnetized' substances like water, glass, sand or iron filings. Patients put their hands inside the vessels, held protruding metal rods or were tied to the machines using cords – to receive a stronger

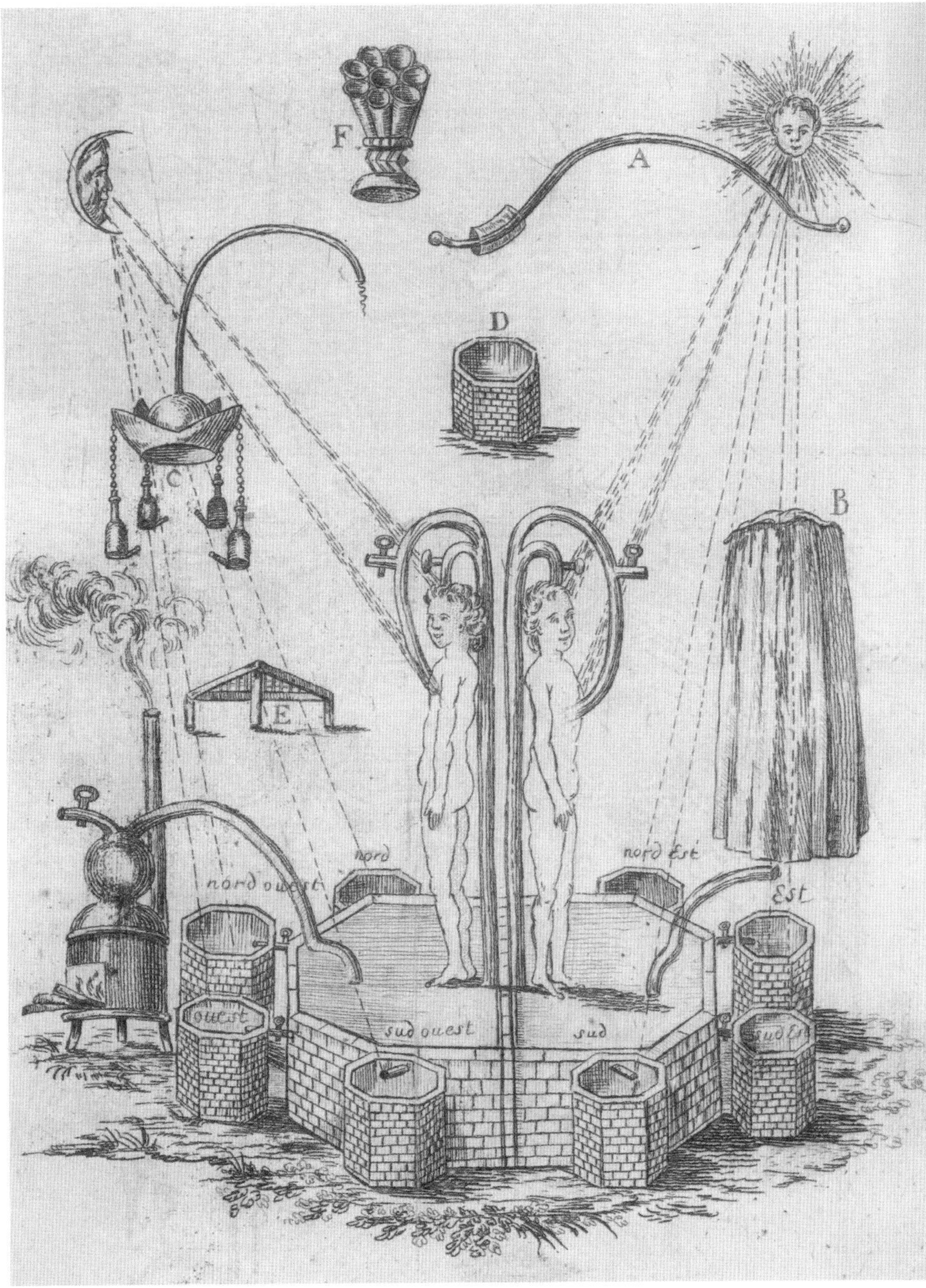

Mesmer's Baquet Moral (_Moral Tub_), French engraving, 18th century

Anton Mesmer's moral tub was a device created to direct the power of animal magnetism to induce spiritual refinement and moral improvement. Inside the tub were iron filings, sulphur and bottles of magnetized water. Protruding iron rods were applied to the clients' heads or other body parts to receive the healing.

'Patients in Paris receiving Mesmer's animal magnetism therapy', coloured etching after C-L. Desrais, late 18th century
Mesmer is depicted bottom left, inducing a crisis, while other patients around the tub hold metal rods, hoping animal magnetism will cure their physical and mental illnesses. The walls of his elegant salons were decorated with astrological characters, creating a mystical atmosphere.

dose of animal magnetism. Magnetizers also cured by gliding their hands close to a patient's body. Mesmer advised practitioners to employ a small wand (note the closeness to classic magic), ideally made of glass or metal. *Mesmer's Aphorisms and Instructions* (1785) explains that nearness, but not touching, produces the strongest effect because 'there exists a fluid betwixt the hand of the conductor and the patient.' As blockages were removed, many patients experienced a crisis, in which they shouted, raved, went catatonic, stared or fainted. Mesmer told his followers how to more reliably induce these powerful altered states. Keep constantly returning to the most afflicted part. Use additional equipment like a magnifying glass. Play emotive music (many salons had a piano for this purpose, while mesmerists claimed that sound conducted magnetism). Increase the number of people in the room, or chain the patient and magnetizer together, if necessary. The placebo effect must have been enormous. Even so, not everyone felt animal magnetism. Many experimented with the dramatic new therapy, but only some experienced sensations, crisis or healing. 'The time passed away without having felt the least sensation,' wrote one investigator in 1785.

Animal magnetism was repeatedly rejected and debunked by scholars and medical practitioners. Scientific societies ruled against it in London, Paris and Berlin. In 1784, Louis XVI (1754–93) directed Royal Commissioners including Benjamin Franklin (1706–90) to investigate. Their report revealed that they watched, astonished, animal magnetism healing sessions for upwards of three hours. To begin with, many patients were tranquil or unconscious, while others were afflicted with slight burnings and pain. Some, though, became convulsed or powerfully affected, which seemed eventually to influence the other patients to also experience a crisis. The faster the piano was played, the quicker and more violent the convulsions. In 1785, France's Royal Society of Medicine issued another report. It charged Mesmer with being a plagiarist, of claiming to invent a theory and practice that had in fact been taken from others, from Paracelsus to French physician Michel-Augustin Thouret (1749–1810).

< **'Robert Macaire mesmerizes an old lady in front of an audience', coloured lithograph by H. Daumier, *c.* 1838**
Robert Macaire was a French fictional crook. Here, he uses animal magnetism to make a woman catatonic.

> **Poster for a mesmerism show in Attleboro, Massachusetts, USA, 1885**
From around the 1830s, mesmerists toured provincial Europe and America. Their entertaining demonstrations helped to inspire interest in faith healing and hypnotism.

John Adams Whipple,
***Hypnotism*, c. 1845**

Here, a 'doctor' is hypnotizing patients in Massachusetts, USA. In 1843, Scottish surgeon James Braid coined the term 'hypnotism' to distinguish altered states induced via fixation and focus from the occult theories of animal magnetism. A few doctors used hypnotism for pain relief before chemical anaesthetics proliferated.

Mesmer's new theory was actually 'an ancient system, abandoned by the learned near a century ago'. In late 1830s England, the medical journal *The Lancet* attacked the mesmerism practised by Dr John Elliotson (1791–1868) of University College Hospital. The eminent periodical uncovered fraud in the display: the subjects had gone into crisis when presented with substitute objects, which were not really magnetized. Never again did animal magnetism convince large numbers of the medical profession. Similar critiques were taken to the public, between the 1830s and 1850s, by showmen who made their livings as anti-mesmerists, travelling around provincial lecture halls and assembly rooms, demonstrating how mesmerists feigned their effects.

Despite this ample discrediting, animal magnetism's influence was vast. It showed the possibility of inducing what at the time was known as artificial somnambulism, a sort of therapeutic semi-sleep and altered state of consciousness that would be widely used in subsequent occultism and magic. It inspired later esoteric practitioners, including theosophy's Helena Blavatsky (1831–91), who created a potent mythology that an elite secret society had chosen Mesmer to teach occult lore. More practically, animal magnetism's effects on nervous conditions underlined how civilized life bred malaises and problems that may somewhat effectively be treated with mystical therapies. Mesmerist performances sensationally demonstrated people's immense suggestibility and began uncovering the hidden depths of their mental lives. Psychology, psychiatry, psychotherapy and hypnotism were built on these revelations. Animal magnetism also inspired the 19th-century faith-healing movement known as New Thought. From here, belief in the power of faith to heal and improve lives spread widely, from Christian science to the Human Potential Movement and Alcoholics Anonymous. Mesmer may, among many other things, have been a plagiarizing pseudo-scientist, but he popularized probably the most widely impactful form of alternative and mystical healing in modern history.

As mysticism became alternative, it linked with radical causes and countercultural movements.

< ***The Flints Hypnotic Skirt Dance*, poster, Chicago, USA, *c.* 1895**
In this music hall act, showman Herbert L. Flint purportedly hypnotized his wife and daughter to undertake a high-energy, graceful and comedic dance. Male audience members (plants) also took part.

> ***Magnétisme et Hypnotisme*, *c.* 1900**
A popular French guide to magnetism and hypnotism for stage magicians.

Animal magnetism directly challenged the ascendancy of elite physicians, by developing healing therapies that were more populist, intuitive, emotive, sensational and egalitarian. But the movement also rocked the political and cultural status quo, particularly in France during the years before the outbreak of revolution in 1789. Historians such as Robert Darnton (b. 1939) and others found that mesmerism fostered revolutionary views, by popularizing universalist-type theories of health that seemed to accord with universalist Enlightenment doctrines of 'natural rights', espoused by radical thinkers such as Jean-Jacques Rousseau (1712–78). More prosaically, animal magnetism salons often functioned as alternative meeting places for dissident elites and polemicists.

During the mid and late 19th century, many adherents of the new esoteric practice of spiritualism were also proponents of disruptive political ideologies such as feminism and socialism. Through the spirit world, these radicals hoped to achieve a human flourishing and equality that was impossible within the

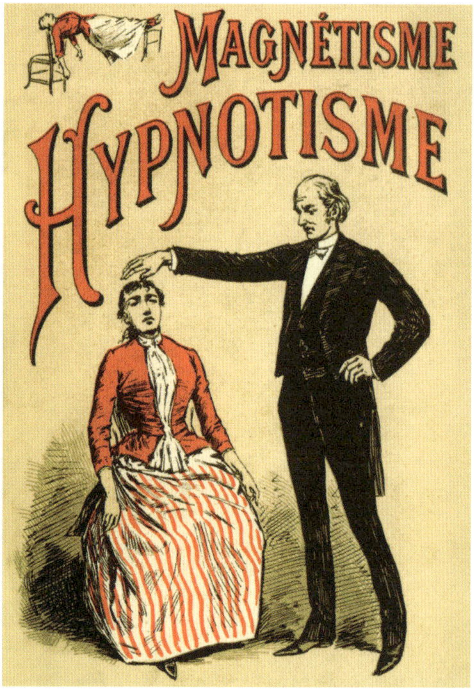

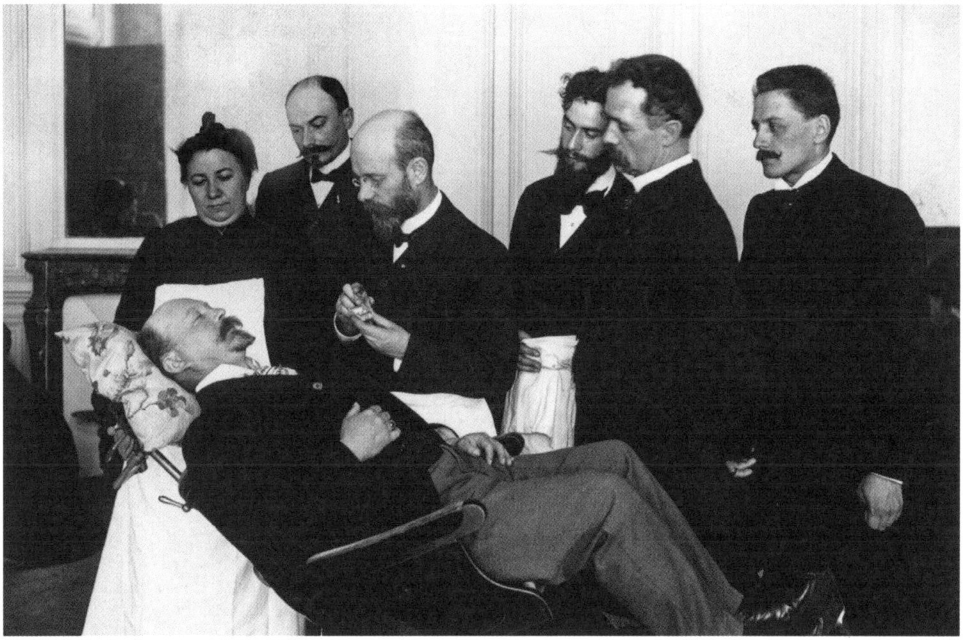

'Doctors observe hypnosis', France, 1890s
Hypnotism became an experimental psychological therapy in the late 19th century. In Paris, neurologist Jean-Martin Charcot's demonstrations influenced a young Sigmund Freud.

confines of industrial capitalism. Other spiritualists believed that their movement would utterly transform prevailing thought and culture. Proof of communications between the living and dead must induce a 'certain revolution of the world's opinions upon the hitherto accepted conceptions of Science, Philosophy, and Religion,' wrote the trance medium and so-called Bishop of Spiritualism J. J. Morse (1848–1919) in his preface to the memoir of another seer, Emma Hardinge Britten (1823–99). Many people were drawn to spiritualism for more personal reasons, too, from bereavement to pure curiosity. Doubts about the literal truth of Christianity were growing. Moral objections to the idea of an eternally punishing hell were increasing. Older beliefs were decaying, but a yearning remained for spiritual answers and meaning.

During this fluctuating and inquiring moment, spiritualism created attractive and positive ways of interacting with the dead. Unlike traditional belief in ghosts and malevolent phantasms, spiritualism saw spirits as benevolent happy beings who came from an entirely pleasant afterlife with wholly good intentions towards the living. In seances, spirits and mediums displayed a huge range of astonishing powers, which were publicized in spiritualist books such as Britten's *Nineteenth Century Miracles* (1884). Some abilities, particularly healing and clairvoyance, overlapped with the conventional offerings of service magicians. Either directly or through a medium, spirits also drew, made music, spoke in tongues, rapped on and pushed tables, and provided wise testimony. Along with various humble people, many great figures purportedly appeared, from Plato and Aristotle to Napoleon Bonaparte. Perhaps the greatest feat of all was materialization, where some or all of the spirit would appear in the seance room.

What soon became known as the Modern Spiritualist Movement began in the late 1840s, with an ordinary haunting in Hydesville, New York State. Within the home of the Fox family, two teenage sisters (Maggie and Kate) heard ghostly raps. They were sent elsewhere, but the raps followed them. In 1849, the sisters put on a paid demonstration at a Rochester hotel, asking the spirits questions about personal prospects and the stock market, and getting raps in response. Imitators soon emerged, with their own spirit guides. Some mediums had seen ghosts, prophetic dreams and premonitions since childhood. Others possessed family traditions of the supernatural. The relatives of Scottish medium Daniel Dunglas Home (1833–86) were apparently seers who possessed the not always welcome gift of second sight, which made them perceive the other world of phantasms and fairies. Many spiritualist mediums had prior experience with mesmerism, clairvoyancy and occult research. English medium and spiritualist lecturer Britten served, when younger, as one of the 'clairvoyant and magnet subjects' of a London occult society, she noted in her autobiography.

Spiritualism blossomed in the late 19th-century era of growing globalization, communications, travel and migration. Around thirty-six monthly spiritualist periodicals spread news of the spirit realm worldwide, according to historian Bret E. Carroll (b. 1961).

William H. Mumler, 'Leading spiritualist Emma Hardinge Britten photographed with the spirit of Beethoven', 1871

Mumler was an infamous spirit photographer, and Britten strongly defended his work. Writing for the Medium *spiritualist journal in 1871, she described the evidence that Beethoven's spirit was present during her photoshoot in Boston, Massachusetts, USA, as 'conclusive'.*

PROFILE
SPIRIT PHOTOGRAPHY

The mysticism of spiritualism was depicted in the new medium of photography. The first claims of spirits being photographed were made in 1860, in the French journal *Revue Spiritualiste*. Soon after, American William H. Mumler (1832–84) began making and selling spirit photographs taken in studios in Boston and New York, including the photos below, dating from 1861 to 1878. He pictured wealthy clients with spirits of their dead relatives, including Mary Todd Lincoln and the spirit of her deceased husband, former president Abraham

Lincoln (below, top right). For some, these images were remarkable proof of the reality of life after death and connection with spirits who could give insights into past, present and future. For others, they were dubious curiosities or frauds, but still interesting and worth looking at. Ghost-hunters and sceptical stage magicians, including American writer and illusionist Milbourne Christopher (1914–84), were instrumental in explaining the double-exposure camera techniques that spirit photographers used to create such ghostly images.

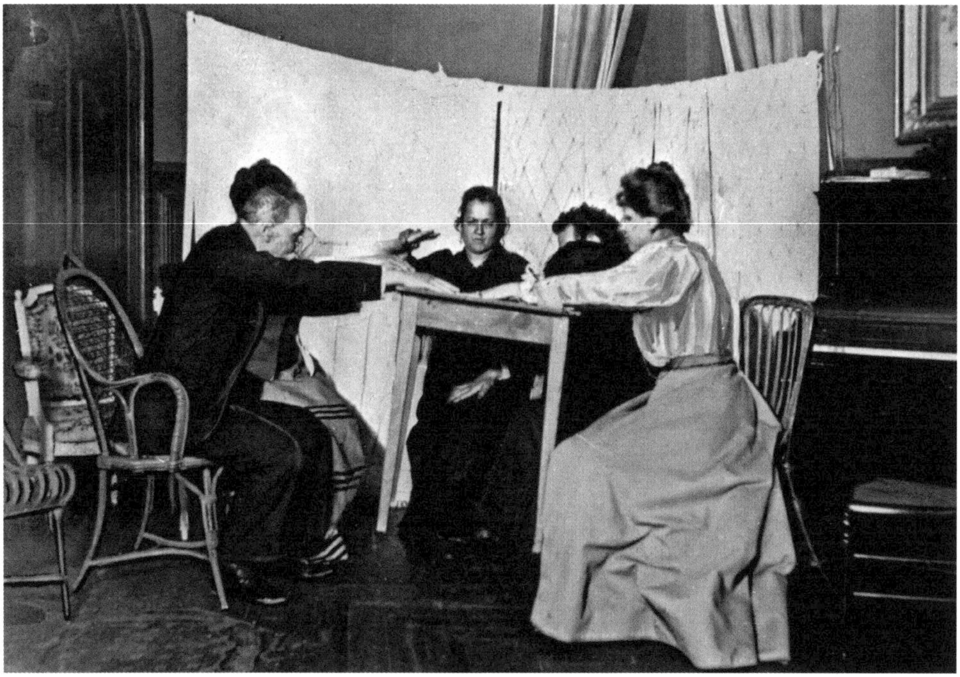

M. G. de Fontenay, 'Seance at the home of Monsieur Blech in Montfort l'Amaury, France', 1897
Fontenay took several photographs of this experiment, and here the table appears to levitate. Such seances were social gatherings, where entertainment mingled with a quest for proof of the afterlife.

Mediums took seances across borders: Mrs Maria B. Hayden (1824–83) was the first to bring them from the USA to Britain in 1852–53. Late Victorian England had between 10,000 and 100,000 spiritualists, historian Alex Owen estimated in her classic study *The Darkened Room* (1989), although even more people experimented or paid attention in less committed ways. The spiritualist movement spread similarly through Europe, Russia, Australia and New Zealand, while smaller numbers of adherents could be found in colonial South Asia and Malaysia. Spiritualism was particularly popular in the USA, where it achieved 'a prominence there unparalleled in any other country,' according to Britten. She estimated that around 34,000 mediums catered to four million earnest American believers, with greater numbers of experimenters. This was likely a considerable exaggeration by a spiritualist partisan. The Federal Census of 1880 recorded only 297 people with occupations linked to spiritualism, but this, likewise, was surely a significant understatement because working as a medium was legally dubious.

Harry Houdini exposing fraudulent seance tricks, New York City, USA, 1925
During the 1920s, Houdini demonstrated how spiritualist mediums exploited stage magic techniques. This image shows how a 'secured' foot can be released and used to ring a bell.

The number of American spiritualists does seem to have been large, swelled by a tsunami of grief following the Civil War of 1861 to 1865. For the 1870s, historian David K. Nartonis (b. 1943) found evidence of spiritualist work in almost 800 different towns and cities.

Debates raged about how far the startling phenomenon of spiritualism could be ascribed to spirits, how much was caused by the mystical powers of the mediums, and what was owed to fraud. Trickery and misrepresentation were notoriously common. Even spiritualism's most partial advocates, including Britten in *Nineteenth Century Miracles*, had to admit that the movement contained legions of 'remorseless swindlers'. Backstreet fakes, according to a report in the 16 March 1876 edition of the *Spiritualist Scientist* journal, typically undertook fraudulent seances involving spirit materializations for ordinary folk curious about the wonders of spiritualism. An interested person would make an application to attend, then be told to come back at a certain time. It would be arranged for the paying attendees to be outnumbered at least two to one by incognito friends or employees of the medium sat at the front, whose supportive reactions

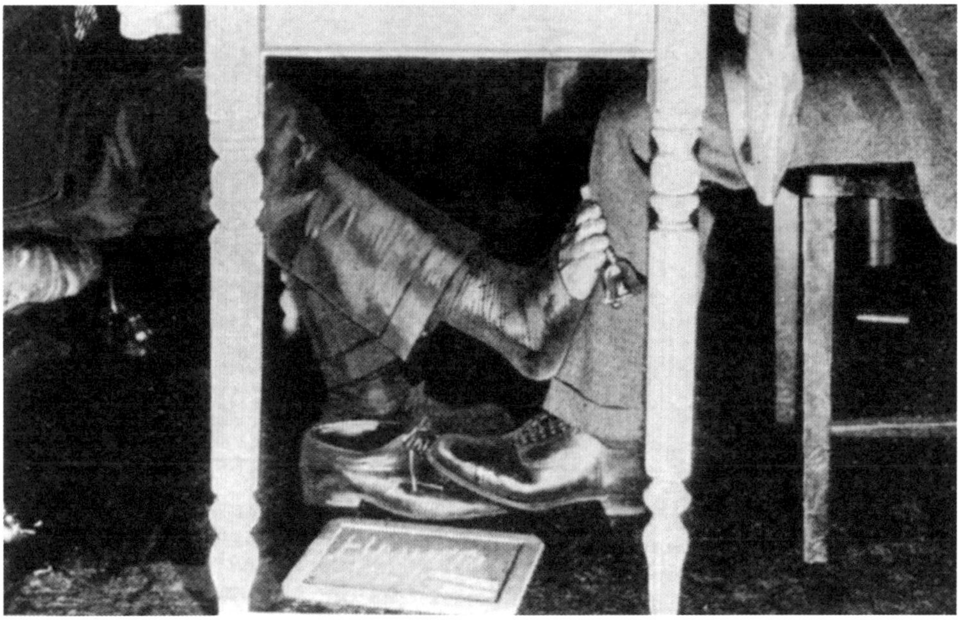

and enthusiasm would ensure the charade passed successfully. Spiritualism was not just blighted by backstreet frauds like this: tricksters found their way to the pinnacle of the movement. The Fox sisters were themselves implicated in trickery. In 1888, Maggie confessed that Kate had made the raps at their home by cracking her knees. Decades earlier, in 1853, British physicist and chemist Michael Faraday (1791–1867) debunked 'table-turning' by devising and employing a device that detected when the medium was applying pressure to the table. And British spiritualist Florence Eliza Cook (1856–1904) made a career out of materializing the spirit of Katie King, despite being repeatedly exposed as a fraud. In 1880, a clergyman attending one of her seances seized the spirit of Katie King, and it was revealed to be none other than Florence herself. Equally, deliberate deception can be easily overstated: 'Often, very often, there was no trickery in the matter,' noted the experienced psychical researcher Frank Podmore (1856–1910) in *The Newer Spiritualism* (1910). Automatic writing and altered states were actions of the subconscious, he thought, during an era before psychoanalysis.

< **'Diagnosing the Fox sisters', USA, *c.* 1851**
At a public seance, Dr Flint diagnoses popping knee joints in an attempt to show how the rappings heard by the Fox sisters were faked. In 1888, Margaret Fox herself demonstrated how the sisters used joint cracking to found modern spiritualism.

> **A woman (probably Florence Cook) posing as the materialized spirit Katie King, London, 1874**
This much-disputed photograph may have been taken at the home of scientist and spiritualist investigator Sir William Crookes, who believed the materialization to be genuine.

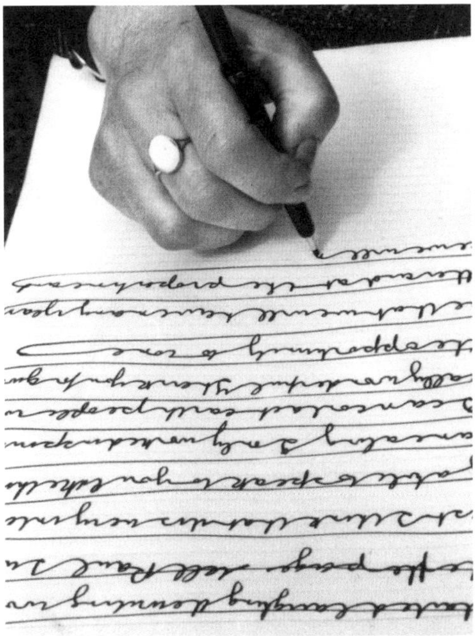

< **Automatic writing, London, 1960s**
Medium Mrs P. Savile claimed to psychically receive information from a being named White Cloud, then convey it through automatic writing.

> **William S. Marriott simulating automatic writing and a spirit guide, 1910**
Marriott was a British stage magician and spiritualist sceptic, who worked to expose the trickery of mediums.

Some spiritualist books and psi websites claim that one well-known Victorian medium was never exposed: Daniel Dunglas Home. 'No well-informed spiritualist will deny that in Home the case is presented at its best,' wrote Podmore in *The Newer Spiritualism*. Admirers and critics agreed that no medium performed remarkable feats so competently and for such distinguished audiences, which included Emperor Napoleon III and Empress Eugené of France, as well as Russia's Tsar Alexander II. Home's 'sittings' began with table vibrations, knocks and sometimes levitation. Quite often, he then paused, to deliver in a trance-like state sermons based on visions of Heaven, God, angels and Jesus. Next, for the higher phenomena, the lights were turned low. Spiritual agencies seemed to carry objects around the room, play musical instruments like the accordion, and even touch or stroke the sitters. Most extraordinary of all, Home himself appeared to levitate, projecting his voice from above where the attendees sat, while mysterious spirit hands also materialized. But these mediumistic displays were not free from doubt and suspicions of trickery. In an article for the

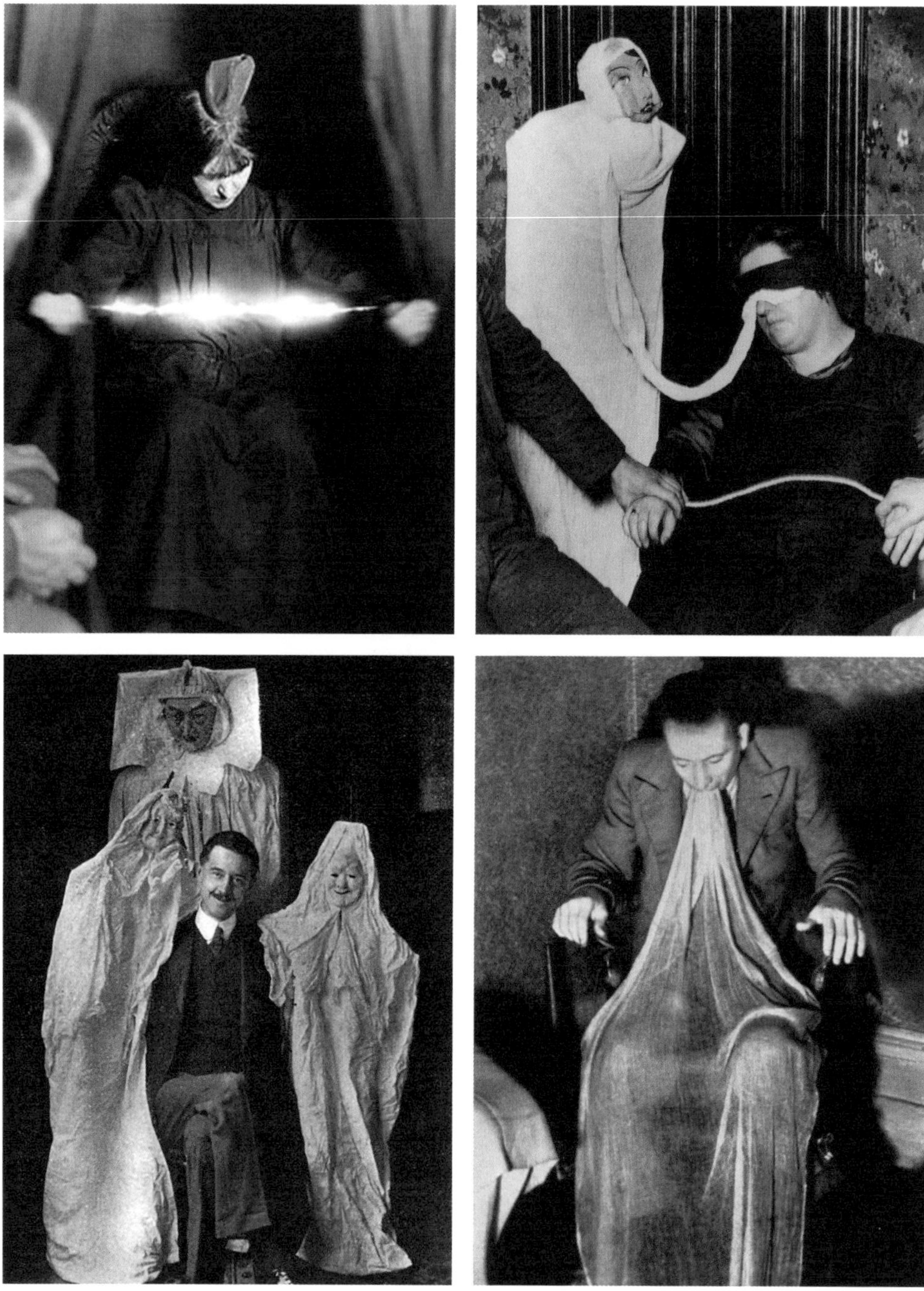

Spiritualist ectoplasm (the materialization of a medium's spiritual energy), fake and purportedly real, 1910s–50s

French medium Eva Carrière (top left) and Scottish spiritualist Helen Duncan (top right) were both ultimately exposed as frauds. British illusionist William S. Marriott (bottom) demonstrates how ectoplasm could be made from cheese cloth, gauze, papier-mâché and coat hangers.

Journal of Psychical Research in 1903, an anonymous author reported attending one of Home's sittings, where they clearly perceived that the spirit hand was in fact connected to the medium's shoulder and arm.

Spiritualism, mixed with large doses of Eastern religion and magic, was the inspiration for theosophy. Helen Blavatsky, theosophy's cigar-smoking matriarch, travelled from Russia through Europe to the USA, where she met collaborator Henry Steel Olcott (1832–1907). Together, they went to India, where Blavatsky became the first well-documented Western woman to take the five precepts of Buddhism. Olcott, meanwhile, was instrumental to a revival of Buddhism in Sri Lanka. Together, they created modern theosophy, which offered special knowledge from spiritually evolved 'Mahatmas', and also supernatural powers inspired by esoteric Buddhism and tantric yoga. Theosophy popularized astral (linked to the cosmos) practices along with other mystical ideas such as auras. With training, adepts could strengthen their astral form. With enough power and skill, they could leave their physical body to travel through the astral plane, a magical realm between the material world and the divine. Some theosophists subdivided the astral plane further. C. W. Leadbeater (1854–1934) thought the Lower Astral was a 'psychic junkyard' of turbulent ghosts and elementals. The Higher Astral, however, was a heavenly 'summerland' populated by happy spirits, he wrote in *The Astral Plane* (1895). From these ideas, Austrian occultist Rudolf Steiner (1861–1925) invented anthroposophy, in which the astral body is a 'soul suit' for interplanetary travel.

Many great minds were drawn to spiritualism. Scientists, authors, politicians, scholars and journalists regularly attended seances, often in the spirit of investigation and curiosity. Nobel Prize winners Marie Curie (1867–1934) and her husband Pierre (1859–1906) were two of many eminent Parisians who witnessed the performances of Italian spirit medium Eusapia Palladino (1854–1918). Pierre came to believe, writing: 'These phenomena really do exist,' in one of the last letters before his death. 'It is no longer possible for me to doubt them. It is incredible but it is so.' For a time, spiritualism made it seem as though it may be possible to document the reality of the other world, beyond our material realm, in a scientific and objective way. Learned societies formed to pursue this new goal, including the Cambridge Ghost Club (est. 1862), the Oxford Phasmatological Society (est. 1879), the London-based Society for Psychical Research (est. 1882) and the American Society for Psychical Research (est. 1885).

Psychical research tried to maintain an open-minded and scholarly approach to things mysterious, anomalous and occult. It conducted testing and enquiry 'without prejudice or prepossession of any kind', as London's Society for Psychical Research described in its 'Objects of the Society' (1882). Proponents saw themselves as treading a middle ground between 'the scornful disdain of the savant and credulous belief of the ignorant,' wrote spiritualist and eminent English physicist Sir William F. Barrett (1844–1925) in his guidebook *Psychical Research* (1911). Psychical research was a rational and calm approach to the 'debatable borderland' lying just beyond the limits of science, a realm long shrouded in darkness and superstition. Its appeal was huge, historians like Andreas Sommer (b. 1972) have shown, across Europe and the USA. Many eminent Victorian and Edwardian scientists were members of the London Society for Psychical Research, including the co-discoverer of biological evolution by natural selection Alfred Russel Wallace (1823–1913), physicist Oliver Lodge (1851–1940) and German physicist Heinrich Hertz (1857–94). Vice president of the Austrian Society for Psychical Research Hans Hahn (1879–1934) was also a member of the Vienna Circle of leading intellectuals and scientists. Psychical research used various observational methods and investigations, writing up reports and proceedings not only on spiritualism but also other mystical and psychic abilities. The attempted science of the magic and the supernatural continued, in laboratory settings during the 20th century, with parapsychology. This, and the development of psychic powers, is the subject of the next chapter.

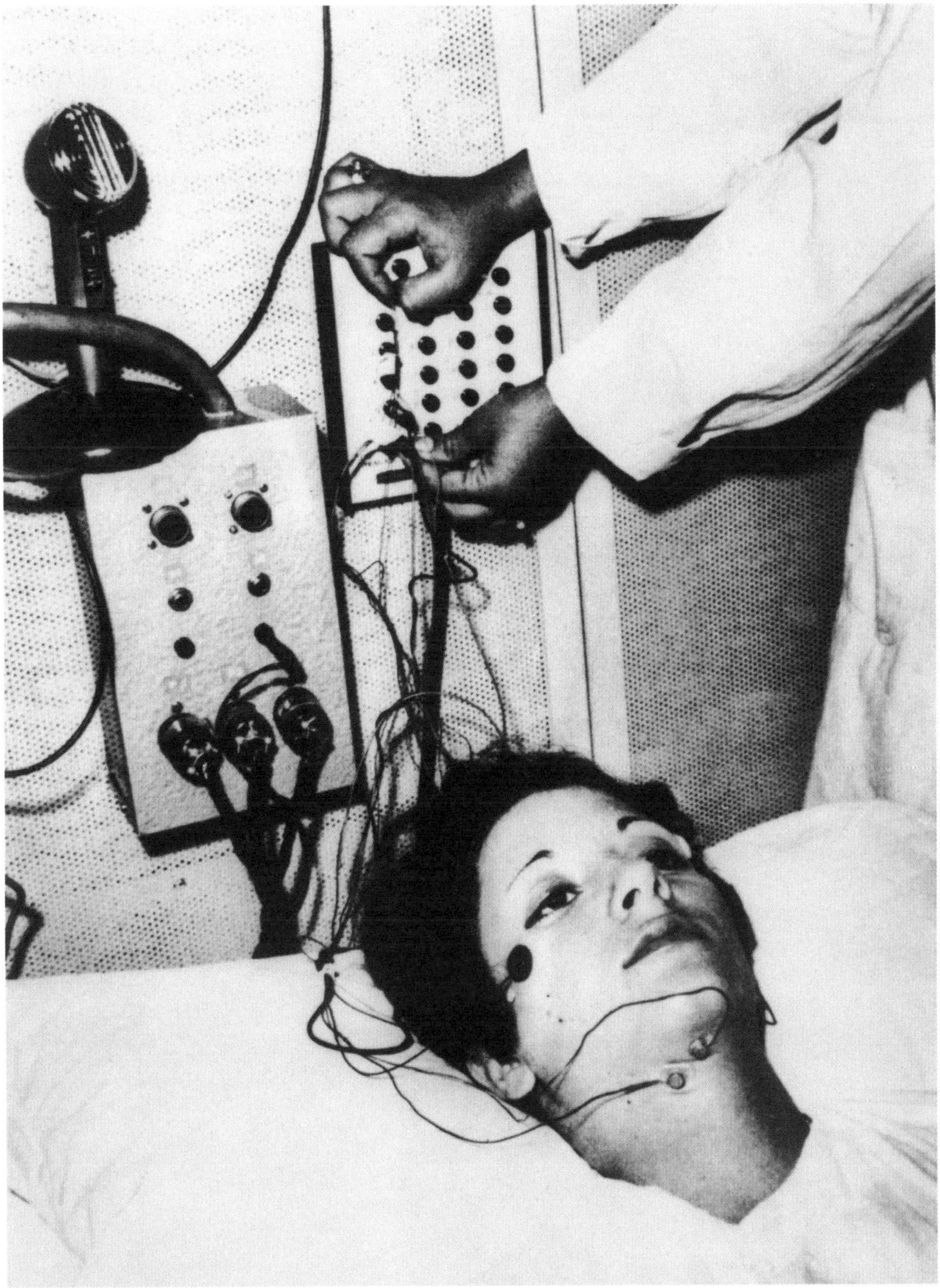

Krippner dream telepathy experiment, Maimonides Medical Center, New York City, USA, 1964

Conducted at the dream laboratory at the Maimonides Medical Center under the direction of psychologist Stanley Krippner and psychiatrist Montague Ullman, this controversial experiment explored whether a 'sender' could through telepathy shape the dreams of a 'receiver'.

'IT IS INDEPENDENTLY ESTABLISHED ON THE BASIS OF THIS WORK ALONE THAT EXTRA-SENSORY PERCEPTION IS AN ACTUAL AND DEMONSTRABLE OCCURRENCE.'

JOSEPH BANKS RHINE,
EXTRA-SENSORY PERCEPTION
(1935)

Psychic powers are mind-based magic. Since the Renaissance, magicians had argued that emotions and beliefs conveyed occult force. During the 20th century, as psychoanalysis revealed human psychology's hidden depths, ideas flourished about brain-driven magic. In the USA, parapsychologists coined 'extrasensory perception' (ESP) for knowledge from beyond the five senses. British magician Dion Fortune popularized 'psychic attack' to denote mind-based occult assaults. Governments from Nazi-era Germany to the Cold War USA funded research programmes, although no conclusive evidence of the existence of psychic powers was produced.

2 PSYCHIC POWERS 2

From the early 20th century, new magic-style powers flourished. Although highly potent, these forces and abilities were less visible and less material than most previous forms of magic. Rituals, objects and ingredients could be useful, but they were not absolutely necessary because the new powers flowed directly from human minds. Proponents claimed that the mysterious cerebral influences emanated from a variety of cognitive processes. Beliefs, deliberate concentration, altered states of consciousness and mental acts of will were key. But so were emotions, personality and intuition, along with subconscious and unconscious brain activity. 'Energy follows thought' became a mantra of this way of understanding mystical forces.

In 1943, Cambridge psychologist Robert H. Thouless (1894–1984) gave brain-based occult abilities a collective name: psi. More commonly, they are known as psychic powers. Psi is plausible mysticism for the modern age. It offers a huge range of extraordinary abilities, but unlike traditional magic is less religious and supernatural and more intellectual, psychological and scientific.

The embryonic ideas behind psychic powers were created in the Renaissance by theorists of natural magic seeking to uncover mysterious and hidden forces. In his *Three Books of Occult Philosophy*, Cornelius Agrippa wrote often of the power of our imagination and emotions, which had tangible effects upon the bodies, minds and spirits of others. He thought that occult influences like these explained why love magic worked, and also how a reputed witch's touch or presence could cause mystical poisoning and sickness. Swiss physician, alchemist and theorist of natural magic Paracelsus agreed that passions and emotions carried magical force. Paracelsus's natural magic was deeply faith-based: those who had faith in 'the light of nature' would obtain 'from nature as much as he believes', he wrote. The mystical power of feelings was, therefore, enhanced when it was combined with psychological acts such as faith, will, belief and intention.

These ideas were kept alive in the writings of 19th-century occultists such as Éliphas Lévi. However, psychic powers were elaborated and became widely

< *page 204*
Polish medium Stanisława Tomczyk seemingly making a pair of scissors levitate, Poland, 1909
During the 1900s and 1910s, psychical researchers in Poland and Britain repeatedly examined Stanisława's purported ability to levitate small objects such as beakers, balls and scissors. Eventually, it was spotted that she used an extremely thin hair or thread attached to her hands.

Selling psychic services, UK and USA, early 21st century

During the late 20th century, psychic healing and readings became more widely available through stalls at New Age festivals and alternative fairs, as well as from psychic practitioners working from their homes and offices. Advertising also became bolder, as esoteric practices and beliefs became more acceptable.

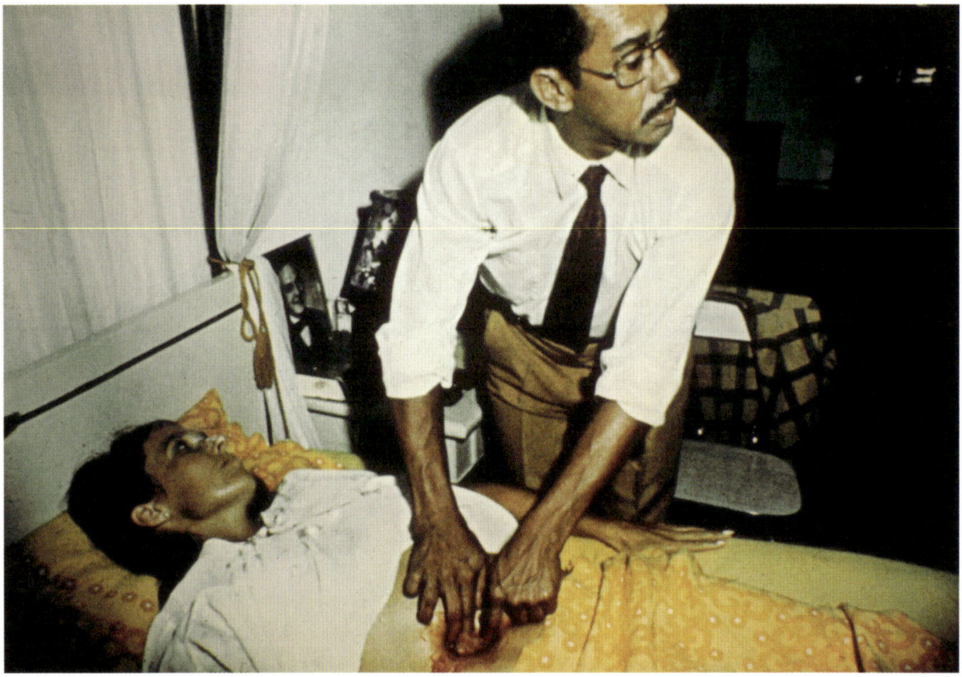

Psychic surgery, Brazil, 1970s
Psychic surgeon Edivaldo Silva treated thousands of patients. While healing, he would go into a trance-like state, his actions purportedly controlled by spirit experts in psychic surgery.

credited during the early 20th century. By the 1920s, telekinesis and other psychic abilities seemed plausible and deserving of close investigation. In *Magic: History, Theory, Practice* (1923), German polymath Ernst Schertel (1884–1958) wrote: 'Today – unlike more than twenty years ago – a person of understanding can no longer pass by the phenomena of the occult.' The discovery of radio, X-rays and the electromagnetic spectrum made some think that invisible but powerful esoteric forces may well exist. Meanwhile, new insights from psychology and psychiatry revealed that the mind was immensely deep, complex and powerful. The psyche, analysts such as Sigmund Freud and Carl Jung (1875–1961) explained, extends far beyond consciousness to include a misty world of unconscious and instinctive mental processes. Within the mysteries of the human mind, magic would be reborn.

Jung's psychological ideas were highly amenable to mystical and magical uses. He developed his understanding of the psyche partly by studying Western grimoires and Eastern mysticism, such as the *I Ching*

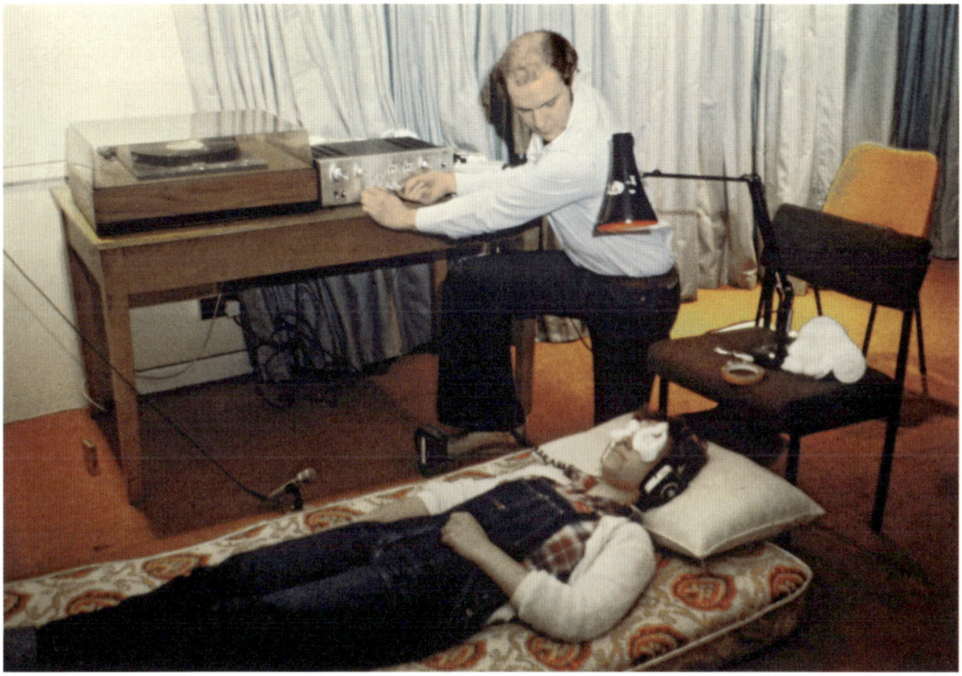

ESP investigation, England, 1979
British parapsychologist Carl Sargent supervises a potential 'receiver' of ESP during a ganzfeld experiment (testing for ESP or telepathy) at the University of Cambridge, UK. Malpractice likely marred the research.

divination manual. Weird or anomalous experiences, he seemed to suggest, were valuable – but not for traditional supernatural reasons. During the early 1950s, Jung explained to television interviewers that dreams could be used to predict the future by revealing insights from the collective unconscious. Jung also made coincidence seem mystically important, with the concept of synchronicity. It meant a significant link between unrelated events: an 'acausal connecting principle'. In texts such as *The Interpretation of Nature and the Psyche* (1952), Jung noted that synchronicity 'originates in the unconscious' yet somehow 'anticipates the external physical process.' This scientific rendering of magical-style intuition and correspondence became influential among esoteric experts and also people with more fleeting mystical interests. The concept also inspired many artists, musicians and storytellers, including a 1983 album by The Police and James Redfield's adventure novel *The Celestine Prophecy* (1993).

Psychic abilities are extremely varied and versatile. During the late 19th century, some psychics claimed

PROFILE
PSYCHIC ABILITIES

Psychic abilities provide abnormal powers as well as knowledge from beyond the five senses. Some psychics claim to have been born with enhanced gifts. Many report that everyone can develop psychic abilities

TELEPATHY
The mind-to-mind conveying of information and emotions is called telepathy and involves a transmitter and a receiver, like a magical radio or phone. These twins are performing a 'thought-reading' trick for a 1950s TV show.

CLAIRVOYANCE
The ability to use a sixth sense or extrasensory perception (ESP) to gain information about people, events or places is called clairvoyance. This fortune-teller is pictured at Louisiana State Fair, USA, in 1938.

PSYCHIC DEFENCE
Various practices aim to defend people, places, animals and property from harmful psychic powers. In the movie *Midnight Offering* (1981), a teenage witch uses her psychic powers to kill off those who get in her way.

PSYCHOMETRY
Psychometry is the ability to mystically discern information about an object's history through touching or sometimes merely seeing it. The history usually focuses on biographical details of a previous owner.

ASTRAL PROJECTION
A deliberate psychic activity causing a person's spiritual being to temporarily separate from their physical body, as seen in Henry John Stock's *The Aspiration of a Soul While Listening to Music* (1881).

AURA READING
Some people believe they can perceive subtle fields of mystical radiation emanating from individuals. These psychic auras are often said to reflect a person's particular physical, emotional and spiritual state.

with the right training and mindset. The range of different psychic abilities is large, yet most are fundamentally based on a combination of will, intention and subconscious mental activity.

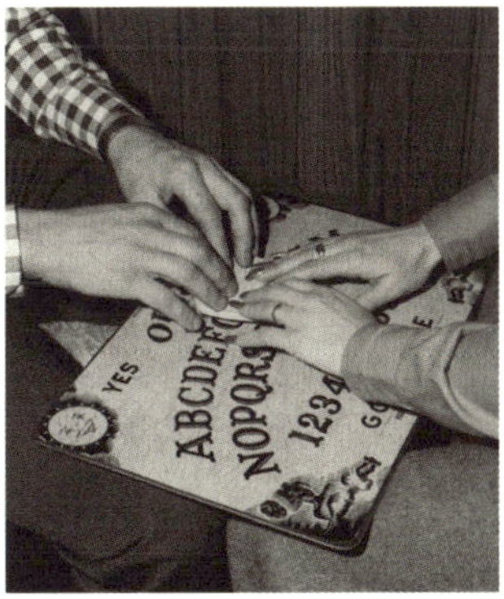

MEDIUMSHIP
Primarily, mediumship makes contact with the spirits of the dead, a practice that can overlap with clairvoyance and dowsing. Psychic mediums sometimes use a Ouija board as a way of communicating with a spirit.

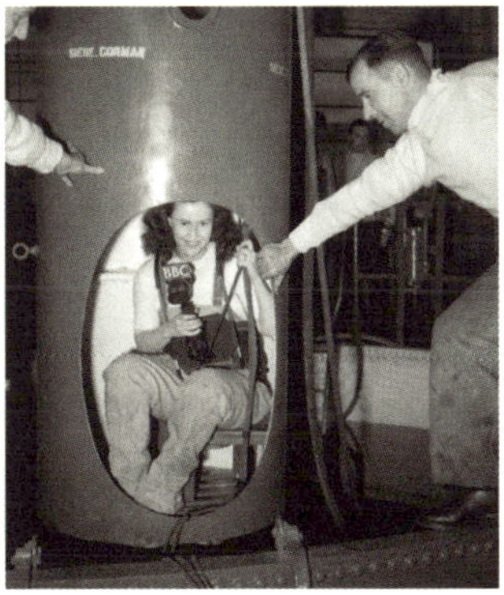

REMOTE VIEWING
This psychic ability seeks to obtain impressions about distant unseen objects. In the 1940s and 1950s, Australians Sydney Piddington and Lesley Pope used the technique to baffle audiences with their 'mind-reading' act.

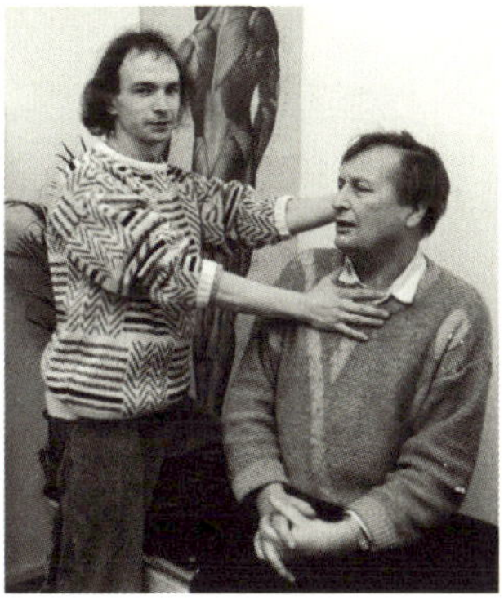

PSYCHIC HEALING
A very wide range of mystical healing practices to help reduce or cure physical, emotional and spiritual problems. Here, the healer touches certain places on the body to psychically heal organs or tissue underneath.

PSYCHOKINESIS / TELEKINESIS
This ability uses intense mental concentration to influence an object without physical touch, as demonstrated by Uri Geller. Telekinesis may alter the workings of an item.

DOWSING
Dowsing uses rods, or sometimes pendulums, to find hidden things such as water sources and minerals. Dowsing can also provide personal insight and identify emotional or energy blockages.

PRECOGNITION / PREMONITION
This branch of ESP provides knowledge of future events. Some psychics claim that precognition, or premonition, is the most common psychic ability after telepathy.

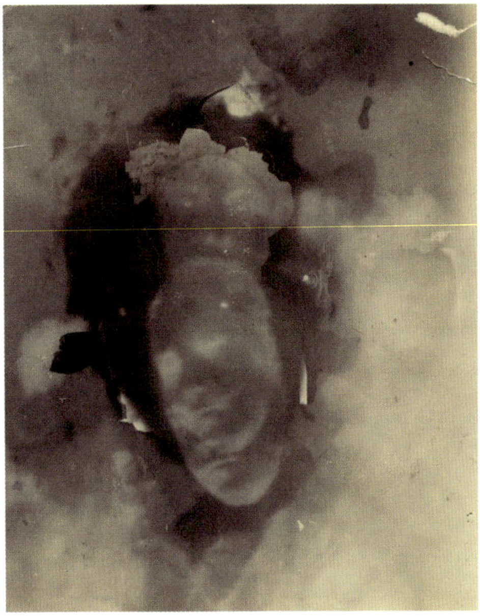
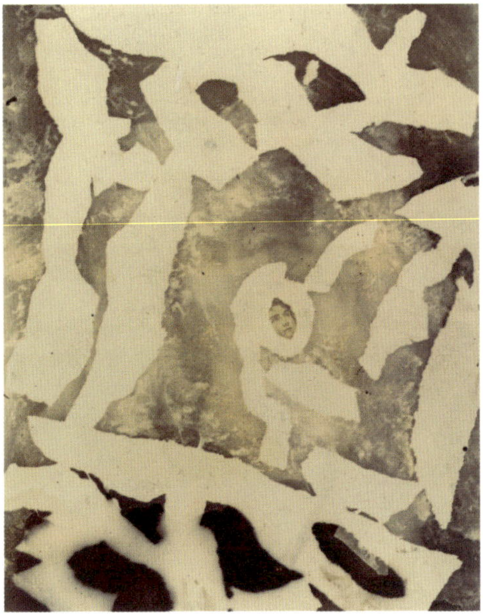

Thoughtographs, UK, 1890s
These allegedly psychic photographs were created by the spiritualist photographer Charles Lacey. With intense concentration, psychics could apparently burn mental images onto photographic negatives.

to be able to burn images from their minds onto photographs with thoughtography. Extrasensory perception (ESP) was conceptualized a few decades later, in the 1930s. The term was coined by parapsychologists at Duke University as a noncommittal way to describe the mental act of receiving information without using the senses. It quickly caught on, American researcher Louisa Rhine (1891–1983) recalled in *ESP in Life and Lab* (1967), because it 'filled a need' by explaining weird and anomalous experiences that mainstream culture dismissed as coincidence or delusion. When Duke University's ESP research was publicized, people flooded forward with stories. A movie-goer from Memphis went into the theatre with the intensifying and eventually unbearable feeling their home was on fire. They drove home to see the surrounding fields burning. A mother was accurately informed of her son's death through a dream, before her husband came to tell her the next day.

Scientific methods seem not to detect the existence of ESP. At Duke University's Parapsychology Research Laboratory (1930–65), studies led by Joseph Banks Rhine (1895–1980) appeared, at first, to produce small

Psychokinesis experiment, Duke University, North Carolina, USA, 1960s
Botanist and parapsychologist Joseph Banks Rhine conducts a 'dice turning test' (rolling a dice by hand), investigating whether mental focus and concentration influence the result.

but real ESP effects, above chance. However, later work suggests these effects were the result of sensory leakage, where participants gained information from the demonstrators or environment. Psychological research that is carefully constructed to make sensory leakage impossible finds no evidence of ESP. The Mind Machine, a steel-cabinet-encased computer created at the University of Hertfordshire, was taken around British shopping centres and museums during the early 2000s. Some 27,856 participants were asked to guess the outcome of four random electronic coin tosses. The results were statistically consistent, possibly, with a tiny ESP effect, but basically within the realms of chance. Although scientific evidence may be lacking, polls and surveys consistently find that between half and two-thirds of Americans say they believe in psychic powers and psi phenomena.

The modern esoteric scene teems with psychic powers. Infamous British magician Aleister Crowley (1875–1947) loathed the term 'psychic' but still used it. 'What I hate to call psychic phenomena,' he spat in his *Confessions* (1969). Gerald Gardner (1884–1964), founder of the Wiccan tradition of modern pagan

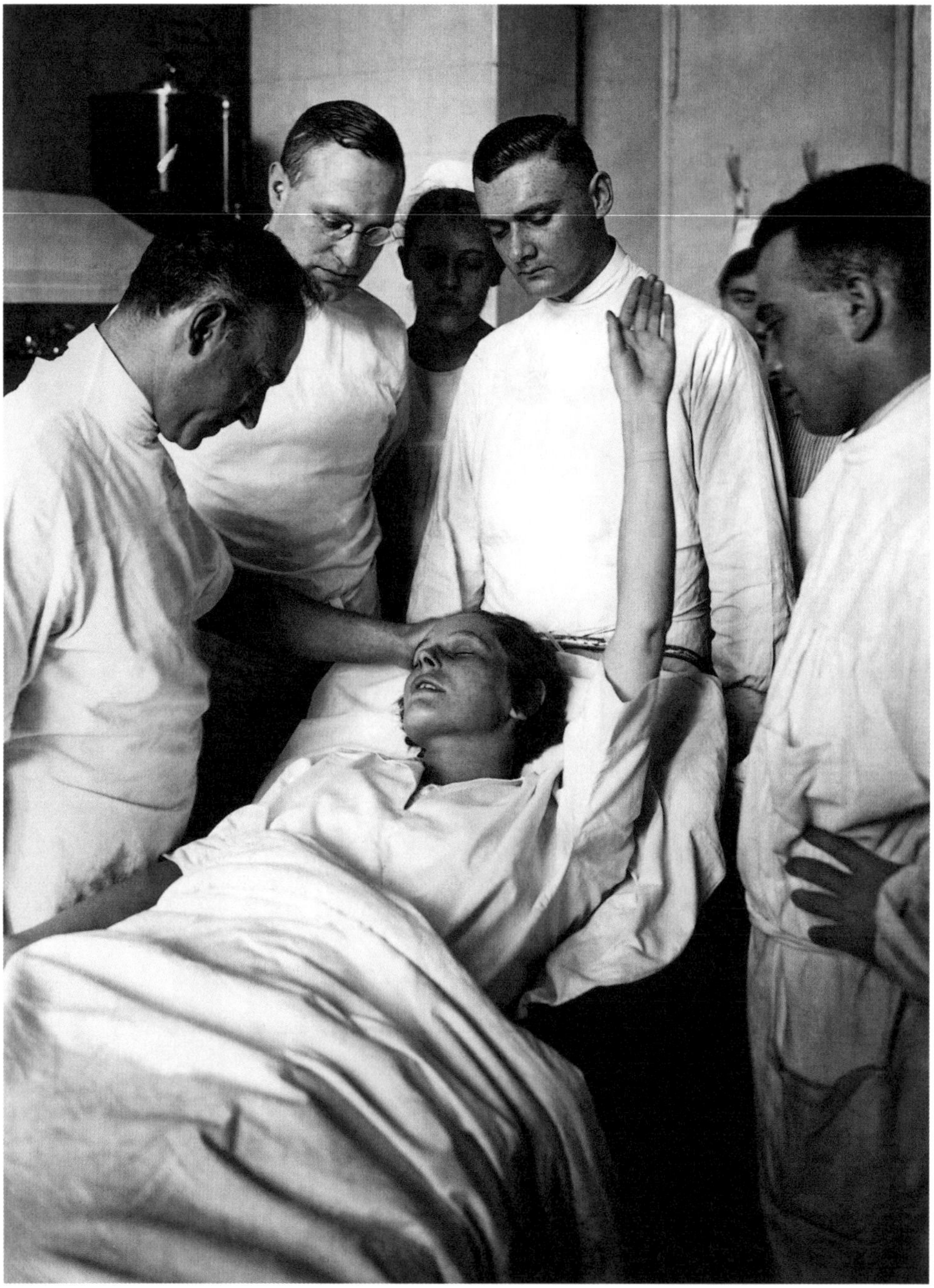

Anaesthesia by hypnosis, Germany, 1926

A doctor is using the hypnotic technique of visual fixation. The aim is to induce a nervous sleep and hypno-analgesia to numb specific body parts. The 1920s saw growing medical and scientific interest in hypnosis and the powers of suggestion, following a lull caused by the uptake of chemical anaesthetics.

witchcraft, wrote often of psychic abilities. But the magician who most used psychic powers was Dion Fortune (1890–1946). Born Violet Mary Firth Evans, Fortune helped establish the style of magic known as Western esotericism, while her Fraternity and Society of Inner Light taught a mystery tradition of inner consciousness and self-regeneration. However, Fortune's most widely influential work concerns dangerous psychic powers. Titled *Psychic Self-Defence* (1930), it explains how to detect and repel mind-driven occult assaults or psychic attacks.

During the interwar period, growing numbers of people were learning telepathy, hypnosis and faith healing. As a result, Fortune thought, psychic attacks were becoming more common. Bad dreams, sleep paralysis, nervous exhaustion and mental breakdown were typical symptoms. Paranormal phenomena may also appear: horrible smells, inexplicable fires, strange slime and weird footprints that go nowhere. Psychic attacks updated traditional ideas of harmful magic, or the 'left-hand path' as many modern mystics call it. Mental harm predominated. The assailant's malice was also downplayed. 'All attacks are not deliberately motivated,' Fortune cautioned. Methods of defence mingled occultism, folklore and mystical Christianity. Running water had 'peculiar electrical qualities' and could be used for deflecting or purifying occult attacks, especially if salt were added. Consecrated bathwater could also break 'an undesirable psychic contact'. The 'Christ-force...should be invoked in every operation of psychic self-defence,' Fortune insisted. The concept of psychic attack later evolved into the notion of psychic or energy vampires, who sap your energy and ruin your mood. This idea has crossed over into popular culture, with energy vampires appearing next to blood-drinkers in the American sitcom *What We Do in the Shadows* (2019–24). The term 'emotional vampire' is also used by therapists and psychologists, such as Dr Al Bernstein (b. 1950), to describe draining people who are hard to deal with. But in the esoteric scene, psychic vampirism is literally believed to do real harm, not only emotionally but also physically and materially.

PROFILE
PSYCHIC TOOLS

Compared with other forms of magic, psychic abilities are highly cognitive and brain-based, emanating more from internal power than external ritual. However, psychics also use a wide variety of mystical tools to focus their minds and develop their abilities. Many of these implements are drawn from the deeper history of magic, although for psychics they often serve subtly different functions. From pendulums to rune stones, psychic tools provide sensory anchoring, ensuring that the mind focuses on the mystical act. Tools may enhance placebo effects, as well as being tactile, soothing and enjoyable to use.

PENDULUM
Used to answer binary 'yes/no' questions, or to locate hidden energies, pendulums are often made of metal, wood or crystals, because these are said to have useful 'energy' qualities.

RUNE STONES
Psychics typically draw runes from a bag in certain numbers (1, 3 or 9) or scatter them on a cloth. Interpretations are often based on orientation and proximity, as well as intuitive response.

DIVINING ROD
In 17th-century Europe, divining rods were used to find criminals and treasure. From the early 20th century, psychics used dowsing in personal readings to help detect subtle energy fields.

SPIRIT / OUIJA BOARD
Spirit boards emerged from late 19th-century American spiritualism, with the Ouija board specifically becoming a commercial hit during the 1890s.

CRYSTALS
Crystal balls are used for scrying and divination. The psychic gazes inside, looking for visions, images and symbols. Other crystals are used for healing, protection and assistance.

TAROT CARDS
Originally developed as playing cards in late medieval Europe, tarot cards have become indispensable psychic tools because of their vivid pictures and archetypal images.

Radiesthesia on a candy bar, California, USA, 1978
At the Berkeley Holistic Health Center, administrators Eddie Bauman and Pamela Wright use the swing of a pendulum to reveal invisible psychic energies. Wright's son is visibly upset when the pendulum answers in the negative when asked if the candy bar is good for him.

Dion Fortune's career encapsulates the close connection, during modern times, between magic and psychology. As Violet Firth, she trained and worked as a psychotherapist during the 1910s and early 1920s. Around the same time, she began learning about the occult and theosophy, above all by working and training with a mysterious service magician and leader of an occult society named Theodore William Carte Moriarty (1873–1923). Our knowledge of him mostly comes from Fortune's *The Secrets of Dr Taverner* (1926), a work of fiction apparently 'founded on fact' and dedicated to the occultist to whom Fortune felt she owed 'the greatest debt of my life'. Dr Taverner's therapies 'began where ordinary medicine ended', specializing in cases of mental illness that were dimly understood or could lead to institutionalization in an asylum. Much classic magic was described in modern terms. 'Psychic interference', for example, was a term Dr Taverner used for 'being possessed by a devil'. A protective spell was described as 'a sphere of influence, a kind of psychic bell jar, over this house to keep out evil entities', while telepathy was like using a 'wireless telephone'.

Radiesthesia is a mystical pseudoscience that uses a hand-held pendulum, fork or rod to discover resources such as precious metals, dangers like harmful radiation and fertile land. It was developed primarily in Germany, which, during the 1920s, was home to hundreds of purportedly scientific radiesthesiologists. Some, like Siegfried Reuter (1876–1945), focused on finding mineral deposits. Others claimed that diseases such as cancer were caused by harmful earth rays that could only be identified using divining tools. Ludwig Straniak (1879–1951) employed a sidereal pendulum, with a Y- or L-shaped stick, to detect purported ley lines and 'earth rays'. He wrote scientific papers about radiesthesia, claiming that the pendulum was pushed by an 'eighth force of nature', hidden in our atmosphere. Straniak also co-founded the Society for Scientific Pendulum Research, which received some Nazi funding. With the establishment of the Third Reich in 1933, German farms and industries began employing experts in radiesthesia to explain how cosmic and electromagnetic forces influenced their business. In 1934, Adolf Hitler (1889–1945) hired radiesthesiologist Gustav Freiherr von Pohl (b. 1873) to search the Reich

Parapsychologist Hans Bender with the Psi-Recorder 70, Germany, 1970s
Bender's machine recorded metal movement and sound in an attempt to scientifically investigate the alleged psychic spoon-bending of Uri Geller and others.

Chancellery to see if it were blighted by harmful 'death rays', historian Eric Kurlander (b. 1973) has shown.

Parapsychology, the scientific and often lab-based study of anomalous powers, found support among some leading Nazis. Publications for the Office of Public Health endorsed the reality of extrasensory phenomena that had formerly been called supernatural. Rudolf Hess (1894–1987) proposed establishing a Central Institute for Occultism during the mid-1930s, to explore parapsychology and fringe or border science. Above all, Nazi parapsychology was undertaken by Hans Bender (1907–91), who finished a doctorate about ESP in 1933, the same year he joined the Sturmabteilung (SA). After publishing various books on parapsychology, in 1941 Bender was appointed as an assistant professor in the Institute of Psychology and Clinical Psychology at Strasbourg's Reich University, recently established to promote Nazi-style science. In 1942, he founded a university-affiliated centre for the study of parapsychology, the Paracelsus Institute, showing the links between psi and the key Renaissance natural magician. Bender asked for support from the Schutzstaffel (SS) and received encouraging words and various confiscated books on astrology. Many senior Nazis were on the institute's governing board.

During the Cold War (*c.* 1947–91), concern that the Communist USSR and China were pursuing cutting-edge research in psi inspired action in the USA. Between the 1970s and 1990s, physicists at Stanford Research Institute received CIA funding to investigate remote reviewing, in which the mind is supposed to perceive distant and unseen objects. Space agency NASA gave support for experiments in psychokinesis: the psychic act of exerting force or influence on an object using thought alone. Meanwhile, between 1977 and 1995, as many as twenty people at a time worked on the United States Army's STAR GATE programme, which investigated anomalous phenomena such as telepathy, remote viewing and psychokinesis. The programme received $2 million a year to continue its work, until it was finally deemed irrelevant in 1995. Unfortunately, none of these investigations found convincing evidence that psi powers objectively exist.

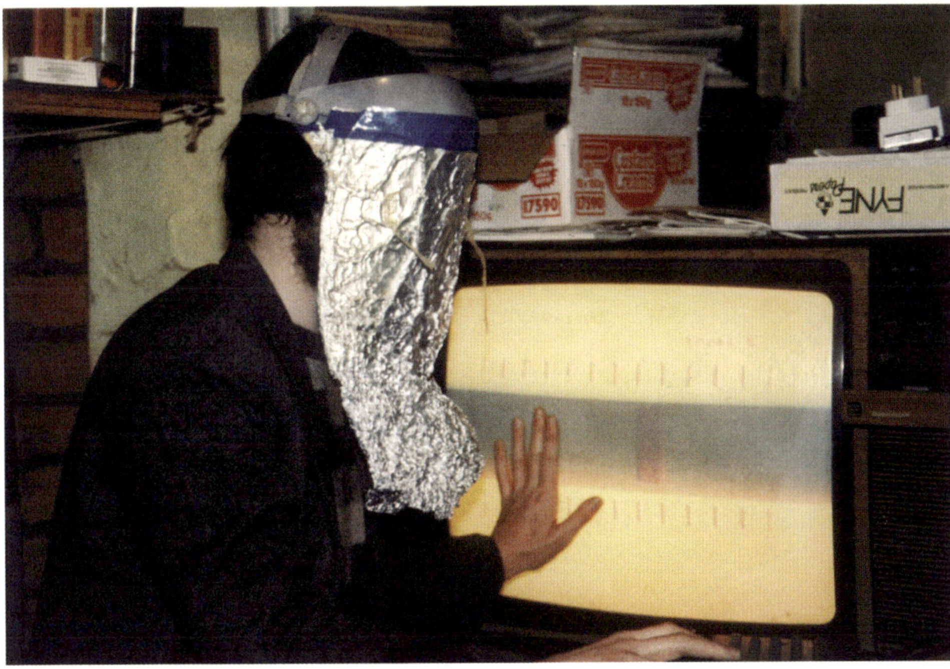

Private parascience experiment, England, 1974

These images show a psychokinesis experiment at the Paraphysical Laboratory (Paralab) of physicist Benson Herbert in Wiltshire, UK. Between the 1960s and early 1990s, Benson modernized parascience using equipment such as high-speed cameras, polygraphs and various home-made devices.

3 WITCHCRAFT, MAGICK & CRYSTALS 3

'WHEN I CALL MYSELF A WITCH, I'M CONSCIOUSLY SETTING MYSELF APART FROM THE STATUS QUO.'

THORN MOONEY,
WITCHES AMONG US (2024)

From the mid-20th century, new and positive forms of witchcraft emerged. Wicca, under the influence of British occultist Gerald Gardner, combined diverse esoteric traditions into a life-affirming neo-pagan religion. During the late 20th and early 21st centuries, many more novel forms of witchcraft were created by countercultural magical practitioners. Aleister Crowley created liberating 'magick', as he preferred to call it, which was further developed from the 1980s by the unpretentious tradition of chaos magick. Meanwhile, New Age practices like crystal healing and reiki brought magic to wider audiences.

WITCHCRAFT, MAGICK & CRYSTALS
3 3

The idea of harmful witchcraft, hexes and bad spells haunts our fears with remarkable persistence. Today, this notion is widely believed in many parts of the world, including sub-Saharan African, Melanesia and South Asia, but you can find flickers of it everywhere. In London in 2019, for example, a mother and her adult son were found guilty of harassing their neighbour, whom they believed to be a malign witch, telling the poor lady's daughter so and pumping religious television shows through the walls late at night. It can be hard to establish how widely people fear harmful witchcraft, because it is a notoriously secretive and sensitive subject. Even so, there is no doubt these ideas are less widespread and less acted on than in the past. Across Europe and the USA, belief seems to have remained quite widespread during the 19th and early 20th centuries, as evidenced by a steady stream of vigilante attacks on alleged witches. These assaults began to decline during the late 19th century and early 20th century, in part because of better policing and law enforcement. Life was improved by running water to individual households, public health provision, environmental regulations and more effective medicines. Historians like Owen Davies have laid primary emphasis on these developments for the decline of belief in harmful witchcraft in Britain and the USA at this time. However, new medical regulations also made it harder for mystical healers to sell magical services. Harmful witchcraft never totally disappeared, but it seems to have reached a low point in Europe and the USA during the early and mid-20th century.

The decline of harmful witchcraft enabled witches to be reborn and recreated as positive and empowering figures. The first new witchcraft movement began in England, probably during the 1940s. Its chief architect was a self-educated ex-colonist and amazingly complex man named Gerald Gardner. Drawing on an enormously rich range of sources, he synthesized Wicca, a neo-pagan and highly religious form of witchcraft. It was organized into covens, structured around the ritual year, and dedicated to a Horned God and Moon Goddess. Gardner outlined a startlingly revisionist thesis about

< *page 222*
Konstantin Savitsky,
***A Witch*, 1879**
The Russian realist painting depicts a marginalized yet powerful figure. Supernatural tropes are low key, including animals and a staff.

Abbé Desnoyers, modern witch-finder (top), and the women he accused (bottom), France, 1926

Desnoyers claimed his parish of Bombon near Melun was infested with witches and convinced some parishioners that their ills were caused by harmful spells. He was successfully prosecuted for fraud and assault after abusively exorcising two alleged witches.

< **Male Wiccan performing the Great Rite, UK, 2008**
This neo-pagan fertility ritual evokes the sacred marriage (Hieros Gamos) of the Horned God (represented by the knife) and the Triple Goddess (represented by the chalice).

> **Gerald Gardner, father of Wicca, England, 1950s**
In his rituals, Gardner used magical swords, daggers, circles, chalices and other items described in historical grimoires.

witches in books, such as the fictional *High Magic's Aid* (1949) and the purportedly factual *Witchcraft Today* (1954), interviews, television programmes and also a museum. Witchcraft, according to him, was not evil magic but an ancient pagan religion, older than Christianity, with its roots in the Neolithic era. Its bad reputation came from stigmatization and persecution by later Christians. Rather than being malefactors, witches worshipped and cast spells overwhelmingly for good. Gardner knew this, he told readers of *Witchcraft Today*, because he was an anthropologist (he was not) who had encountered the last remnants of the ancient and primordial cult. In a corner of the New Forest, in southern England, he claimed he met and was initiated into the last surviving coven. Some scholars, including Philip Heselton (b. 1946) and Ethan Doyle White, think that a group identifying with witches may well have existed, albeit based on modern ideas about witchcraft rather than an unbroken ancient tradition. Others, however, judge Gardner's origin claims to be a potent myth analogous to other religious creation stories, rather than the literal truth. It seems unlikely that Gardner was inducted into a preexisting coven, but it cannot be ruled out.

Smithing among the Dayak people, Sarawak, Malaysia, early 20th century
Dayak smiths produce a wide array of tools for daily life but also forge blades and other sacred objects believed to hold spiritual power. When he lived in Malaysia, Gerald Gardner was inspired by Dayak beliefs, amulets, tattoos and weaponry.

Wicca combined a great variety of concepts and traditions in a completely new way. Renaissance ceremonial magic helped shape the rituals, which drew particularly on the *Lesser Key of Solomon*. The magic of the occult revival was also influential: Gardner met Aleister Crowley in 1947 and was inducted into his magical society the Ordo Templi Orientis. Other elements were taken from deeper history: the word 'wicca' comes from the Old English term for a male sorcerer. Folklore, too, was an inspiration, both oral and written, invented and traditional. Gardner took ideas from *Aradia, or The Gospel of Witches* (1899) by American folklorist Charles Godfrey Leland (1824–1903). Colonial encounters across Borneo, Malaya and beyond were also important: socializing with Dayak people in the early 20th century shaped Gardner's conviction that magic and the occult were normal and natural. Another source was spiritualism and psychical research, which Wicca's founder investigated during trips back to England in the 1930s.

Gardner's idea that witchcraft was in fact a fertility-focused pagan religion had its origins in 18th-century

PROFILE
NEW WITCHCRAFTS

Witchcraft today is an incredibly diverse, expressive and vibrant spirituality. Across the world, self-identified witches have created many thousands of novel versions of the craft, by intuitively blending folklore with religion, magic, philosophy, feminism, history, politics and aesthetics. Many modern witches are neo-pagan, but practitioners also profess different faiths and none. Christian Witchcraft has emerged on a small scale during recent decades, for example. Despite many differences, modern forms of witchcraft commonly emphasize positive spell casting, female independence and a spiritual reverence for nature.

CEREMONIAL
Often drawing on the historical grimoire tradition, ceremonial witchcraft is a deep and serious form of spiritual practice that uses highly structured rituals and complex symbolism. Rituals are adjusted according to the problem requiring resolution.

COSMIC
Astrology, planetary alignments and the lunar cycle are vital in the spells of cosmic witches, who use energies from beyond Earth, particularly from planets and stars. Some work with planetary deities and spirits residing in space.

WICCA
Wicca is a coven-based form of positive witchcraft that totally rejects the image of the witch as a harmful figure. Wicca emerged during the 1940s and 1950s, then evolved into different branches. Dianic Wicca honours only the female goddess.

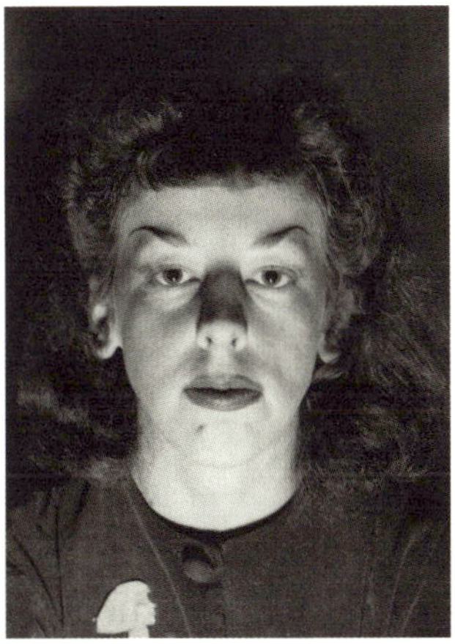

ART
Creativity is nurtured in art witchcraft, which works magic through painting, drawing, sculpture, music, textiles and collage to focus and express the 'intention' that empowers spells. Rosaleen Norton, seen here, was an artist and self-identified witch.

URBAN
Urban witchcraft adapts magical practice to city life. Some urban witches use magic politically, to reduce crime or promote social justice, as at this March For Our Lives event in 2018. Others seek natural magic in parks, waterways and their own garden.

SECULAR
A non-religious witchcraft practice that does not include concepts of deities. Secular witches emphasize psychology, mindset, energy and nature in their practice. Although they reject gods, many embrace the supernatural reality of magic.

HEDGE
The solitary practice of hedge witchcraft is based on the image of the traditional wise woman, but without the Christian parts of historical white magic. It has spread internationally through conferences, books, personal networks and online media.

GREEN
The natural world is prized by green witches. Plants, soil and rocks feature prominently in spells, corresponding with the magical elements of earth, water, air and fire. Outdoor settings are common for the rituals of green witches.

HEREDITARY
Hereditary witchcraft draws on inherited magical identity, experience and knowledge. This can include relatives with magical identities, but it can also come from broader history and tradition. In this respect, anyone can be a hereditary witch.

D'Raven Ashly, Wiccan Celtic Priestess, New York City, USA, 2022
Ashly performs at WitchsFest USA, one of hundreds of annual festivals for modern witches held across Europe, North America, Australasia and online.

German and 19th-century French scholarship. Yet it was in England, during the early 20th century, that the notion achieved its greatest form, through the dubious scholarship of Margaret Murray (1863–1963). In articles and books such as *The Witch-Cult in Western Europe* (1921) and *The God of Witches* (1931), the forceful writer argued that a witch religion had worshipped a Horned God, who Christian observers called 'the Devil'. It was an enchanting thesis for a radical age, accepted not only at the fringes of society but by illustrious publishers like Oxford University Press. Murray's propensity for malpractice, however enchanting, is evident in the purportedly historical magical artefacts she gave to institutions like the British Museum.

Wicca soon spread and changed. After World War II, Gardner founded a coven in the grounds of a nudist club at the Hertfordshire village of Bricket Wood. In 1951, he began working with Cecil Williamson (1909–99), a fascinating collector and also likely inventor of occult objects. Together, they set up a new witchcraft museum in Castletown, on the Isle of Man. From 1953, Gardner began working with Doreen Valiente (1922–99)

< **Sybil Leek, the 'White Witch of Burley', with her jackdaw Hotfoot Jackson, New Forest, England, 1964**
Leek was a Wiccan High Priestess and service magician who sold useful spells and herbs.

> **Patricia Crowther, Wiccan High Priestess, Sheffield, 1971**
Crowther blows a ritual horn, probably as the calling to gather to begin a ceremony or to honour the masculine Horned God.

to write a 'Book of Shadows', codifying and refining Wicca's rituals. Other women were welcomed into the craft, including Eleanor Bone (1911–2001) and Patricia Crowther (1927–2025), who along with other witches soon began creating new types of Wicca. Many were feminist and excluded the ritual nudity Gardner had taken from his interests in nudism and the erotic magick of Crowley. Meanwhile, the 1980s and 1990s saw the emergence of solitary types of modern witchcraft. Hedge witchcraft was based on the spell-crafting image of the old wise woman, but without the Christian white magic. Today, there are many varieties of witchcraft, from trans and nonbinary witchcraft to fairy witchcraft, and much more. Some witches identify as pagan, neo-pagan, New Age or spiritual, but not all.

Modern witches are highly diverse, but all reject negative witchcraft stereotypes of harm and depravity. Instead, modern witchcraft is an empowering identity and a positive magical practice. Witchcraft books tell readers to do magic responsibly, with good intentions and never to substitute magic for clinical medicine. Many witches, including Susan Bowes in *The Wiccan Handbook* (2021), contend that magic only works if 'your

Evelyn De Morgan,
***The Love Potion*, 1903**

Despite the presence of a black cat at her feet, this witch is depicted as a learned scholar whose leather-bound books include magical classics by Agrippa and Paracelsus. In her elegant study, she enacts love magic by pouring a potion into a chalice, while the couple embraces in the background.

intention is pure and your wish is to do good selflessly.' Historical witchcraft, black or grey or white, was much more aggressive. Love magic, for example, was extremely coercive. It tried to force a specific person to be overcome with desire, against their will. The love magic of modern witches is quite different. It attracts kinds of love, rather than enflaming specific people. Today, modern witchcraft is full of cathartic and soothing magic, detailed in books such as *Spellwork for Self-Care* (2012) and artist Sam McKechnie's *Gentle Spells & Kind Magic* (2022). It provides daily magic to guard your home or improve your luck, sleep, self-esteem, relationships and even personal finances. Much witchcraft today is designed to enhance people's lives, by unlocking remarkable powers hidden in all of us and connected with nature.

Despite the changes and innovations, the ancient and transcultural idea of harmful witchcraft remains in the early 21st century. When things are going wrong in people's lives, and when normal methods fail to provide solutions, some individuals still begin to wonder whether they may be suffering from malicious mystical forces, directed by an ill-disposed person. Cornish solitary witch Gemma Gary (b. 1987), in a guidebook to her own brand of *Traditional Witchcraft* (2015), notes that: 'Old beliefs in the power of the curse and of ill-wishing are still very much alive.' Some people in the West of England, as elsewhere, may consult a white witch or esoteric practitioner when intractable problems arise. Healers take various approaches: some removing the harm; others sending it back. But according to Gary, this magical defence is less aggressive than in the past because victims generally no longer want to know who precisely is responsible.

During the early 20th century, ceremonial magic was made enormously more creative and liberating by Aleister Crowley. From an early interest in the occult at Cambridge University, he became a leading member of the Golden Dawn. Crowley left the order following a failed takeover, then proceeded to devise his own remarkably liberated Thelema school of magick, as he preferred to call it. The term 'Thelema' means 'will' in

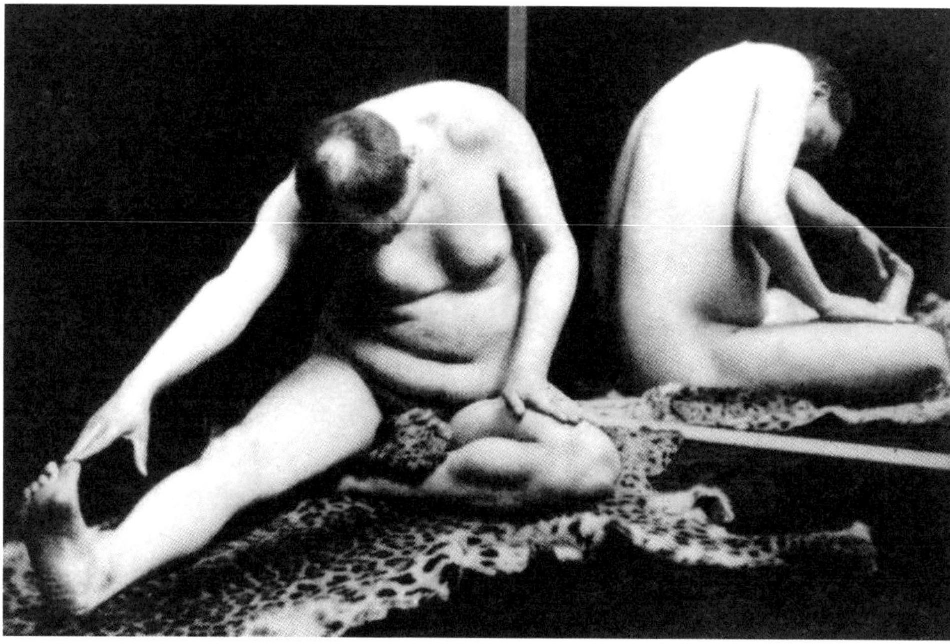

Aleister Crowley performing 'the parallelogram' yoga pose, from *Equinox*, 1912
Crowley the libertine provocateur covers his genitals with a leopard skin rug.

ancient Greek and summed up in a single word the essence of Crowley's teaching. Thelema expanded upon the Hermetic Qabalah that Crowley learned from the Golden Dawn, to include many more traditions and sources, such as the Chinese divination classic the *I Ching*, which the magus used daily. Obscenities, fables, parables, poetry, blasphemy and paradoxes littered Crowley's magickal writings. So did dry humour, irony, exhibitionism and self-abasement. A 1912 issue of his periodical *Equinox*, for example, shows Crowley doing yoga poses naked, with his privates painted over. 'An elderly, corpulent gentleman of sedentary habit has been good enough to pose', it explains, 'so that none need feel debarred from devoting himself to the Great Work on the ground of physical infirmity.' This issue of *Equinox* also contains a portion of the sacred text of Thelema: the *Book of the Law*, known alternatively as the *Liber Al vel Legis*. Written in Cairo in 1904, by Crowley with corrections by his wife Rose Edith Kelly (1874–1932), it was attributed to the gods Ra-Hoor-Khuit, Nuit and Hadit. They, in turn, were based loosely on ancient Egyptian deities, but with significant innovations in symbolism and character. Each god dictates a chapter of remarkable aphorisms.

Crowley's magick unlocked the potential for human flourishing. 'Every man and every woman is a star,' was the third precept of the *Book of the Law*. The text certainly contained some practical or operative elements. Beginning and ending with the word 'abracadabra', the *Liber Al*'s third section explains how to make a magical cake that can be used to defeat enemies or to increase the practitioner's strength. Generally, though, the focus of Crowley's magick was more internal and psychological. It explored the 'untrodden regions of the mind', as he wrote in his diary. Drugs, sex, complex magic and literature were all present. Ultimately though, it came down to will. Magick, for Crowley, burned with the psychology of Friedrich Nietzsche (1844–1900). It only works if you develop the will to believe. Practise will billions of times, advises Crowley's *The Book of Lies* (1913). 'Not until then is that which is done well done.' The will was central to becoming and creating. It was the meaning of life as well as magick. 'Though hast no right but to

Symbolic paintings representing Aleister Crowley's magical organization A∴ A∴, 1909
Dedicated to spiritual enlightenment and the perfection of humanity, the Argenteum Astrum (Silver Star) blended ceremonial magic with Buddhism and yoga.

do thy will,' states the forty-second precept of the *Book of the Law*. Pure will, focused on result not purpose, was a thing 'in every way perfect'.

Crowley was inspirational beyond the magical scene. His bald head appeared on the cover of The Beatles' *Sgt. Pepper's Lonely Hearts Club Band* (1967). His symbols and ideas influenced *Led Zeppelin III* (1970) and *IV* (1971). Ozzy Osborne sang about 'Mr Crowley' (1980), as did David Bowie in 'Quicksand' (1971) and Iron Maiden in 'The Number of the Beast' (1982). *Blood Sugar Sex Magik* (1991), by the Red Hot Chili Peppers, is also somewhat influenced by Crowley.

Crowley's liberating example was one of the sparks that helped to create chaos magick. Coursing with creative energy, the new magical school was formed, between the late 1970s and 1990s, by punks who laughed at themselves and others. They wanted powerful effects: 'magick', in the old-style spelling preferred by Crowley. Yet chaos magicians rejected anything pompous, serious or hierarchical. Chaos was a pop culture buzzword and meant energized disorder. In the postmodern moment, when grand narratives were failing, chaos magick incorporated any symbol or system. Even a brand logo or a song, if it helped. Anything, to elicit strong but temporary belief.

< **Eight-pointed symbol of chaos magick**
Known most often as the Star of Chaos, this symbol evokes the flexible and postmodern nature of this magical tradition. Chaos magick is defined by infinite possibilities, not fixed truths.

> **Civil disobedience and chaos magick, Chile, 2022**
Like anarchism, chaos magick is profoundly anti-dogmatic. In recent decades, niche movements such as anarcho-arcanism and mystical-anarchism have fused magic with radical politics and civil disobedience.

< **Gnosticism symbol, from Bernard de Montfaucon's *L'Antiquité Expliquée, et Représentée en Figures*, 1719**
This lion-headed serpent is Chnoubis, a Gnostic deity and daemon known for healing and protection.

> **Magic gold and heliotrope pendant, Roman, 3rd to 4th century** CE
This amulet features Chnoubis, a Gnostic deity and daemon known for healing. It is engraved with protective magic words and magic names.

Fun and irreverence surged through chaos magick. Its anti-dogmatic spirit began with Peter Carroll's (b. 1953) *Liber Null* (1978), meaning a book of void or nothing, which combined multiple traditions. Carroll's *Psychonaut* (1982) was a magickal tome for psychological explorers with a sense of humour. Chaos magick was flexible and funny. Yet it also aimed for amazing experiences and great effects. Many practitioners practised gnosis, switching from normal consciousness to altered states and back again. Despite the jokes, they appreciated the profundities of mysticism. As practitioner Phil Hine (b. 1963) notes in the guidebook *Condensed Chaos* (1995): 'Magic is a doorway through which we step into mystery, wildness, and immanence.'

The most accessible forms of modern magic come from the New Age. It is a vague but useful term, which since the mid-20th century has been used to refer to the idea that we have entered a novel era of metaphysical understanding, a change that occurs once every 2,000 years as the Earth moves into a different constellation of the zodiac. Specifically, we have left the Epoch of Pisces (dark and light fishes) for the Age of Aquarius (water). In practice, the New Age movement is often associated with metaphysical thinking and mystical practices that began to flower during the 1960s in

Different coloured quartz stones, believed to energize and balance the body's chakras

Crystal healers often describe clear quartz as a 'master healer' that helps the crown chakra clear mental fog and promote clarity. Purple amethyst is supposed to foster intuition and spirituality by resonating with the crown and third-eye chakras. Blue crystals are said to assist the throat chakra, which governs communication and expression. Green crystals such as aventurine and green calcite supposedly energize the heart chakra, promoting love and emotional healing. Rose quartz also resonates with the heart chakra for love and compassion towards others and oneself. Yellow citrine is believed to resonate with the solar plexus chakra, promoting confidence and energy.

West Coast America, before spreading more widely across the world. It is typically regarded, with some hostility but justification too, as being self-focused and consumer orientated. People experiment, change and choose what they like, from what has been described as a 'spiritual supermarket'. The movement is ambivalent about science, recognizing its prestige but also asserting its limits, sometimes using scientific and pseudoscientific approaches, at other times rejecting them. The influence of the New Age movement is shallower but wider than modern neo-paganism.

The New Age is often defined as a movement of new spiritual and religious practices. However, magical-style techniques play a large role in providing immediate and tangible benefits. Crystals are probably the most prominent form of New Age mysticism, with many celebrity fans, including Adele (for stage fright), Kim Kardashian (after a robbery) and Victoria Beckham (for positive energy). Mystical shops (high street and online) and festivals are major suppliers of crystals, including the alternative medicine fairs pioneered by London's Kensington Exhibition Centre from 1977. In Britain, some colleges offer training in the use of crystals through beauty therapy programmes. In 1975, Bob Dylan was iconically pictured reading *Crystal Magick* (1968) by Carlyle A. Pushong (1916–92). This scarce book, by a learned but low-profile occultist, is not really about crystal healing in the modern sense: it primarily concerns the older practice of using crystals for divination, or scrying, through a complex mix of ideas from Hinduism, Kabbalah and various magical traditions. Modern crystal magic is more talismanic and fulfilment-orientated, based on concepts of energy. In the USA, teachings and writings by Marcel Vogel (1917–91) – an IBM researcher on quartz screens who became an expert quartz healer – were influential in the early days. Interviewed for *Yoga Journal* in 1985, Vogel explained that beneficial healing intent could be transmitted and amplified, from one person to another, using quartz crystals.

Crystal healing should probably be called crystal magic or crystal mysticism, because it concerns many

Divination with a crystal ball, late 20th century
Crystal balls have been used for scrying and fortune-telling since antiquity. Industrial glass-making from the later 19th century enabled their mass production.

other matters as well as health. Guidebooks recommend crystals to help with confidence and all manner of situations and problems, including graduations, dates, careers and above all sleep. As many proponents note, crystals have been used magically in virtually all recorded civilizations. Yet the range and affordability of crystals are totally new. Crystals are also activated, charged, energized, cleansed, reenergized and used in new ways, drawn from New Age and non-Western traditions. They are first cleansed of unwanted energy, using methods such as pure mental intention or via exposure to running water, smoke, sunlight or sound, or being buried or even placed in a bowl of rice, salt or flowers. After this, crystals are fed, programmed and charged by sunlight, moonlight, burying or contact with powerful objects. Finally, they can be worn, carried around, kept near, held or applied to the human body. Belief is an important but subtle component of crystal magic. In *Crystal Healing* (2005), practitioner Judy Hall (1943–2021) advises: 'Belief in the process speeds things up, but you do not have to believe, merely to keep an open mind.' She and other crystal practitioners

< **Crystal readings, New York City, USA, 2020**
Some crystal readers scry for visions in crystal balls. Others intuitively select healing crystals that resonate with their clients' problems and 'vibrations'.

> **Crystal pendulum, England, 2000**
Crystal practitioners often intermingle new wellness trends with old magic.

also lay great stress on intuition and listening to one's inner voice, to guide one's approach to crystals.

Crystal magic appeals for very many reasons. It is extremely tactile, beautiful and enjoyable. It is hyper-commodified, convenient, undemanding and soothing. It is also highly personalized, around each user's precise concerns and needs. But crystals may resonate for deeper reasons, too. In a 1961 lecture, novelist Aldous Huxley (1894–1963) explained: 'The reason for our high estimation of precious stones' is 'because we see these things in our visionary experience.' Geometric shapes and structures, of intense colour, are buried in every mind. Crystals, beautiful and perfect, evoke this.

Crystals seem to help some people, psychologically and psychosomatically, by providing support in crucial moments of personal difficulty. 'My life changed because of these magical allies,' writes practitioner Kathy Banegas (b. *c.* 1970) in *Practical Crystals* (2023), describing how this holistic therapy helped her feel like herself again after painful experiences of illness, bereavement and stress. Similar benefits can be seen

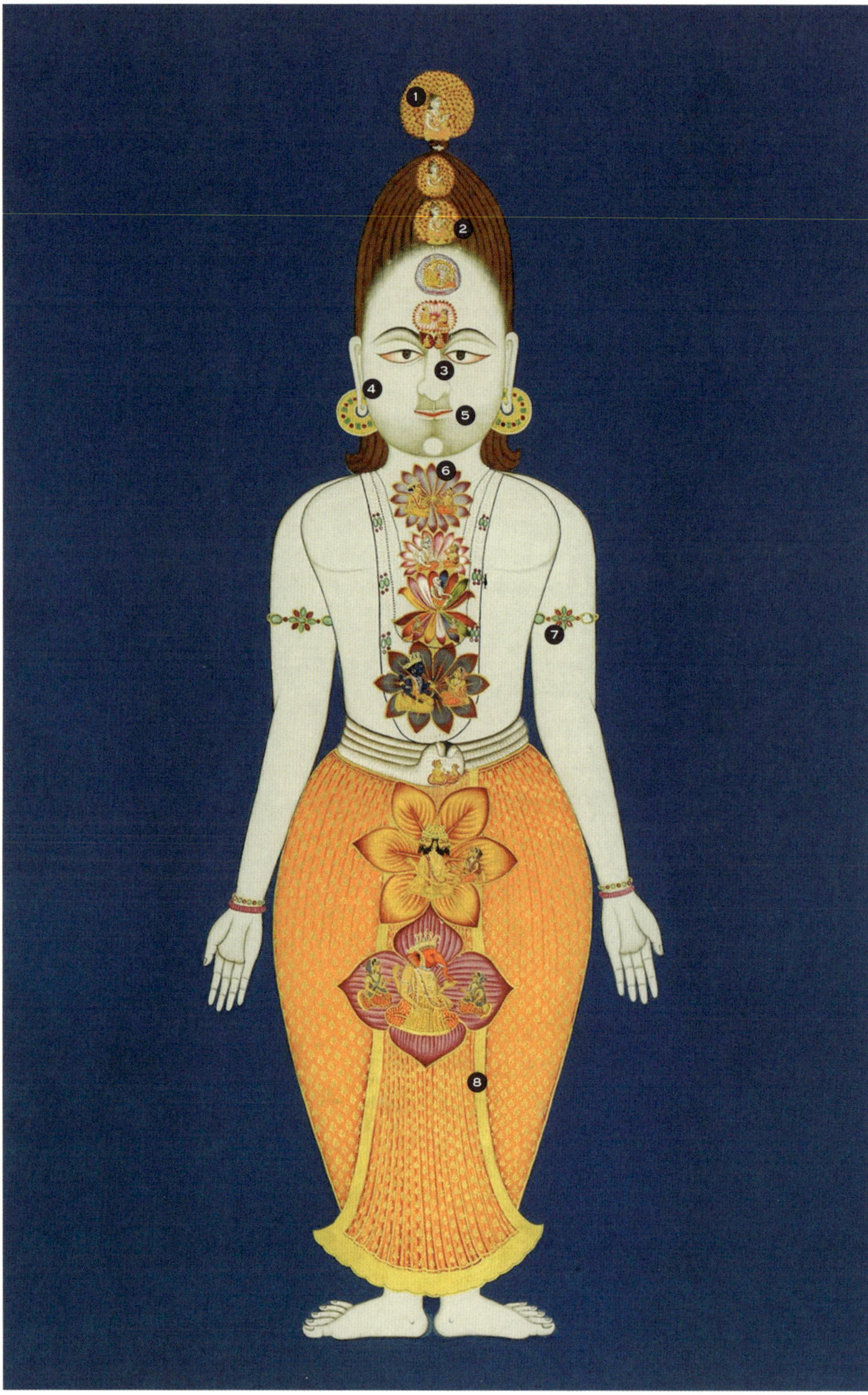

DECODING
CHAKRAS OF THE SUBTLE BODY

Through purification, postures and breathing exercises, Hindu yogis (practitioners of yoga) empowered energy centres in the body called 'chakras'. When fully activated, these chakras gave yogis supernatural powers akin to or surpassing magicians and even gods. Flight or seeing and hearing from vast distances could apparently be achieved. The yogi depicted here, from the *Nath Charit*, attributed to Bulaki (1823), has fully activated all of his chakras.

1.

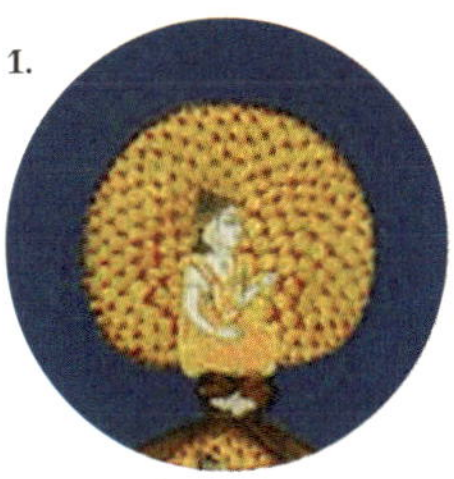

LIFE AXIS
The chakras sit on the *sushumna nadi* (central energetic channel), through which *prana* (life force) flows, from the base of the spine to the crown of the head.

2.

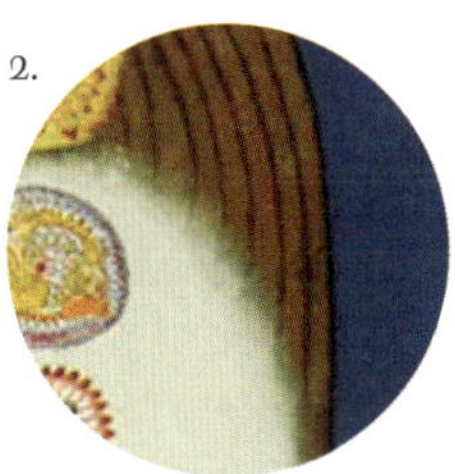

JATA
Matted locks (*jata*) emulate Lord Shiva, the patron god of the Nath monastic order. Long *jata* indicate years spent in spiritual discipline (*tapasya*).

3.

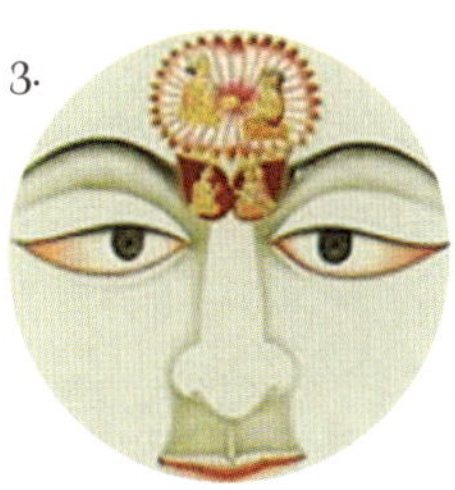

EYES
Inward-turned or crossed eyes show the practice of *shambhavi mudra* (eyebrow-centre gazing). It is a meditation technique in Hatha yoga.

4.

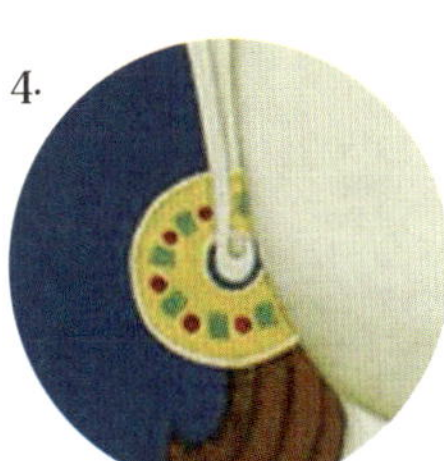

EARRINGS
Kundal sacred earrings were given to those joining the Nath order to signify commitment to the physically exacting Hatha yoga practice.

5.

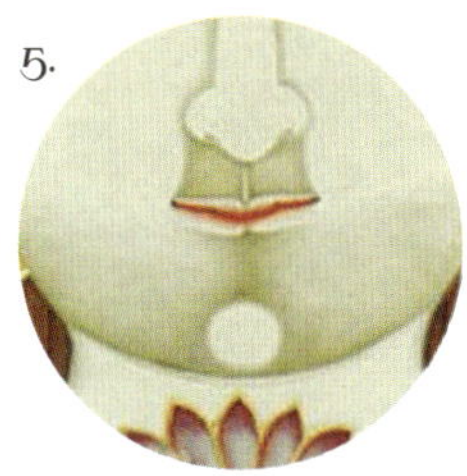

SKIN
Skin is covered with sacred ash. Known as *raksha*, consecrated ash is believed to increase spiritual power and protect against harmful forces.

6.

LOTUS FLOWERS
Glowing lotus flowers represent the chakras or energy centres along the spine of the subtle body (the non-physical energy system).

7.

BAJUBAND
Talismanic ornaments for the upper arms signify authority and also provide strength and protection from harmful forces such as the evil eye.

8.

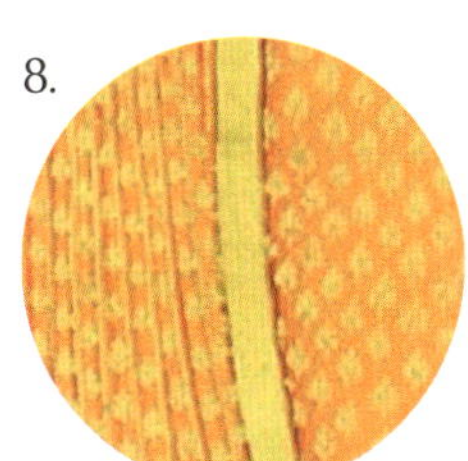

SAFFRON ROBE
The robe signifies the yogi's vows of *sannyasa* (external renunciation) and *vairagya* (inner detachment), in pursuit of spiritual liberation.

in reiki healing, developed from Buddhist roots in late 19th-century Japan, although it now displays major Hindu influences, too. Reiki channels an invisible healing force through energy centres in the human body called chakras. Healers generally place their hands on, or glide them slightly above, a patient's body, perhaps focusing on each chakra for a few minutes, to restore the proper flow of energy. Some criticize this low-risk alternative therapy for being pseudoscientific. However, metaphysical and pseudoscientific therapies can have valuable placebo effects. Numerous small-scale clinical trials indicate that reiki mildly reduces perceptions of pain for various conditions, including childbirth, cancer and osteoarthritis. Other studies find it slightly decreases some unpleasant menopause symptoms, and marginally diminishes patient anxiety for difficult treatments like haemodialysis. Some clinical trials, however, find no effect. The jury is still out, but it seems plausible that reiki makes quite a lot of people feel a little bit better.

Magic is rising. The recent revival of alternative mysticism has helped to inspire the German philosopher Jürgen Habermas (1929–2026) to reclassify the rich countries of Europe, along with Australia, Canada and New Zealand, as 'postsecular' societies, which no longer lack religion and mysticism. Since the 1980s, other commentators have written of a wider 're-enchantment of the world'. A key indication of this re-enchantment is the growing size of the wellness market for complementary and mystical therapies, which includes many practices that could be classified as loosely magical. In 2025, the Future of Wellness survey conducted by management consultancy firm McKinsey valued the wellness market at $2 trillion globally, making it slightly less than 2 per cent of the world economy. Wellness therapies, products and experiences are particularly connected with women and younger adults from Gen Z, the latter of whom, as a cohort, experience worse health and more burnout than previous generations. As we have seen throughout this book, as times get harder and other solutions fade, magic revives and returns.

>> *pages 246–47*
Practising modern witchcraft, Toronto, Canada, 1973
The altar features ritual candles, knives (athames), two figurines (Horned God and Moon Goddess), a brazier, a chalice and a Book of Shadows.

Reiki healing, Mexico City, Mexico, 2010

Crystal healing often features in reiki and here the practitioner wears a quartz bracelet. Clear quartz is said to be the master healer, able to cleanse and balance energy. The client appears calm and soothed.

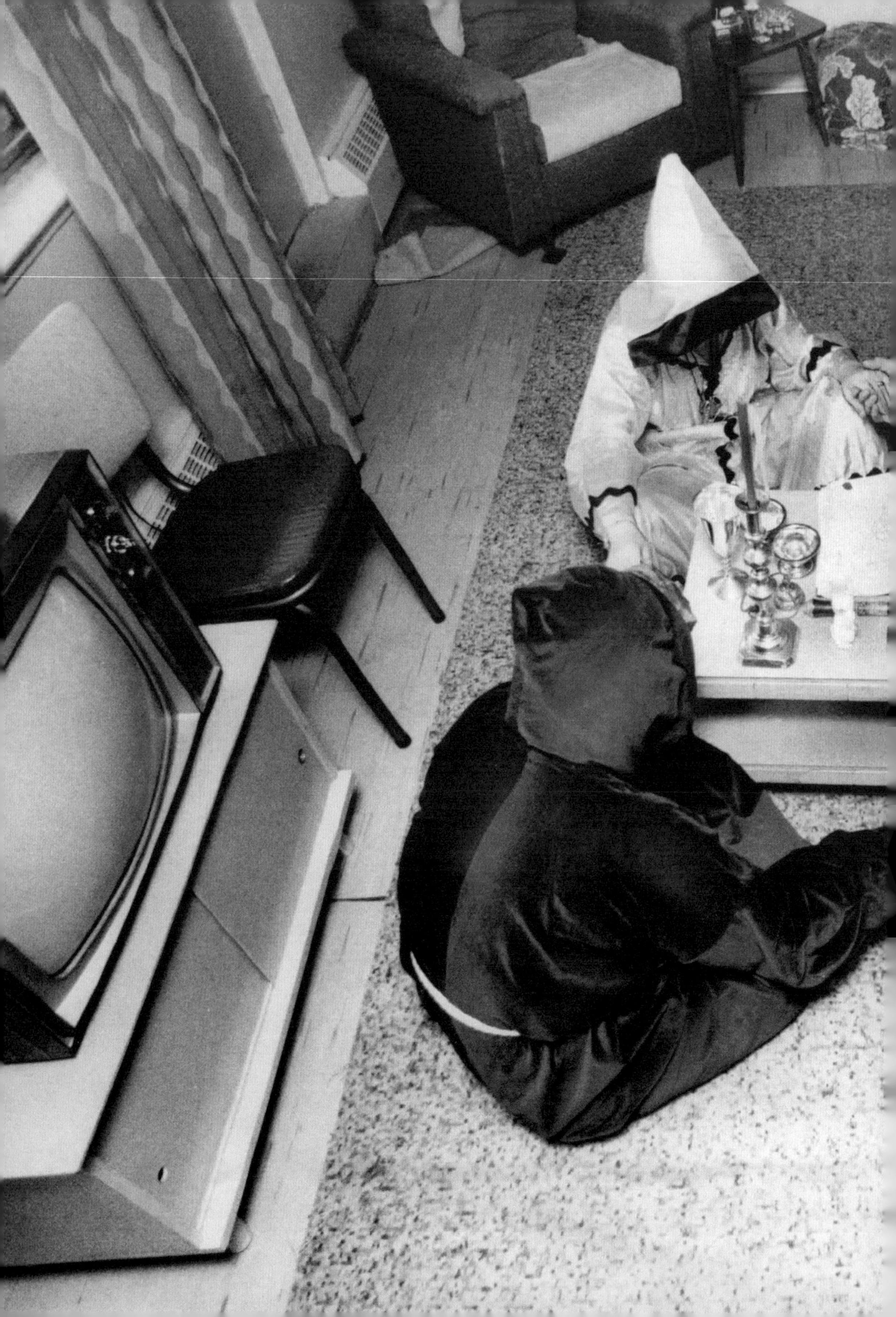

FURTHER READING

WEBSITES AND ONLINE RESOURCES

Esoterica, videos about Western Esotericism by Dr Justin Sledge, YouTube, www.youtube.com/@TheEsotericaChannel [accessed 11 March 2026].
Grimoire Magick, online archive of manuscripts, https://booksofmagick.com/ [accessed 11 March 2026].
Ireland's National Folklore Collection, digital archive, www.duchas.ie/en [accessed 11 March 2026].
Twilit Grotto: Archives of Western Esoterica, grimoire collection compiled by Dr Joseph H. Peterson, https://esotericarchives.com/ [accessed 11 March 2026].

GENERAL HISTORIES AND SURVEYS

Bailey, Michael D., *Magic and Superstition in Europe: A Concise History from Antiquity to the Present* (Lanham, MD: Rowman & Littlefield Publishers, 2007).
Gosden, Chris, *The History of Magic: From Alchemy to Witchcraft, from the Ice Age to the Present* (London: Viking, 2020).
Holland, Heidi, *African Magic: Traditional Ideas that Heal a Continent* (Johannesburg: Penguin South Africa, 2001).
Hutton, Ronald, *The Witch: A History of Fear, from Ancient Times to the Present* (London: Yale University Press, 2017).
Ryan, W. F., *The Bathhouse at midnight: An Historical Survey of Magic and Divination in Russia* (University Park, PA: Pennsylvania State University Press, 1999).
Scot, Reginald, *The Discoverie of Witchcraft* (1st ed 1584: Mineola, NY: Dover Publications, 1972).
Shah, Idries, *Oriental Magic* (St Albans: Paladin, 1973).
Thomas, Keith, *Religion and the Decline of Magic: Studies in Popular Beliefs in Sixteenth and Seventeenth-Century England* (London: Weidenfeld & Nicolson, 1971).

PSYCHOLOGY OF MAGIC

Dunbar, Robin, *How Religion Evolved: And Why It Endures* (New York: Oxford University Press, 2022).
Hutson, Matthew, *The 7 Laws of Magical Thinking: How Irrationality Makes Us Happy, Healthy and Sane* (New York: Hudson Street Press, 2012).
Kuhn, Gustav, *Experiencing the Impossible: The Science of Magic* (Cambridge, MA: The MIT Press, 2019).
Macknik, S. L., Martinez-Conde, S., and Blakeslee, S., *Sleights of Mind: What the Neuroscience of Magic Reveals About Our Everyday Deceptions* (New York: Henry Holt and Co., 2010).
Subbotsky, Eugene, *Magic and the Mind: Mechanisms, Functions, and Development of Magical Thinking and Behavior* (New York: Oxford University Press, 2010).
Vyse, S. A., *Believing in Magic: The Psychology of Superstition,* updated edn (New York: Oxford University Press, 2014).

FAIRIES AND MAGICAL BEINGS

Bourke, Angela, *The Burning of Bridget Cleary: A True Story* (New York: Viking, 2000).
Hultkrantz, Å. (ed.), *The Supernatural Owners of Nature: Nordic Symposion on the Religious Conceptions of Ruling Spirits (Genii loci, Genii speciei) and Allied Concepts* (Stockholm: Almqvist & Wiksell, 1961).
Johnson, Marjorie T., *Seeing Fairies: From the Lost Archives of the Fairy Investigation Society, Authentic Reports of Fairies in Modern Times* (Charlottesville, VA: Anomalist Books, 2014).
Kirk, Robert, *The Secret Commonwealth: Of Elves, Fauns and Fairies* (1st edn 1691: New York: NYRB Classics, 2019).
Maarouf, Mohammed, *Jinn Eviction as a Discourse of Power: A Multidisciplinary Approach to Moroccan Magical Beliefs and Practices* (Leiden: Brill, 2007).
Rieti, Barbara, *Strange Terrain: The Fairy World in Newfoundland* (St John's, NL: Memorial University of Newfoundland, 1991).
Young, Simon, and Houlbrook, Ceri (eds), *Magical Folk: British and Irish Fairies: 500 AD to the Present* (London: Gibson Square Books, 2018).

ANCIENT MAGIC

Betz, Hans Dieter (ed.), *The Greek Magical Papyri in Translation, Including the Demotic Spells*, updated edn (Chicago, IL: University of Chicago Press, 2022).
Cogan, Mordechai, 'A Lamashtu Plaque from the Judaean Shephelah', *Israel Exploration Journal*, vol. 45, no. 2/3 (1995), pp. 155–61.
Edmonds, Radcliffe G. III, *Drawing Down the Moon: Magic in the Ancient Greco-Roman World* (Princeton, NJ: Princeton University Press, 2019).
Finkel, Irving, *The First Ghosts: Most Ancient of Legacies* (London: Hodder & Stoughton, 2021).
Luck, Georg, *Arcana Mundi: Magic and the Occult in the Greek and Roman Worlds* (Baltimore, MD: Johns Hopkins University Press, 2006).
Ogden, Daniel, *Magic, Witchcraft and Ghosts in the Greek and Roman Worlds: A Sourcebook* (New York: Oxford University Press, 2009).

COMMUNITY EXPERTS

Auray, Christophe, *Magie et Sorcellerie dans le Fermes Bretonnes* (Rennes: Éditions Ouest-France, 2006).
Davies, Owen, *Popular Magic: Cunning-Folk in English History* (London: Hambledon Continuum, 2003).
Evans-Pritchard, E. E., *Witchcraft, Oracles and Magic Among the Azande* (Oxford: Clarendon Press, 1937).
Favret-Saada, Jeanne, *Deadly Words: Witchcraft in the Bocage*, trans. Catherine Cullen (Cambridge: Cambridge University Press, 1980).
Ogungbile, David O. (ed.), *African Indigenous Religious Traditions in Local and Global Contexts: Perspectives on Nigeria* (Lagos: Malthouse Press, 2015).
Somé, Malidoma Patrice, *Of Water and the Spirit: Ritual, Magic and Initiation in the Life of an African Shaman* (New York: G. P. Putnam's Sons, 1994).
Stanmore, Tabitha, *Cunning Folk: Life in the Era of Practical Magic* (London: Penguin, 2024).

GRIMOIRES AND CEREMONIAL MAGIC

Agrippa, Cornelius, *Three Books of Occult Philosophy Written by Henry Cornelius Agrippa of Nettesheim*, trans. John Freake (1st edn 1533: London: Gregory Moule, 1651).
Conybeare, F. C., 'The Testament of Solomon', *Jewish Quarterly Review*, vol. 11 (1898), pp. 1–45.
Davies, Owen, *Grimoires: A History of Magic Books* (Oxford: Oxford University Press, 2009).
Harms, Daniel, Clark, James R., and Peterson, Joseph H. (eds), *The Book of Oberon: A Sourcebook of Elizabethan Magic* (Woodbury, MN: Llewellyn Publications, 2019).
Oron, Michael, *Rabbi, Mystic or Impostor? The Eighteenth-century Ba'al Shem of London*, trans. E. Levin (London and Liverpool: The Littman Library of Jewish Civilization and Liverpool University Press, 2020).
Peterson, Joseph H., *The Grimorium Verum: A Handbook of Black Magic* (Scotts Valley, CA: CreateSpace Independent Publishing Platform, 2007).
Waite, A. E. (ed.), *The Hermetic and Alchemical Writings of Aureolus Philippus Theophrastus Bombast, of Hohenheim, called Paracelsus the Great*, vols 1 and 2 (London: James Elliott & Co., 1894).

HARMFUL WITCHCRAFT

Ashforth, Adam, *Witchcraft, Violence and Democracy in South Africa* (University of Chicago, 2005).
Briggs, Robin, *Witches and Neighbors: The Social and Cultural Context of European Witchcraft* (New York: Viking Press, 1996).
Davidson, L. S., and Ward, J. O. (eds), *The Sorcery Trial of Alice Kyteler* (New York, 1993).
Davies, Owen, *Witchcraft, Magic and Culture: 1736–1951* (Manchester: Manchester University Press, 1999).
Drage, William, *Daimonomageia: a Small Treatise of Sicknesses and Diseases from Witchcraft and Supernatural Causes* (London: J. Dover, 1665).
Evans-Pritchard, E. E., *Witchcraft, Oracles and Magic among the Azande* (Oxford: Clarendon Press, 1937).
La Fontaine, Jean, *Witches and Demons: A Comparative Perspective on Witchcraft and Satanism* (New York: Berghahn Books, 2016).
Roper, Lyndal, *The Witch Craze: Terror and Fantasy in Baroque Germany* (New Haven, CT: Yale University Press, 2004).
Suggett, Richard, *A History of Magic and Witchcraft in Wales* (Cheltenham: The History Press, 2008).
Waters, Thomas, *Cursed Britain: A History of Witchcraft and Black Magic in Modern Times* (London: Yale University Press, 2019).

FORTUNE-TELLING AND DIVINATION

Cicero, Marcus Tullius, *On Old Age, On Friendship, On Divination*, trans. W. A. Falconer (Cambridge, MA: Harvard University Press, 1923).
Davies, Owen, *A Supernatural War: Magic, Divination, and Faith During the First World War* (Oxford: Oxford University Press, 2018).
Peek, Philip M. (ed.), *African Divination Systems: Ways of Knowing* (Bloomington, IN: Indiana University Press, 1991).
Smith, Richard J., *Fortune-tellers and Philosophers: Divination in Traditional Chinese Society* (Boulder, CO: Westview Press, 1991).
Wilhelm, Hellmut, and Baynes, Cary F. (eds), *The I Ching or Book of Changes* (Princeton, NJ: Princeton University Press, 1992).

MESMERISM AND SPIRITUALISM

Animal Magnetism: Report of Dr Franklin and Other Commissioners (Philadelphia, PA: H. Perkins, 1837).
Britten, Emma Hardinge, *Autobiography of Emma Hardinge Britten* (Manchester: Mrs M. Wilkinson, 1900).
Carroll, Bret E., *Spiritualism in Antebellum America* (Bloomington, IN: Indiana University Press, 1997).
Home, D. D., *Incidents in My Life* (New York: Bolt & Williams, 1872).
Owen, Alex, *The Darkened Room: Women, Power, and Spiritualism in Late Victorian England* (Chicago, IL: University of Chicago Press, 2004).
Poyen, Charles, *The Progress of Animal Magnetism in New England* (Boston, MA: Weeks, Jordan & Co., 1837).
Winter, Alison, *Mesmerized: Powers of Mind in Victorian Britain* (Chicago, IL: University of Chicago Press, 1998).

POLITICAL MAGIC

Abbott, Elizabeth, *Haiti: The Duvaliers and their Legacy* (New York: McGraw-Hill Book Company, 1988), p. 110.
Barnett, Donald L., and Njama, Karari, *Mau Mau from Within: An Analysis of Kenya's Peasant Revolt* (New York: Monthly Review Press, 1966).
Dikötter, Frank, *Dictators: The Cult of Personality in the Twentieth Century* (London: Bloomsbury Publishing, 2020).
Geschiere, Peter, *The Modernity of Witchcraft: Politics and the Occult in Postcolonial Africa*, trans. Peter Geschiere and Janet Roitman (Charlottesville, VA: University of Virginia Press, 1997).
Kurlander, Eric, *Hitler's Monsters: A Supernatural History of the Third Reich* (New Haven, CT: Yale University Press, 2017).
Whitehead, Neil L., *Dark Shamans: Kanaimà and the Poetics of Violent Death* (Durham, NC: Duke University Press, 2002).
Young, Francis, *Magic in Merlin's Realm: A History of Occult Politics in Britain* (Cambridge: Cambridge University Press, 2022).

MAGICAL PROTECTION

Hoggard, Brian, *Magical House Protection: The Archaeology of Counter-Witchcraft* (New York: Berghahn Books, 2019).
Kedar, Dorit, 'Who Wrote the Incantation Bowls?' (Ph.D. Freie Universität Berlin, 2018).
Young, Francis (ed.), *A Medieval Book of Magical*

Stones: The Peterborough Lapidary (Cambridge: Texts in Early Modern Magic, 2016).
Black, George F., *Scottish Charms and Amulets* (Edinburgh: Neill & Co., 1894).
Ghose, Madhuvanti, *Vanishing Beauty: Asian Jewelry and Ritual Objects from the Barbara and David Kipper Collection* (Chicago, IL: Art Institute of Chicago, 2016).

MAGICAL FOLKLORE

Grimm, Jacob, and Wilhelm, Grimm, *The Complete Fairy Tales of the Brothers Grimm*, trans. Jack Zipes (New York: Bantam Books, 1987).
Grose, Francis, *A Provincial Glossary: With a Collection of Local Proverbs and Popular Superstitions* (London: 1787).
Hutton, Ronald, *The Stations of The Sun: A History of the Ritual Year in Britain* (Oxford: Oxford University Press, 1996).
Luzel, F. M., *Celtic Folk-Tales from Armorica*, trans. Derek Bryce (Lampeter: Llanerch Enterprises, 1985).
Norman, Mark, *Black Dog Folklore* (Penzance: Troy Books, 2015).
Opie, Ioana, *A Dictionary of Superstitions* (Oxford: Oxford University Press, 1992).

PERFORMANCE MAGIC

Copperfield, David, Wiseman, Richard, and Britland, David, *David Copperfield's History of Magic* (New York: Simon & Schuster, 2021).
During, Simon, *Modern Enchantments: The Poetic of Visual Magic* (Cambridge, MA: Harvard University Press, 2002).
Maskelyne, John Nevil, and Devant, David, *Our Magic: The Art in Magic, the Theory of Magic, the Practice of Magic* (New York: E. P. Dutton & Company, 1911).
Professor Hoffmann, *Modern Magic: A Practical Treatise on the Art of Conjuring* (London: George Routledge & Sons, 1876).
Steinmeyer, Jim, *Hiding the Elephant: How Magicians Invented the Impossible and Learned to Disappear* (New York: Carroll & Graf Publishers, 2003).

MODERN WITCHCRAFT AND ALTERNATIVE MAGIC

Baker, Phil, *City of the Beast: The London of Aleister Crowley* (London: Strange Attractor Press, 2021).
Doyle White, Ethan, *Wicca: History, Belief, and Community in Modern Pagan Witchcraft* (Brighton: Sussex Academic Press, 2016).
Gary, Gemma, *Traditional Witchcraft: A Cornish Book of Ways* (Penzance: Troy Books, 2015).
Howard, Michael, *Modern Wicca: A History from Gerald Gardner to the Present* (Woodbury, MN: Llewellyn Publications, 2009).
Hutton, Ronald, *The Triumph of the Moon: A History of Modern Pagan Witchcraft* (Oxford: Oxford University Press, 1999).
Josephson-Storm, Jason Ā., *The Myth of Disenchantment: Magic, Modernity, and the Birth of the Human Sciences* (Chicago, IL: University of Chicago Press, 2017).
Kaczynski, Richard, *Perdurabo: The Life of Aleister Crowley* (Berkeley, CA: North Atlantic Books, 2010).

SOURCES OF QUOTATIONS

9 Gardner, Gerald, *The Meaning of Witchcraft* (London: The Aquarian Press, 1959).

47 Grose, Francis, appendix on 'Popular Superstitions', *A Provincial Glossary: With a Collection of Local Proverbs and Popular Superstitions* (London: 1787).

75 Favret-Saada, Jeanne, *Deadly Words: Witchcraft in the Bocage*, trans. Catherine Cullen (Cambridge: Cambridge University Press, 1980)

93 Kirk, Robert, *The Secret Commonwealth: Of Elves, Fauns and Fairies* (1st edn 1691: New York: NYRB Classics, 2019), p. 23.

115 Agrippa, Cornelius, *Three Books of Occult Philosophy Written by Henry Cornelius Agrippa of Nettesheim*, trans. John Freake (1st edn 1533: London: Gregory Moule, 1651), p. 352.

141 Quoted in: Abbott, Elizabeth, *Haiti: The Duvaliers and Their Legacy* (New York: McGraw-Hill Book Company, 1988), p. 110.

159 Professor Hoffmann, *Modern Magic: A Practical Treatise on the Art of Conjuring* (London: George Routledge & Sons, 1876), p. 546.

177 *Animal Magnetism: Report of Dr Franklin and Other Commissioners* (Philadelphia, PA: H. Perkins, 1837), p. 12.

205 Joseph Banks Rhine, *Extra-Sensory Perception* (Boston, MA: Bruce Humphries Publishers, 1935), p. 218.

223 Thorn Mooney, *Witches Among Us: Understanding Contemporary Witchcraft and Wicca* (Woodbury, MN: Llewellyn Publications, 2024).

SOURCES OF ILLUSTRATIONS

Every effort has been made to locate and credit copyright holders of the material reproduced in this book. The author and publisher apologize for any omissions or errors, which can be corrected in future editions.

a: above, **b**: below, **c**: centre, **l**: left, **r**: right

1 Bridgeman Images; 2 Birmingham Museums Trust/ Birmingham Museum & Art Gallery. Presented by Sir John Holder, 1912; 3 Bridgeman Images; 4 Library of Congress, Washington DC; 6–7 Alfonso Vicente/Alamy; 8 Wellcome Collection, London; 11 Victoria and Albert Museum, London; 12 Abbas/Magnum Photos; 13 Wellcome Collection, London; **14al** Director's Fund. Art Institute of Chicago; **14ac** Zts/Dreamstime.com; **14ar** The Metropolitan Museum of Art, New York. Rogers Fund, 1954; **14bl** Museum of V. M. Vasnetsov; **14bc** Rijksmuseum, Amsterdam; **14br** Dinah Maria Mulock Craik, *The Fairy Book, The Best Popular Fairy Stories*, 1913; **15al** Sabena Jane Blackbird/Alamy; **15ac** Gift of Comtesse Robert de Veyrac, 1976. The Metropolitan Museum of Art, New York; **15ar** Gift of Florence and Herbert Irving, 2015. The Metropolitan Museum of Art, New York; **15bl** Culture Club/Bridgeman/ Getty Images; **15bc** Arthur Mee and Holland Thompson, *The Book of Knowledge*, vol. II, New York, 1912. Illustration by Elenore Abbott; **15br** *Round about our Coal Fire, or, Christmas Entertainments*, 1734; 17 Wellcome Collection, London; 18 John Stewart Kennedy Fund, 1913. The Metropolitan Museum of Art, New York; **19l** Heritage Image Partnership Ltd/Alamy; **19r** Gift of A. Hyatt Mayor, 1960. The Metropolitan Museum of Art, New York; **20l** NPL – DeA Picture Library/Bridgeman Images; **20c** Harris Brisbane Dick Fund, 1991. The Metropolitan Museum of Art, New York; **20r** The Bothmer Purchase Fund, 1987. The Metropolitan Museum of Art, New York; **21al** The Trustees of the British Museum, London; **21ac** Science History Images/Alamy; **21ar** Werner Forman/ Universal Images Group/Getty Images; **21bl** Musée du Louvre, Dist. GrandPalaisRmn. Photo Christian Décamps; **21bc** NPL – DeA Picture Library/Bridgeman Images; **21br** Purchase, Rogers Fund and Schimmel Foundation Inc. Gift, 1984. The Metropolitan Museum of Art, New York; **22l** Ajayamdr/Shutterstock; **22r** Pictures From History/ Universal Images Group/Getty Images; 23 Album/Alamy; 24 Heritage Image Partnership Ltd/Alamy; **25l** dpa picture alliance/Alamy; **25r** Gift of Bruce Ferrini. The Cleveland Museum of Art (2000.201); 26–27 Erich Lessing/ Bridgeman Images; **28a** University of Tübingen. Photo Juraj Lipták; **28b** Fadil Aziz/Alcibbum Photograph/Getty Images; 30 © Oxford University Museum of Natural History; **31l** Purchase, 1886. The Metropolitan Museum of Art, New York; **31r** The Trustees of the British Museum, London; 32 Pictures From History/imageBROKER/ Shutterstock; 33 The Trustees of the British Museum, London; 34–35 The Metropolitan Museum of Art, New York. Gift of Edward S. Harkness, 1935; 36 Bridgeman Images; 38 The Trustees of the British Museum, London; **39l** The J. Paul Getty Museum, Los Angeles (Ms. Ludwig I 14, fol. 358v, 83.MA.63.358v); **39r** Universal History Archive/Getty Images; 40–41 Fine Art Images/Bridgeman Images; 43 Ira Berger/Alamy; 44 Bridgeman Images; 46 From the British Library archive/Bridgeman Images; 49 Shawn.ccf/Alamy; **51al** Everett Collection Inc./ Dreamstime.com; **51ac, ar** Mary Evans Picture Library; **51cl** Daniel Wiedemann/Dreamstime.com; **51c** istock/ Gianluca Fabrizio; **51cr** Kaido Rummel/Dreamstime.com; **51bl** Yongyut Serasoot/Dreamstime.com; **51bc** Everett Collection Inc./Dreamstime.com; **51br** Elena Sergeeva/ Dreamstime.com; 52 Niday Picture Library/Alamy; **53l** Image © National Museums Scotland; **53r** World History Archive/Alamy; 54 National Museums Scotland; **55l** GrandPalaisRmn (musée du Louvre). Photo Stéphane Maréchalle; **55r** Gift of Marshall and Marilyn R. Wolf, 2018. The Metropolitan Museum of Art, New York; **56al** Purchase, Edward S. Harkness Gift, 1926. The Metropolitan Museum of Art, New York; **56ac** Science & Society Picture Library/SSPL/Getty Images; **56ar** The Khalili Collections; **56bl** Purchase, Edward S. Harkness Gift, 1926. The Metropolitan Museum of Art, New York; **56bc** Gift of Edward S. Harkness, 1917. The Metropolitan Museum of Art, New York; **56br** Gift of Henry H. Getty, Charles L. Hutchinson, and Norman W. Harris. Art Institute Chicago; **57al** Science Photo Library; **57ac** Rogers Fund, 1912. The Metropolitan Museum of Art, New York; **57ar** Rogers Fund, 1944. The Metropolitan Museum of Art, New York; **57bl** National Museums Scotland; **57bc** Wellcome Collection, London; **57br** SSPL/Getty Images; **58l** Collection of the Smithsonian National Museum of African American History and Culture, Gift in honour of Marion Kumala Lockard; **58r** The Picture Art Collection/Alamy; **59l** Gift of Robert T. Moffatt. Museum of Fine Arts Boston; **59r**, 60 The National Museum, Denmark Photo John Lee; **61l, c** National Museum of Denmark. Photo Lennart Larsen; **61r** Purchase, The Bothmer Purchase Fund and Lila Acheson Wallace Gift, 1994. The Metropolitan Museum of Art, New York; 62–63 The Khalili Collection; **64a** Rijksmuseum, Amsterdam; **64b** Bequest of George C. Stone, 1935. The Metropolitan Museum of Art, New York; **65l** Museum purchase, Fowler McCormick, Class of 1921, Fund. Princeton University Art Museum (2001-215.2 a-b); **65r** Museum purchase, Fowler McCormick, Class of 1921, Fund. Princeton University Art Museum (1996-290); 66 Jim Ekstrand/Dreamstime.com; **67al** Basement Stock/ Alamy; **67ac** National Museums Scotland; **67ar** Simon Evans/Alamy; **67cl** Ryedale Folk Museum, Hutton-le-Hole; **67c** Alex Ramsay/Alamy; **67cr** PA Images/Alamy; **67bl** Man Vyi; **67bc** Zoonar GmbH/Alamy; **67br** Anasife/ Dreamstime.com; **68l** Jack Sparticus/Alamy; **68r** Richard Butner; **69l** Yale Center for British Art, Paul Mellon Collection (B1977.14.12152); **69r** Heinrich Cornelius, *Agrippa von Nettesheim*, 1578; 71 National Museums Scotland; 72–73 John G. Johnson Collection, 1917. Philadelphia Art Museum; 74 Alan Gignoux/Alamy; 77 Richard Pierrin/AFP/Getty Images; **78l** Wellcome Collection, London; **78r** The Metropolitan Museum of Art/Art Resource/Scala, Florence; 79 The Huntington Library, Art Museum, and Botanical Gardens/Bridgeman Images; 80 Wellcome Collection, London; 82 National Museum of Denmark. Photo Roberto Fortuna; **83l** The Hunt Museum, Limerick; **83r** David E. Apter, *Magic charm seller*, (detail), 1965. Gift of David E. Apter, M.A. (HON.), 1969. Yale University Art Gallery; **84l** The Trustees of the British Museum; **84r** Bayerische Staatsbibliothek Munich; 85 Penlee House Gallery and Museum, Penzance/ Bridgeman Images; **86al** mofles/istock; **86ac** Michael Turner/Dreamstime.com; **86ar** Jorge Bernal/AFP/Getty Images; **86bl** fototrav/Istock; **86bc** Chip Somodevilla/ Getty Images; **86br** Robert Gilhooly/Alamy; **87al** The State Library Victoria; **87ac** Library of Congress, Washington, DC; **87ar** The Picture Art Collection/Alamy; **87bl** Cleveland Public Library, Puckett Collection: Folk Beliefs of African Americans in the Southern United States; **87bc** The Library of Congress, Washington, DC; **87br** Historic Collection/Alamy; 88 The Metropolitan Museum of Art, New York. Thomas J. Watson Library;

89l, c Musée du Louvre, Dist. GrandPalaisRmn. Photo Georges Poncet; **89r** National Museums Scotland; **91** Maurice Ascani/Gamma-Rapho/Getty Images; **92** Wellcome Collection, London; **95** Museum Purchase, 1900. The Metropolitan Museum of Art, New York; **96** Antonio Siwiak/Alamy; **97** Kevin Higgins; **98** Kevin Britland/Alamy; **99al** Chris Alan Selby/Alamy; **99ac** Plentn; **99ar** John Hamilton; **99bl** Poliphilo; **99bc** George7378/Dreamstime.com; **99br** Nalidsa Sukprasert/Dreamstime.com; **100a** John Holmes/Alamy; **100b** Image navi - QxQ images/Alamy; **102l** The Picture Art Collection/Alamy; **102r** The Stapleton Collection/Bridgeman Images; **103l** *Konst och Konstnärer*, 1910–1914; **103r** Herman Hofberg, *Svenska folksägner*, 1882; **104l** Impaint/Alamy; **104c** steeve-x-art/Alamy; **104r** The Picture Art Collection/Alamy; **105al** Alternativity; **105ac** Pseudopanax; **105ar** Christie's Images/Bridgeman Images; **105bl** W. Ramsay Smith, *Myths & legends of the Australian aboriginals*, 1932. Illustration by Alice Woodward; **105bc** CPA Media Pte Ltd/Alamy; **105br** steeve-x-art/Alamy; **107al** Justin Long/Alamy; **107ar** adrian davies/Alamy; **107b** levers2007/istock; **108–109** Bridgeman Images; **111** The Trustees of the British Museum; **112** University of Tübingen, Tübinger Hausbuch; **114** Look and Learn/Bridgeman Images; **117** Jörg Bittner Unna; **118–119** From the British Library archive/Bridgeman Images; **120** The Khalili Collections; **122** Wellcome Collection, London; **123l** Folger Shakespeare Library/Folger Imaging Department; **123r** Bibliothèque nationale de France; **124** Folger Shakespeare Library/Folger Imaging Department; **127** History and Art Collection/Alamy; **128l, c** The Picture Art Collection/Alamy; **128r** Wellcome Collection, London; **129al** Thomas Frognall Dibdin, *A Bibliographical, Antiquarian and Picturesque Tour in France and Germany*, 1821. University of Calilfornia Libraries; **129ac** Wellcome Collection, London; **129ar** Gift of Henry Walters, 1917. The Metropolitan Museum of Art, New York; **129bl, bc** Wellcome Collection, London; **129br** From the British Library archive/Bridgeman Images; **130** Maurice Kaye/Daily Mirror/Mirrorpix/Getty Images; **131** Harry Price/Mary Evans Picture Library; **132–133, 134l** Wellcome Collection, London; **134r** Tux-Man; **135** Bridgeman Images; **136** Fuzzypeg; **139** Charles Walker CollectionA/Alamy; **140** The J. Paul Getty Museum, Los Angeles; **143** Gift of Bashford Dean, 1914. The Metropolitan Museum of Art, New York; **144–145** W. Moses Willner Fund. Art Institute of Chicago; **146l** Photo Scala, Florence/bpk, Bildagentur für Kunst, Kultur und Geschichte, Berlin; **146r** Ray/Shutterstock; **147** Gift of Diandra and Michael Douglas. Los Angeles County Museum of Art (M.81.271.13); **148** Peter Newark American Pictures/Bridgeman Images; **149** From the British Library archive/Bridgeman Images; **150** SZ Photo/Bridgeman Images; **152** Gallen-Kallela Museum, Finland; **153** Photo Scala, Florence/bpk, Bildagentur für Kunst, Kultur und Geschichte, Berlin; **155** Stephen Maturen/Getty Images; **156–157** Digital image, The Museum of Modern Art, New York/Scala, Florence. © 2026 Remedios Varo, DACS/VEGAP; **158** Unidentified photographer. Courtesy of Archives of Ontario; **161** From the British Library archive/Bridgeman Images; **162** Professor Hoffmann, *Modern Magic: A Practical Treatise on the Art of Conjuring*, 1904. Boston Public Library; **163l** Granger - Historical Picture Archive/Alamy; **163r** Associated Press/Alamy; **164–165** Album/Alamy; **166l** Potter and Potter Auctions, Inc., Chicago; **166r** Brinsley Nicholson, *The Discoverie of Witchcraft by Reginald Scot*, 1886. Princeton Theological Seminary Library; **167** Bibliothèque nationale de France; **168** Universal Art Archive/Alamy; **169l** Musée Carnavalet, Histoire de Paris; **169r** Bridgeman Images; **170–171** Library of Congress, Washington DC; **173** Phil Franke; **174** Heritage Art/Heritage Images/Getty Images; **176** Nationalmuseum, Sweden; **179** Gift of Mrs. Carl Joseph Ulmann, 1929. The Metropolitan Museum of Art, New York; **180–181** The Stapleton Collection/Bridgeman Images; **182** Rijksmuseum, Amsterdam; **183l** Ebenezer Sibly, *A Key to Physic*, 1794; **183r** Jean-Loup Charmet/Science Photo Library; **185** Chronicle/Alamy; **186** Wellcome Collection, London; **187l** Paris Musées, Maison de Balzac; **187r** Library of Congress, Washington, DC; **188** Gilman Collection, Gift of The Howard Gilman Foundation, 2005. The Metropolitan Museum of Art, New York; **190l** Library of Congress, Washington, DC; **190r** Chronicle/Alamy; **191** Bettmann/Getty Images; **193** Alpha Stock/Alamy; **194, 195al, ac, b** The J. Paul Getty Museum, Los Angeles; **195ar** Gainew Gallery/Alamy; **196** Tallandier/Bridgeman Images; **197, 198** Chronicle/Alamy; **199l** The Paul Kaye Collection/Mary Evans Picture Library; **199r** Mary Evans Picture Library; **200al** Jimlop collection/Alamy; **200ar** Harry Price/Mary Evans Picture Library; **200bl** Mary Evans Picture Library; **200br** Chronicle/Alamy; **203** John Cutten/Mary Evans Picture Library; **204** Mary Evans Picture Library; **207a** UrbanImages/Alamy; **207b** Steve McCurry/Magnum Photos; **208–209** Guy Lyon Playfair/Mary Evans Picture Library; **210al** Daily Mirror/Mirrorpix/Getty Images; **210ac** Granger - Historical Picture Archive/Alamy; **210ar** Everett Collection/Bridgeman Images; **210bl** Charles Walker Collection/Alamy; **201bc** steeve-x-art/Alamy; **210br** Ken Howard/Alamy; **211al** Bettmann/Getty Images; **211ac, bl** PA Images/Alamy; **211ar** Penta Springs Limited/Alamy; **211bc** Guillaume Souvant/AFP/Getty Images; **211br** Pinacoteca di Brera, Milan/With permission of the Italian Ministry of Culture/Bridgeman Images; **212** Gilman Collection, Gift of The Howard Gilman Foundation, 2005. The Metropolitan Museum of Art, New York; **213** Duke University Archives Photographic Collection: Visitors, Rhine, Dr and Indian visitor, 1963 October; **214** SZ Photo/Scherl/Bridgeman Images; **216** John Greim/Shutterstock; **217al** Malivan_Iuliia/Shutterstock; **217ac** Svitlyk/Shutterstock; **217ar** Dorling Kindersley ltd/Alamy; **217bl** Evgenii Leontev/Shutterstock; **217bc** FotoHelin/Shutterstock; **217br** Bigc Studio/Shutterstock; **218** Roger Ressmeyer/Corbis/VCG/Getty Images; **219** Institut für Grenzgebiete der Psychologie und Psychischen Gesundheit (IGPP). Photo Leif Geiges; **221** Chronicle/Alamy; **222** Heritage Image Partnership Ltd/Alamy; **225** Sueddeutsche Zeitung Photo/Mary Evans Picture Library; **226l** Jack Cox - Travel Pics Pro/Alamy; **226r** Postcard of *Magicians Room, The Witches Mill, Castletown, I.O.M*; **227** Wellcome Collection, London; **228l** Louise Oligny/Gamma-Rapho/Getty Images; **228c** Dmytro Zinkevych/Dreamstime.com; **228r** David Lewis Hodgson/Mary Evans Picture Library; **229al** Mitchell Library, State Library of New South Wales and Courtesy ACP Magazines Ltd; **229ac** Shauna Hundeby/Alamy; **229ar** Harry Kerr/BIPs/Getty Images; **229bl** Steve Hawkins Photography/Alamy; **229bc** Louise Oligny/Gamma-Rapho/Getty Images; **229br** Richard Splash/Alamy; **230** Ira Berger/Alamy; **231l** PA Images/Alamy; **231r** Trinity Mirror/Mirrorpix/Alamy; **232** De Morgan Foundation/Bridgeman Images; **234** Smith Archive/Alamy; **235** Harry Price/Mary Evans Picture Library; **236l** BNP Design Studio/Alamy; **236r** Martin Bernetti/AFP/Getty Images; **237l** Bibliothèque nationale de France; **237r** Christie's Images/Bridgeman Images; **238al** Peter Hermes Furian/Dreamstime.com; **238ar** Amnachphoto/Dreamstime.com; **238cl** Viktoriya89/Dreamstime.co; **238cr** Infinityphotostudio/Dreamstime.com; **238bl** Martin Novak/Dreamstime.com; **238br** Vvoevale/Dreamstime.com; **240** Bridgeman Images; **241l** Jon Bilous/Alamy; **241r** Adrian Sherratt/Alamy; **242–243** The Picture Art Collection/Alamy; **245** Chico Sanchez/Alamy; **246–247** Harold Barkley/Toronto Star/Getty Images

INDEX

Illustrations are in **bold**.

ACKNOWLEDGMENTS

Many thanks to everyone who has helped me research, write and create this beautiful book. At Thames & Hudson, I have benefitted immensely from the talent and dedication of Jane Laing, Sadie Butler, Becky Gee, Agatha Smith, Jo Walton and, above all, my excellent editor Florence Allard. My family have also been tremendously helpful and extremely patient while I completed this fun but challenging project. My daughter Mary inspired me with her ideas, enthusiasm, questions and kindness. My son John both distracted and encouraged me, when writing seemed difficult. As always, my wife Helen was exceptionally supportive, generous and wonderful.

ABOUT THE AUTHOR

Dr Thomas Waters teaches history at Imperial College London and is the author of *Cursed Britain: A History of Witchcraft and Black Magic in Modern Times* (2019). He studied at Leeds and Oxford, and has been researching and teaching about the history of magic for more than twenty years in both universities and the wider community.

***Front cover, centre* 'Zauberei' ('Wizardry'), coloured lithograph from *Hokus Pocus* or *Magic Picture Book*, Dutch, late 19th century**
This illustration is from a prop book that showed different images, or none, depending on how the holder flicked the pages. Look and Learn/Valerie Jackson Harris Collection/Bridgeman Images.

***Front and back covers, corners* Details from a symbolic painting for Aleister Crowley's magical organization A.˙. A.˙., 1909**
These four details represent the magical elements of air (yellow), water (blue), earth (green) and fire (red). Harry Price/Mary Evans Picture Library.

***Back cover, above* Noblewoman's amulet box, late 19th–early 20th century**
Known as 'ga'u', protective talismans such as this one contained texts consecrated by Buddhist monks. The Metropolitan Museum of Art, New York. John Stewart Kennedy Fund, 1915.

***Back cover, below* Gem, engraved with a scorpion and protective magical words, Roman, 100–250 CE**
On the reverse, this gem reads ωιθθμ, εν χινιαμ, βων, a variant of the Greek magic phrase ωρθμενχινιαμβων, which is found on other scorpion amulet gems. The J. Paul Getty Museum, Villa Collection, Malibu, California.

***Page 1* Abracadabra from *The Ingoldsby Legends, or Mirth and Marvels*, 1864**
The earliest known reference to abracadabra appears in a 2nd-century CE Roman medical text, which reports that wearing a triangular abracadabra amulet around the neck gradually reduces fevers like malaria.

***Page 2* Edward Burne-Jones, *The Wizard*, 1898**
In this Pre-Raphaelite masterpiece, a wizard uses a convex mirror to reveal to a young woman a ship sinking in a storm. The painting has often been linked with Prospero and Miranda from Shakespeare's The Tempest.

***Page 4* Zan Zig performing tricks, 1899**
Born in New Orleans, to a fortune-teller mother, the American stage magician Harry Robenstein (aka Zan Zig) was talented but unstable. In 1897 he lost an eye in a stage accident and, in 1899, a finger. At the 1893 Chicago World's Fair, Zan Zig performed a fake 'séance', during which an audience member died of a heart attack.

***Pages 6–7* Pieter van Laer, *Self-Portrait with Magic Scene*, *c.* 1635–37**
This self-portrait depicts the artist as a sorcerer, recoiling from the devil's skeletal claws. The working magician, suddenly mauled or taken by the devil, was a popular motif in early modern European folklore, literature and religious teaching.

First published in the United Kingdom in 2026 by Thames & Hudson Ltd, 6–24 Britannia Street, London WC1X 9JD

First published in the United States of America in 2026 by Thames & Hudson Inc., 500 Fifth Avenue, New York, New York 10110

For image copyright information, see pages 251–252

EU Authorized Representative:

Interart S.A.R.L.
19 rue Charles Auray, 93500 Pantin, Paris, France
productsafety@thameshudson.co.uk
interart.fr

A CIP catalogue record for this book is available from the British Library

Library of Congress Control Number 2026937556

ISBN 978-0-500-03048-6
01

Printed and bound in China by C&C Offset Printing Co. Ltd

MIX
Paper | Supporting responsible forestry
FSC www.fsc.org FSC® C008047